HOSPITAL AND CLINICAL PHARMACY

For B.Pharm Course

RANDHIR SINGH DAHIYA
[M. Pharm., Ph. D]
Associate Professor,
Maharishi Markandeshwar College of Pharmacy,
Maharishi Markandeshwar University,
Mullana, Ambala, 135001.

DINESH LUTHRA
[M. Pharm., Ph. D (Pursuing)]
Assistant Professor,
Surya School of Pharmacy,
Surya Educational and Charitable Trust,
Rajpura, Punjab, 140401.

Price ₹ 160.00

Hospital and Clinical Pharmacy　　　　　　　　　　　**ISBN 978-93-81595-99-2**

Second Edition : August 2015
© : Authors

The text of this publication, or any part thereof, should not be reproduced or transmitted in any form or stored in any computer storage system or device for distribution including photocopy, recording, taping or information retrieval system or reproduced on any disc, tape, perforated media or other information storage device etc., without the written permission of Authors with whom the rights are reserved. Breach of this condition is liable for legal action.

Every effort has been made to avoid errors or omissions in this publication. In spite of this, errors may have crept in. Any mistake, error or discrepancy so noted and shall be brought to our notice shall be taken care of in the next edition. It is notified that neither the publisher nor the authors or seller shall be responsible for any damage or loss of action to any one, of any kind, in any manner, therefrom.

Published By :　　　　　　　　　　　　　　　　　　　　　　　**Printed By :**
NIRALI PRAKASHAN　　　　　　　　　　　　　　　　　　　**Repro India Ltd,**
Abhyudaya Pragati, 1312, Shivaji Nagar,　　　　　　　　　　**Mumbai.**
Off J.M. Road, PUNE – 411005
Tel - (020) 25512336/37/39, Fax - (020) 25511379
Email : niralipune@pragationline.com

☞ DISTRIBUTION CENTRES

PUNE
Nirali Prakashan : 119, Budhwar Peth, Jogeshwari Mandir Lane, Pune 411002, Maharashtra
Tel : (020) 2445 2044, 66022708, Fax : (020) 2445 1538
Email : bookorder@pragationline.com, niralilocal@pragationline.com
Nirali Prakashan : S. No. 28/27, Dhyari, Near Pari Company, Pune 411041
Tel : (020) 24690204 Fax : (020) 24690316
Email : dhyari@pragationline.com, bookorder@pragationline.com

MUMBAI
Nirali Prakashan : 385, S.V.P. Road, Rasdhara Co-op. Hsg. Society Ltd.,
Girgaum, Mumbai 400004, Maharashtra
Tel : (022) 2385 6339 / 2386 9976, Fax : (022) 2386 9976
Email : niralimumbai@pragationline.com

☞ DISTRIBUTION BRANCHES

JALGAON
Nirali Prakashan : 34, V. V. Golani Market, Navi Peth, Jalgaon 425001,
Maharashtra, Tel : (0257) 222 0395, Mob : 94234 91860

KOLHAPUR
Nirali Prakashan : New Mahadvar Road, Kedar Plaza, 1st Floor Opp. IDBI Bank
Kolhapur 416 012, Maharashtra. Mob : 9850046155

NAGPUR
Pratibha Book Distributors : Above Maratha Mandir, Shop No. 3, First Floor,
Rani Jhanshi Square, Sitabuldi, Nagpur 440012, Maharashtra
Tel : (0712) 254 7129

DELHI
Nirali Prakashan : 4593/21, Basement, Aggarwal Lane 15, Ansari Road, Daryaganj
Near Times of India Building, New Delhi 110002
Mob : 08505972553

BENGALURU
Pragati Book House : House No. 1, Sanjeevappa Lane, Avenue Road Cross,
Opp. Rice Church, Bengaluru – 560002.
Tel : (080) 64513344, 64513355,Mob : 9880582331, 9845021552
Email:bharatsavla@yahoo.com

CHENNAI
Pragati Books : 9/1, Montieth Road, Behind Taas Mahal, Egmore,
Chennai 600008 Tamil Nadu, Tel : (044) 6518 3535,
Mob : 94440 01782 / 98450 21552 / 98805 82331,
Email : bharatsavla@yahoo.com

niralipune@pragationline.com | www.pragationline.com
Also find us on www.facebook.com/niralibooks

PREFACE ...

Hospital and Clinical Pharmacy gathers texts on the key features of pharmaceutical services within and from hospital based pharmacies. The book gives an introduction to the service, of benefit to preregistration graduates and to undergraduates. It also aims to benefit recently qualified pharmacists undertaking further studies or gaining wider training rotational roles.

The book has been structured on functional lines, i.e. there are chapters on purchasing, supply, medicines information, and so forth. We have included some chapters on education and training and impact of information technology on pharmacy functions where skills are required and indeed specialist post should develop. Each chapter attempts to describe the ground to be covered, providing definitions where these assist.

It is our sincere wish that this book be equal to the task of providing the readers with a thorough grounding in hospital pharmacy. The reader of this book is urged to go beyond the material as well as topics covered in this book to ensure their adequacy for practice specific issues. "Read it, study it and by all means go beyond it".

We hope readers benefit from the book and provide the readers with a wide knowledge base of hospital pharmacy practice and skills required for the developing roles of pharmacist.

Dr. Randhir Singh Dahiya
Dinesh Luthra

ACKNOWLEDGEMENT ...

It is a great privilege to express my gratitude and admiration to the highly esteemed and venerable Chancellor of Maharishi Markandeshwar University, Mullana, Ambala Sh. Tarsem Kumar Garg. He has been the sole inspiration behind this uphill task.

We also take this opportunity to wish our gratefulness to Dr. Pawan Krishan, Dr. S. L. Bodhankar and Ms. Sarabjit Kaur, who guided and helped us in writing this book.

It is also important to mention here that this book would not have been successful without the noted help from my colleagues and friends Dr. Vipin Saini, Dr. Manish Gautam, Dr. Anurag Kuhad, Dr. Jitender Bariwal and Mr. Girish Gupta.

On the personal front we are grateful to our family and friends for their encouragement, support and blessings.

This book is dedicated to Late. Sh. Harish Kumar Luthra.

Last but not the least many thanks to Nirali Prakashan, for giving us the opportunity to get our book published.

Dr. Randhir Singh Dahiya
Dinesh Luthra

CONTENTS ...

1.	**Hospital Organisation**	1.1 - 1.24
	1.1 Introduction	1.1
	1.2 Duties of Medical Superintendent (MS)	1.1
	1.3 Duties of Deputy Medical Superintendent (DMS)	1.2
	1.4 Functions of a Hospital	1.2
	1.5 Classification of a Hospital	1.3
	1.6 Hospital Pharmacy	1.9
	1.7 Functions of Hospital Pharmacy	1.9
	1.8 Objectives of Hospital Pharmacy	1.10
	1.9 Bulk Stores	1.12
	1.10 In-patient Pharmacy	1.16
	1.11 Role of Hospital Pharmacist	1.18
	1.12 Pharmacy and Therapeutic Committee	1.19
	1.13 Functions and Scope	1.21
	1.14 Hospital Budget	1.21
	1.15 Preparation of Budget	1.22
	1.16 Instructions on Hospital Budgeting	1.22
	Summary	1.23
2.	**Hospital Formulary**	2.1 - 2.6
	2.1 Hospital Formulary	2.1
	2.2 Need for Hospital Formulary	2.1
	2.3 Benefits of Drug Formulary System	2.1
	2.4 Preparation of Formulary	2.4
	Summary	2.6
3.	**Drug Information Services**	3.1 - 3.20
	3.1 Introduction	3.1
	3.2 Need of Drug Information Service	3.1
	3.3 Drug Information Centre (DIC)	3.7
	3.4 Medication Errors	3.12
	Summary	3.19
4.	**Nuclear Pharmacy**	4.1 - 4.14
	4.1 Introduction	4.1
	4.2 Classification of Isotopes	4.2
	4.3 Radiopharmaceutical Preparation	4.3
	4.4 Production of Radiopharmaceutical	4.4
	4.5 Methods of Production of Artificial Radionuclides	4.4
	4.6 Preparation of Radioisotopes in laboratory	4.5
	4.7 Therapeutic Application of Radiopharmaceuticals	4.7

	4.8	Diagnostic Applications			4.9
	4.9	Permissible Radiation Dose Level			4.11
	4.10	Radiation Hazards and their Prevention			4.12
	Summary				4.13
5.	**Central Sterile Supply Management**		**5.1**	**–**	**5.10**
	5.1	Introduction			5.1
	5.2	Objectives of Central Sterile Supply Department (CSSD)			5.1
	5.3	Functions of Central Sterile Supply Department (CSSD)			5.2
	5.	Types of Materials			5.3
		5.4.1 Materials for Containers			5.3
		5.4.2 Materials for Closures			5.3
	5.5	Objectives of Sterilization			5.3
	5.6	Packaging Process			5.4
	5.7	Packaging Concept for Sterile Products			5.4
		5.7.1 Primary Packaging Containing the Product			5.5
		5.7.2 Secondary Packaging			5.5
		5.7.3 Transport Packaging			5.5
	5.8	Need of Packing of Sterile Goods			5.5
	5.9	Sterilization Methods			5.5
	5.10	Supply of Sterile Materials			5.9
	Summary				5.9
6.	**Drug Store Management and Inventory Control**		**6.1**	**–**	**6.10**
	6.1	Drug Store Management			6.1
	6.2	Storage at Cool Temperature			6.3
	6.3	Purchasing			6.3
		6.3.1 Methods of Purchasing			6.3
		6.3.2 Inventory			6.4
		6.3.3 Inventory and its Functions			6.5
		6.3.4 Inventory Control			6.5
		6.3.5 Objectives of Inventory Control			6.6
		6.3.6 Need for Inventory Control			6.6
	6.4	Inventory Control Operation			6.8
		6.4.1 Causes of Inventory Imbalance			6.8
		6.4.2 Purchase Order (PO)			6.8
	6.5	Procurement			6.9
		6.5.1 Procurement Procedures			6.9
	6.6	Distribution of drugs			6.10
	Summary				6.10

7.	**The Prescription**		**7.1**	**-**	**7.12**
	7.1	Introduction			7.1
	7.2	Information required on Prescription			7.1
	7.3	Handling of the Prescription			7.5
	7.4	Patient Medication Profile			7.6
	7.5	Filling Prescriptions			7.7
	7.6	Medication Errors			7.9
		7.6.1 Causes of Medication Errors			7.9
		7.6.2 Categories of Medication Errors			7.10
		7.6.3 Prevention of Medication Errors			7.11
	Summary				7.11
8.	**Drug Distribution Services**		**8.1**	**-**	**8.16**
	8.1	Introduction			8.1
	8.2	In-patient Drug Distribution Services			8.1
		8.2.1 Floor or Ward Stock System			8.1
		8.2.2 Individual Prescription Order System			8.2
		8.2.3 Combination of the Above Mentioned Systems			8.2
		8.2.4 Unit Dose System (UDS)			8.2
	8.3	Types of UDS			8.4
	8.4	Unit Dose Process			8.4
		8.4.1 Physician's Medication Order			8.4
	8.5	Methods of Sending the Physician's Orders to the Pharmacy			8.6
	8.6	Patient Medication Profile			8.6
	8.7	Instruction Labels			8.7
	8.8	Medication Delivery to Patients			8.8
	8.9	Charging Policy			8.8
	8.10	Dispensing of Drugs to Ambulatory Patients			8.9
	8.11	Outpatient Dispensing			8.10
	8.12	Location and Layout of Outpatient Dispensing			8.11
	8.13	Emergency Medication Supplies			8.11
	8.14	Dispensing of Controlled Drugs			8.12
		8.14.1 Labelling			8.12
	8.15	Responsibilities of a Pharmacist in Drug Dispensing			8.13
	8.16	Valid Prescription and Dispensing Requirements			8.13
	8.17	Record keeping			8.14
		8.17.1 Records in Drug Distribution System			8.14
	8.18	Pharmacy Service when the Pharmacy is Closed			8.14
	8.19	Automated Medicine Storage and Distribution Devices and Prescription-filling Systems			8.15
	Summary				8.16

9. Manufacturing Unit Hospital 9.1 – 9.18

9.1	Introduction	9.1
9.2	Policy Making of Manufacturable Items	9.1
9.3	Parameters for Buying the Hospital Medicines	9.2
9.4	Demand and Costing	9.2
9.5	Estimation of Demand	9.3
9.6	Personal Requirements	9.3
9.7	Sterile Manufacturing	9.3
9.8	Facilities and Requirements	9.4
	9.8.1 Environmental Control	9.4
	9.8.2 Traffic Control	9.4
	9.8.3 Housekeeping	9.5
	9.8.4 Surface Disinfection	9.5
	9.8.5 Air Control	9.5
	9.8.6 Horizontal Laminar Flow Hood Vertical Laminar Flow Hood	9.6
9.9	Sterile Product Areas	9.6
	9.9.1 Clean- up Area	9.6
	9.9.2 Preparation Area	9.6
	9.9.3 Aseptic Area	9.7
	9.9.4 Quarantine Area	9.7
	9.9.5 Labelling and Packaging Area	9.7
9.10	Manufacturing Process for Sterile Products	9.7
	9.10.1 Equipments Cleaning	9.7
	9.10.2 Preparation of Solution	9.7
	9.10.3 Filtration Membrane	9.8
	9.10.4 Filling of Product	9.8
	9.10.5 Sterilization	9.8
9.11	Sterility Testing	9.9
	9.11.1 Membrane Filtration and Direct Transfer	9.9
	9.11.2 Direct Inoculation	9.9
	9.11.3 Pyrogens Testing	9.9
	9.11.4 Test Animals	9.10
	9.11.5 Procedure	9.10
	9.11.6 Interpretation of Results	9.10
	9.11.7 Detection of Particulate Matter	9.11
9.12	Clarity Testing	9.11
	9.12.1 Visual Methods	9.11
	9.12.2 Automated Visual Inspection	9.11
9.13	Non-sterile Manufacturing	9.11
	9.13.1 Specific requirements for manufacturing of non sterile products are	9.12
	9.13.2 Requirement of equipment for external preparations are recommended for the manufacture of external preparations, i.e. ointments, emulsion, lotions, solutions, pastes, creams, dusting powders and such identical products used for external applications whichever is applicable	9.13

      9.13.3 The following equipments are commended for the manufacture of oral/internal use preparations, i.e. syrups, elixirs, emulsions and suspensions, whichever is applicable.   9.13
- 9.14 Bulk Compounding Formula Record   9.13
- 9.15 Production Planning and Control (PPC)   9.14
- 9.16 Steps of Production Planning and Control   9.15
- 9.17 Production Control   9.15
- 9.18 Batch Manufacturing Records   9.16
- Summary   9.17

10. Incompatibilities   10.1 - 10.24
- 10.1 Introduction   10.1
- 10.2 Physical Incompatibility   10.1
- 10.3 Chemical Incompatibility   10.5
- 10.4 Therapeutic incompatibility   10.19
- Summary   10.23

11. Communicable Diseases   11.1 - 11.52
- 11.1 Introduction   11.1
- 11.2 Infectious Agents   11.1
- 11.3 Factors related to Diseases   11.4
- 11.4 Factors related to Host   11.4
- 11.5 Varicella Zoster Virus Infection (Chicken Pox and Shingles)   11.5
- 11.6 Measles   11.6
- 11.7 Influenza   11.6
- 11.8 Diphtheria   11.9
- 11.9 Tetanus   11.10
- 11.10 Pertussis or Whooping Cough   11.10
- 11.11 Tuberculosis   11.12
- 11.12 Poliomyelitis   11.15
- 11.13 Cholera   11.18
- 11.14 Rabies   11.19
- 11.15 Leprosy   11.21
- 11.16 Typhoid Fever   11.24
- 11.17 Malaria   11.26
- 11.18 Syphilis   11.29
- 11.19 Filariasis   11.32
- 11.20 Gonnorhea   11.35
- 11.21 Hepatitis   11.36
- 11.22 Acquired Immunodeficiency Syndrome (AIDS)   11.45
- Summary   11.49

12. Definition of Dosage Forms   12.1 - 12.6
- 12.1 Introduction   12.1
- 12.2 Aerosols   12.1
- 12.3 Applications   12.1
- 12.4 Capsules   12.1

12.5 Collodions		12.1
12.6 Creams		12.1
12.7 Dusting Powder		12.1
12.8 Ear Drops		12.2
12.9 Elixirs		12.2
12.10 Emulsions		12.2
12.11 Enemas		12.2
12.12 Eye Drops		12.2
12.13 Gargles		12.2
12.14 Gels		12.2
12.15 Granules		12.3
12.16 Implants		12.3
12.17 Inhalations		12.3
12.18 Injections		12.3
12.19 Insufflations		12.3
12.20 Irrigation Solutions		12.4
12.21 Linctuses		12.4
12.22 Liniments		12.4
12.23 Lotions		12.4
12.24 Lozenges		12.4
12.25 mixtures		12.4
12.26 Mouthwashes		12.4
12.27 Nasal Drops and Sprays		12.4
12.28 Ointments		12.5
12.29 Oral Emulsions		12.5
12.30 Oral Liquids		12.5
12.31 Paints		12.5
12.32 Parenteral Preparations		12.5
12.33 Pastes		12.5
12.34 Pastilles		12.5
12.35 Pessaries		12.6
12.36 Pills		12.6
12.37 Poultices		12.6
12.38 Powders (Oral)		12.6
12.39 Suppositories		12.6
12.40 Suspensions		12.6
12.41 Syrups		12.6
12.42 Tablets		12.6
13. Latin		**13.1 - 13.4**

***

1

HOSPITAL ORGANISATION

1.1 INTRODUCTION

A hospital is an establishment where ailing patients receive medical and surgical treatment. Pregnant women often deliver their babies in a hospital.

The organisation of a hospital depends not on its nomenclature but on the number of beds. A 200-bed hospital will require a different kind of organisation compared to 25/50-bed hospital or a 500-bed hospital.

Unfortunately, in India, a private practicing physician/gynecologist terms his dispensary as a Medical Centre or a Hospital. In return, what they offer to their patients is a prescription in lieu of their fee, and that is that.

An average hospital caters to the traumatic requirements of the sick. The name given to such hospitals is General Hospital where a patient stays until he recovers and is fit for discharge. The general hospitals provide treatment, rehabilitation, obstetrics, advice for exit from drug abuse, and the screening of cancer, etc. In comparison, short-term hospitals a doctor examines a patient and admits him/her depending on his/her condition treated, and then discharged to revisit at defined intervals. Besides the long-term and short-term hospitals, there are primary health centers and municipal dispensaries. Since these are under the control of government, they employ qualified doctors.

Non-clinical doctors are qualified doctors, but their function is to take care of hospital organisation/administration while clinicians tend to the traumatic conditions of the patients. However, one can write a lot about hospital organisation, but the ground reality is that in India there are very few hospitals that employ qualified hospital administrators or MBAs in Hospital administration. This could be because of the budgetary constraints.

In India, the administration, call it organisation, is under the control of Medical superintendents and Deputy Medical Superintendents. More than this written in the books published in India is either exaggeration or plagiarism. In some hospitals, medical superintendents call themselves as Directors—Job content remaining the same. Back to Medical Superintendents (MS) and Deputy Medical Superintendents (DMS)

1.2 DUTIES OF MEDICAL SUPERINTEDENT (MS)

1. He/She is the overall in charge of the hospital for its organisation and development in all aspects.

2. To supervise training, efficiency in the standard of investigation, diagnosis, treatment and management of the patients in the hospital
3. To create psychiatric team of workers for the benefit and welfare of the patients;
4. To be in charge of the department of psychiatry to oversee postgraduate education in psychiatry, clinical psychology, psychiatric social work, and psychiatric nursing;
5. To motivate and organize research work;
6. To provide patient care in the concerned specialty; and
7. Any other duty assigned by the authorities from time to time.

1.3 DUTIES OF DEPUTY MEDICAL SUPERINTENDENT (DMS)

1. To assist the MS in supervision of psychiatric neurological, and medical investigation besides the treatment of patients;
2. To deputize for MS when he is absent;
3. To assist the MS in the teaching of psychiatry and neurology to undergraduate, postgraduate students and nursing sisters;
4. To carry out research in psychiatry and allied subjects under the supervision of MS;
5. These duties will be optional depending upon the qualification of the incumbent:
    (a) Take charge of the electroencephalograph department;
    (b) To build up the side of the hospital work;
6. To guide the physicians and other technical staff in the professional and other administrative duties;
7. To supervise training of ward attendants and other medical auxiliaries;
8. To arrange for case demonstration and seminars; and
9. To execute such other duties as assigned to him by MS from time to time.

1.4 FUNCTIONS OF A HOSPITAL

A hospital as mentioned above is as formal institution developed by the society for patient care, intended to meet the complex health needs of its members.

- Individual : Sick or injured has access to centralized medical knowledge and technology.
- Society : It protects the family from many of the disruptive effects of caring for the ill in the home and making the problems less disruptive for the society as a whole.

The functions of a hospital are:
1. Patient Care
2. Health Education
3. Medical Research
4. Training

5. The above given points are explained in detail as follows :
   (a) The principal function of a hospital is the treatment and care of patients.
   (b) To lower the incidence of diseases through early detection and treatment;
   (c) To raise the quality of law and general standards of medical practice;
   (d) To introduce regular review, analysis and improved monitoring of patient care;
   (e) To create avenues for a common link between general public and policy makers;
   (f) To participate in and put into practice, the safety programmes of the hospital;
   (g) To develop maintain an effective system of clinical and administrative records and reports;
   (h) To estimate the needs for facilities, supplies and equipments and then utilize these facilities for evaluation, control and maintenance;
   (i) To provide the means and methods by which persons can work together in groups with the object of care of hospital, department, patient and community;
   (j) To participate in the financial plan for the operation of the hospital; and
   (k) To initiate, utilize and participate in research projects designed for improvement of patient care and other hospital services.

1.5 CLASSIFICATION OF A HOSPITAL

There are different ways to classify a hospital, as a single hospital may fall into more than one class. Broadly, hospitals are classified:
1. Types of services
2. Ownership
3. Medicinal systems
4. Cost based
5. Bed capacity

(1) Types of services

Based upon the type of services and areas, the types of hospitals are:

(a) Teaching cum research Hospital:

The main objective of these hospitals is teaching while research and health care is secondary e.g. Post Graduate Medical Education And Research Institute, Chandigarh; All India Institute of Medical Sciences, New Delhi; Christian Medical College, Ludhiana, and the like

(b) General Hospital:

For general hospitals, the main objective is to provide medical care, training and research is secondary, e.g. Primary Health centers.

(c) Special Hospitals:

These hospitals mainly concentrate on particular disease or area e.g. cancer, heart diseases, dental, psychiatry and maternity.

(2) Ownership:

Based upon of ownership the hospitals can be classified as:

- **(a) Government Hospitals:** These are the hospitals run by the central government, state government, corporations and municipalities e.g. All India Institute of Medical Sciences, District Hospitals, Army Hospitals, and Railways Hospitals.
- **(b) Semi-government Hospitals:** These are the hospitals, which are under the administration of private management or a charitable trust but the Government finances these partially, e.g. King Edward Memorial Hospital (KEM Hospital).
- **(c) Non-Government Hospitals:** Charitable trusts, churches, etc. administer non-profit hospitals. Examples: Mahatma Gandhi Rugnalaya Pune, Ramakrishna Mission Hospital, Kolkata, Christian Missionary Hospital Vellore, Stephens Hospital Delhi, Philadelphia Mission Hospital Ambala, Brown Hospital Ludhiana.

(3) Medicinal based hospitals:

Particular system of medicine followed determines the category of the hospital.

- Allopathic Hospitals
- Ayurvedic Hospitals
- Homeopathic Hospitals
- Unani Hospitals
- Naturopathy
- Acupuncture Hospitals

Size based Hospitals:

- Very small Hospitals
- Small hospitals
- Medium Hospitals
- Large Hospitals

(4) Cost based Hospitals:

- Elite hospitals
- Budget Hospitals
- Private nursing Homes

Elite Hospitals

These hospitals are the symbol of high-tech medical development. The room rates vary between 300–3000 per day. The deluxe rooms comprise refrigerator, TV and telephone. Excepting the medical care, they are like five-star hotels. However, even these elite institutions reserve a particular percentage of their capacity for the poorer sections and subsidize a particular percentage of their accommodation. Jaslok hospital in Mumbai has 25 per cent reservation for the poorer section and 30 per cent at half the rates. Out of the 680 beds of Mumbai Hospitals, 315 are free and 112 are subsidized. Batra hospital, New Delhi and Escorts Hearts Research Institute New Delhi, are also expensive hospitals.

Budget Hospitals

These hospitals cater to the medical requirements of low-income group..

Private Hospitals/Nursing Homes

These medical centers are there in all the metropolitan cities and towns in India, owned by either a single or a group of private practitioners or husband-wife team. They are proprietary or partnership concerns, general nursing homes, with facilities for general surgery. Some nursing homes offer specialized care for cardiac, pediatric, orthopaedic or ophthalmology. The treatment in nursing homes is too expensive.

Teaching Hospitals

Hospitals can be teaching hospitals or research centers whereto attachment of a medical college is mandatory. They can be integrated hospitals where many medical and surgical departments integrate or alternative systems of medicine are accepted as a part of the group, e.g. Mool Chand Khairati Ram Hospital who offer Ayurvedic and Homoeopathic remedial systems. AIIMS, New Delhi, Guru Teg Bahudur Hospital, Delhi, PGIMS, Chandigarh, Lady Harding Medical College, New Delhi, Vardman Medical College, New Delhi ; Maulana Azad Medical College, New Delhi are teaching hospitals.

Organisational Structure of the Hospital

Organisational Structure (OS) is the framework that defines formal reporting relationships between different levels of management of an organisation. OS is the mechanism that operationalizes the management of the orgnisation.

The most important body of a hospital is the governing body or board of directors or board of trustees. This is the major decision making body of the hospital. It comprises various outstanding personalities in the field of medical education, research and administration. The following block diagram depicts the organisational structure of a hospital.

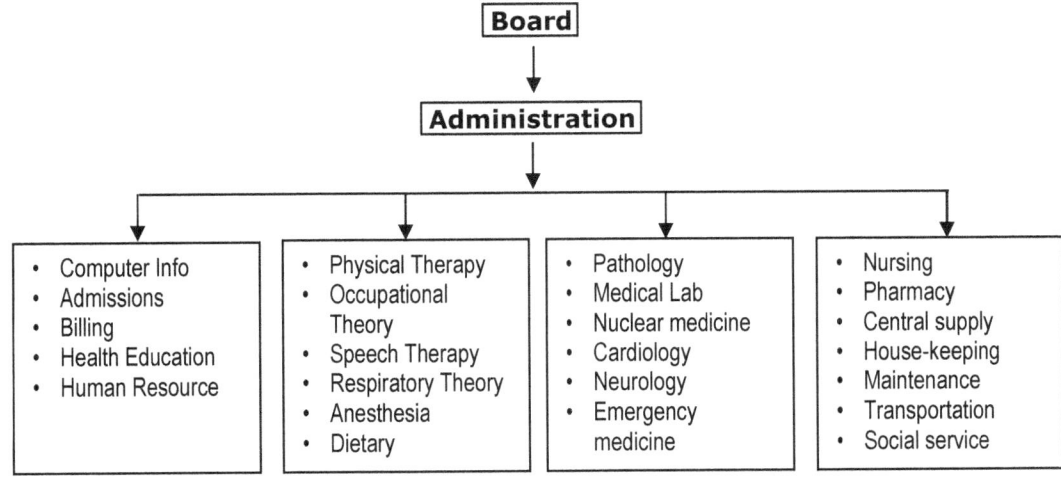

Information Service

For details, see chapter under the title "Drug Information Centre"

Therapeutic Services

For details read the chapter on "Drug Information Centre". Also read Duties of Medical and Deputy Medical Superintendents.

Therapeutic services can be further categorised into the following divisions:

1. Physical Therapy—provides treatment to improve large muscle mobility.
2. Occupational Therapy — treatment goal is to help patient regain fine motor skills.
3. Speech/Language Pathology—identify, evaluate, treat speech/language disorders.
4. Medical Psychology—concerned with mental well-being of patients.
5. Respiratory Therapy — treats patients with lung disease.
6. Cardiac Therapy —treats patients with heart diseases.

Diagnostic Services

The activities of this service relate to the diagnosis made by a physician or nurse practitioner or other health professional. Diagnostic service determines the cause(s) of illness or injury.

It includes the following sections:

1. Medical Laboratory—studies body tissues;
2. Medical Imaging — radiology, MRI, CT, Ultra Sound; and
3. Emergency Medicine -provides emergency diagnosis and treatment.

Support Services

Support services are very important part of the hospital for the functioning and maintenance of the hospital. Actually, the clinical department would not be able to function without the supporting services. Amongst the supporting services are the nursing department, the dietary services, laboratory services, the medical records department, the blood banks, the central sterile supply and the social service department. There are other services clinically essential to the operation of the hospital such as the maintenance and engineering divisions.

Nursing Service

The nursing service is similar to any other large service in the hospital. At the head is a director of nursing (Staff Nurse) who is generally an experienced nurse with administrative talent. The administrative nursing service carries ultimate administrative authority and responsibilities in one or more health facilities provided to individuals and families. Staff nurses participate in formulating policy and devising procedures to the achievement of objectives and in developing and evaluating programmes and services.

The nursing team consists of workers with varying degrees of nursing skill as directed by the profession. Today's nursing practitioner well knows to relate to patients' sensitivities, and help the patients accordingly.

The following principles govern the Nursing service :
1. Nursing care encompasses health promotion, the care and prevention of disease or disability, rehabilitation, teaching, counselling and emotional support as well as the care of illness.
2. Nursing care is an integral part of total health care and is planned and administered in combination with related medical, educational and welfare services.
3. Nursing personnel respect individuality, dignity, and right of every person; regardless of race, color, creed, and national origin, social or economic status.

Dietetic Services

This is an essential service of an institution to apply the principles of nutrition to the preparation of palatable and appropriate food. An adequate numbers of dietitians and technical and clerical personnel look after the dietetics. In addition to purchasing, planning and preparation of menus for patients and employees.

The dieticians are responsible:
- For recording dietary history of patients such as those with food allergies and those unable to accept a limited diet regimen;
- Interviewing patients regarding their food habit;
- Counseling patients and their families about normal and modified regimens; and
- Encouraging patients to participate in planning their own normal and modified regimen and participate in appropriate ward rounds and conferences.

Medical Records Department

Every hospital is liable to maintain adequate medical records of their patients. These records should be accessible for compiling information to enable another practitioner to assume care of the patient at any time. A completed medical record is one which includes identification and sociological data, personal family history, history of present illness, physical examination; special examination such as consultations, clinical laboratory data, x-rays and other examinations; provisional and working diagnosis, medical and surgical treatment, gross and microscopic pathological findings; progress notes, final diagnosis, conditions on discharge; follow up and autopsy findings.

The purpose of medical records is :
1. To serve as a basis for planning and for continuity of patient care;
2. To provide a means for communication among the physician and any professionals contributing to the patient's care;

3. To serve as a basis for review, study and evaluation of the care rendered to the patient;
4. To assist in protecting the legal interest of the patient, hospital and responsible practitioner;
5. To furnish documentary evidence for the course of the patient's illness and treatment during each hospital stay; and
6. To provide data for use in research and education

Pathology Service

A pathologist directs the pathology services, which include blood tests, body and fluid testing, tissue pathology and cytology besides health screening and monitoring tests.

Blood Bank

Blood is of essential nature as a therapeutic agent and most hospitals operate a blood bank. This service is generally under the supervision of a licensed physician. Most hospital's blood bank operates as an adjunct to the local Red Cross Blood Programme.

Radiology

Radiology is the most important of the scientific and therapeutic facilities of the hospital. The department is under the supervision of a qualified physician who has also obtained adequate training and experience in general radiology. The department of radiology generally consists of radiologists, physicists, technicians; radiographers, radiotherapists, isotopharmacists, nurses and secretarial personnel. Radiology includes Ultrasound, CT, MRI, and X-ray.

Medical Social Service Department

The medical social service department is an important liaison between the hospital and the patient and his community. The social worker represents a discipline whose professional focus is on social aspects of the patient and his family. Social service personnel generally provide information relating to medical social study of appropriate patients; social therapy and rehabilitation of patients and follow up reports of discharged patients.

Central Service Department

The central service department furnishes all supplies required for the nursing units. These supplies include sterile linen, sterile kits, operating rooms packs, needles, syringes and other medical surgical supplies. In addition, the personnel in this department clean, inspect, repair, assemble, and sterilize special treatment trays for the various nursing units.

Central sterile supply room: Central sterile supply room is a centralized system practising total decontamination and gives professional support and service for improved patient care by maintaining high processing standards.

The objectives of the department generally encompasses the following:
1. Maintain accurate and current inventory of supplies and equipment in the department;
2. Maintain an accurate record of the effectiveness of the various processes of cleaning, disinfecting and sterilization; and
3. Assume total responsibility for processing hospital items, thereby assuring that all of them receive the same degree of cleaning and sterilization.

1.6 HOSPITAL PHARMACY

The hospital pharmacy is a department, which procures stores, compounds drugs, checks for quality, dispenses, manufactures, packs and distributes to in-patients and outpatients. Qualified pharmacists perform these duties. It is an important department, which caters to the needs of physicians, nurses and other staff members of the hospital.

The modern system of hospital pharmacy also provides drug information and drug monitoring services. The pharmacy should be located in the hospital premises so that patients and staff can easily approach it. In the multi-storey building of a hospital, the pharmacy should be located on the ground floor specifically the dispensing unit. There should be adequate space for routine manufacturing of stock solutions, bulk powders, ointments, etc. The manufacturing room should be adjacent to the pharmacy. Medical stores of a pharmacy should be as the number and variety of medications expand to treat more acutely ill patients and to fill the increasing volume and diversity of prescriptions for outpatients, many hospital pharmacies are implementing a just-in-time (JIT) inventory delivery system from vendors. A JIT system supplies items as close to the time of use as possible in an effort to reduce large inventories, decrease space requirements, and lessen financial outlay.

The growth and emphasis on JIT delivery and stock in the pharmacy means there is less volume of individual items, but more deliveries more often. This may reduce the amount of space required for bulk storage, but increases the amount of space needed for vendor bins, carts, pallets, and totes.

1.7 FUNCTIONS OF HOSPITAL PHARMACY

1. Dispensing of outpatient and discharge prescriptions;
2. Supply and distribution of inpatient medications and maintenance of ward medication stocks;
3. Clinical pharmacy review services to inpatient areas;
4. Drug information and adverse drug reaction reporting;
5. Preparation of specialized sterile pharmaceuticals;
6. Preparation and sterilization of injectable drugs when manufactured in the hospital;
7. Dispensing of drugs including narcotics, chemicals and pharmaceutical preparations;

8. Dispensing and sterilization of parenteral preparations manufactured in the hospital;
9. Planning, organizing and directing pharmacy policies and procedures in accordance with established policies of the hospital;
10. Management and purchase for the requirements of the stores. maintenance of specifications of quality and source for purchase of all drugs, chemicals, antibiotics, biological and other pharmaceuticals preparation used in the hospital;
11. Proper storage of drugs with specifications and maintenance of records;
12. Discarding the expired drugs and containers with damaged labels;
13. Maintenance of an approved stock of antidotes and other emergency drugs;
14. Implementation of decisions of Pharmacy and Therapeutic committee (PTC)
15. Cooperation in teaching students in nursing and medical training programme;
16. Collection and circulation of information regarding the drugs to physicians, interns and nurses;
17. Preparation of periodic reports for submission to the administrator of the hospital;
18. Support for clinical medication trials;
19. Establishment and maintenance of "Drug Information Centre" which will provide information regarding medications to the physicians, nurses or any other competent person who deals in drugs;
20. Providing drug-monitoring services by studying various effects of drugs administered to the patients especially the indoor patients from 'Patients charts' maintained in the wards.

1.8 OBJECTIVES OF HOSPITAL PHARMACY

1. To ensure the availability of the right medication at reasonable cost;
2. To develop the scientific and professional aspects of the practice of hospital pharmacy including consulting role, teaching role and participation in the field of research;
3. To teach hospital pharmacists the ethics for hospital pharmacy to assume responsibility for professional practice;
4. To utilize the resources of hospital to help in improvement of the department and profession as a whole;
5. To develop the administrative or management skills and other aspects essential to the hospital pharmacists in his role as a department head;
6. To attract a greater number of qualified pharmacists in hospital practice; and
7. To coordinate with other departments of a hospital.

Table 1.1: Area for the hospital pharmacy vis-a-vis number of beds

1.	Store room	100 B-450A
		300 B-1000 A
		7000 B-2400 A
2.	Dispensary	100 B-350 A
		300 B-500 A
		700 B-800 A
3.	Office	100 B-110 A
		300 B-150 A
		700 B-200 A
4.	Manufacturing compressed tablets and capsules	For Tablets
		700 B-900 A
		For Capsules
		700 B-200 A
		300 B-250 A
5.	Manufacturing under aseptic conditions for eye drops, eye lotions and other preparations for the external use	700 B-250 A
6.	Parenterals	300 B-600 A
		700 B-600 A

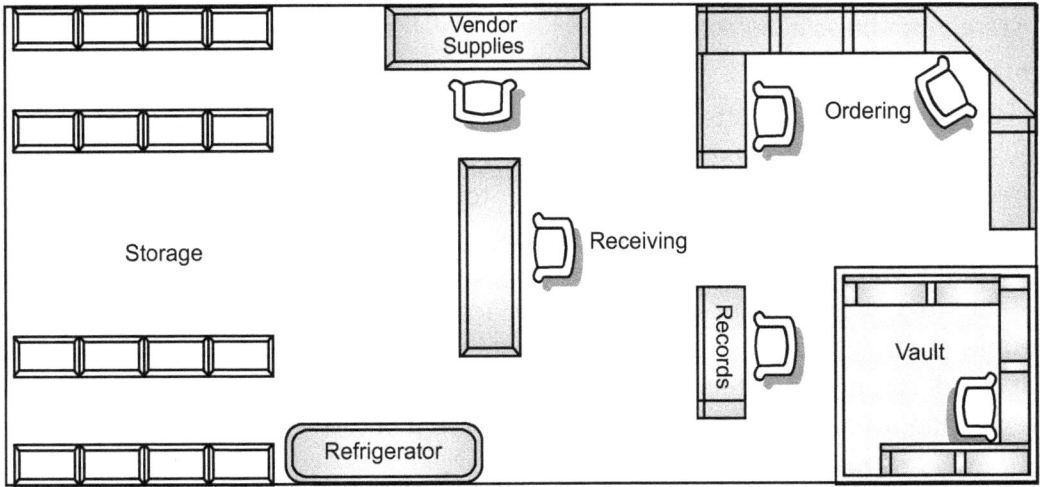

Fig. 1.1: Layout of Hospital Pharmacy

1.9 BULK STORES

The clinical work area in Bulk Stores has four functions to support inventory management:

- Ordering
- Receiving
- Storing
- Distribution

Ordering

This area provides the link to pharmaceutical vendors for JIT delivery and stock. This requires a number of computers and printers for direct link with the prime vendors and other areas of the pharmacy for inventory control. Since inventories are to a minimum with JIT, their close monitoring is necessary to ensure that adequate supplies are always available. Electrical and data access is necessary for the equipment.

Receiving

In the "breakout area," supplies are removed from their outer containers or vendor bins. This process will require a large worktable, preferably mobile and height-adjustable area. There should be allocation of space for receptacles used for packaging materials sorted for recycling.

In addition to this, work center there should be a hand-washing sink, a storage area for JIT vendors, and a large reusable trash receptacle on casters. If vendors do not supply bar codes, the pharmacy should provide code to the stock. This may require a separate workstation for a computer and the bar coding equipment as well as storage for bar coding supplies.

Storing

General Storage: After the items are "broken" out of their outer containers, they are stored in the general storage area. Pharmaceuticals must be separated and stored by category (for example, orals, topical, liquids; eye drops, eardrops, virginals; nasal sprays, injectables, etc). Expiration dates of perishable drugs must be of prime concern, and stock rotated as required. A separate area also is required for outdated, obsolete, or recalled pharmaceuticals, returnable to vendors. This requires shelving of various depths and heights to accommodate the variety of items that need sorting by category. General storage will also require a refrigerator, a freezer, and utility carts for moving supplies throughout the pharmacy.

Controlled Substance Storage

Narcotics and other government-controlled substances are stored in a vault or locked room in the pharmacy, usually located away from the primary entrance, but in a highly visible location. The vault is a separate room with walls and a door to restrict access to controlled substances with schedules II through V. Schedule II narcotics remain inside the vault until needed. Daily supplies of schedule III through V narcotics; there should be separate and secure storage for such drugs both in the outpatient and in-patient pharmacies. Within the vault, there may be a refrigerator, a workstation with computer support for inventory control, and storage. Outside the vault, a small workstation may accommodate staffs who monitor access to supplies from the vault.

Distribution

Bulk Stores is responsible for restocking both outpatient and in-patient pharmacies.

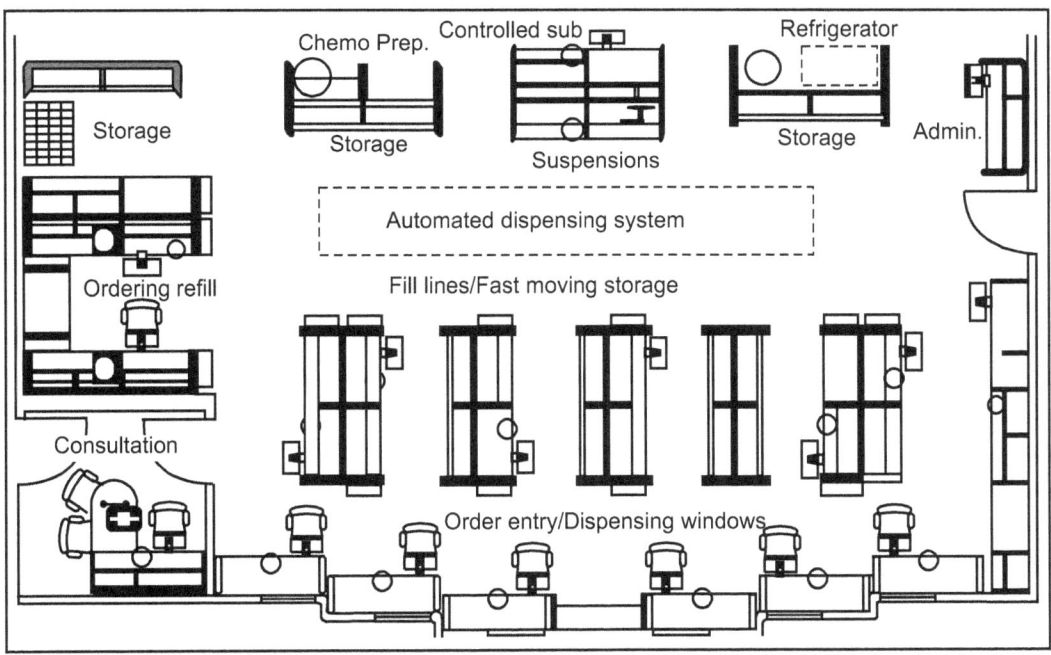

Fig. 1.2: Outpatient Pharmacies

Outpatient Pharmacy

Pharmacists and technicians in the Outpatient Pharmacy are responsible for filling outpatient prescriptions and for providing pharmacy stock to clinics and off-site centers. The Outpatient Pharmacy functions much like a retail pharmacy. It has completely different products and distribution systems than the Inpatient Pharmacy. The size of the Outpatient pharmacy is contingent on the number of outpatients served by the hospital.

The clinical work area in the Outpatient Pharmacy has into four functions to support inventory management:
- Ordering
- Receiving
- Storing
- Distribution

Ordering

This area provides the link to Bulk Stores for delivery of stock. This requires an administrative station with computers and printers. Electrical and data access is necessary for the equipment inventory.

Receiving

Bulk stores supply on a daily basis or several times a day. This area should be in close proximity to Bulk Stores.

Storing

Active Stores

The supplies received from The Bulk Stores supply for filling outpatient prescriptions and for supplying outpatient clinics and off-site centers. As in Bulk Stores, the pharmacy staff sorts pharmaceuticals by category (orals, topical, liquids, eye drops, shelving of various depths and heights to accommodate the variety of items that need a sorting by category. This area will also require a great deal of space to store the volumes of paper products needed to fill prescriptions—printer paper, prescription labels, prescription bags, warning labels or containers, as well as hard copies of prescriptions.

Manufacturing

The manufacturing area provides the compounding and manufacturing of special prescriptions for outpatients that are not available commercially. This area requires a work counter, computer, storage cabinet, and sink with an area for drying glassware.

Prepackaging

In the prepackaging area, the staff sorts medications in both liquid and tablet form and package in smaller containers for outpatient use.

Manufacturing and Prepackaging may be located in a self-contained room.

Distribution

Order Entry

Prescriptions come into order entry as hard copies at the dispensing windows (handed from patient to pharmacy staff), electronically via computers (from physician to pharmacy staff), or by automated phone-in system (from patients requiring refills). The staff feeds the information into the computer system for warnings of interactions with other drugs and for potential allergic reactions by the patient. Once these get a warnings free signal, the computer generates a label on a printer with the name of the patient and medication required. The size of this area and the number and layout of stations has an impact how they receive the prescription information. Workspace will require computers, printers, telephones, fax machines and/or scanners, and some paper storage. Some pharmacies utilize a computerized queuing system to triage the prescription information—triggering the sequence of filling prescriptions based on priority factors. This requires an administrative support station for computers and printers.

Filling

Fill lines are workstations where pharmacists or technicians manually fill prescriptions. At the beginning of the fill line, the pharmacy uses the prescription label as the "picking list." They fill the container with the appropriate items, and at the end of the fill line, the pharmacist checks the filled prescription against the computer and does a visual check as well. Then they put the filled prescription into a paper bag, which is placed alphabetically on shelving close to the dispensing window.

Each fill line may have two computers, one linked to order entry to print the prescription labels, and the other, used by the pharmacist, to check the accuracy of the filled prescriptions. Fill lines require a work counter with shelving for storage of fast moving items along with shelves and bottle drawers below the work surface. The number of outpatient prescriptions filled will determine the need of fill lines and the computers.

The fill station can assume different configurations. If the work performed at the fill area needs separation from patient contact, the configuration is often a straight line located away from the order entry/dispensing window. This results in more privacy for the staff and may speed up the time necessary to fill prescriptions. If the pharmacy wishes to promote patient contact between staff and patient, the configuration may take the form of a pod. This is often an L-shaped workstation. One staff member enters the order, fills the prescription from shelving located next to the window, and dispenses it to the patient. This configuration offers the maximum privacy for the patient and promotes consultation. Fill lines accomplish 80 per cent of the filling, but there are other work counters that need to be accommodated. Controlled substances require a separate work counter with locked storage. This area is typically located away from the fill line to facilitate the privacy and concentration required. The preparation of suspensions requires a sink and distilled water. Here the staff adds a predetermined amount of water to a powder to create a suspension. Some pharmacies may also require chemotherapy stock. This station will require a hazardous waste receptacle.

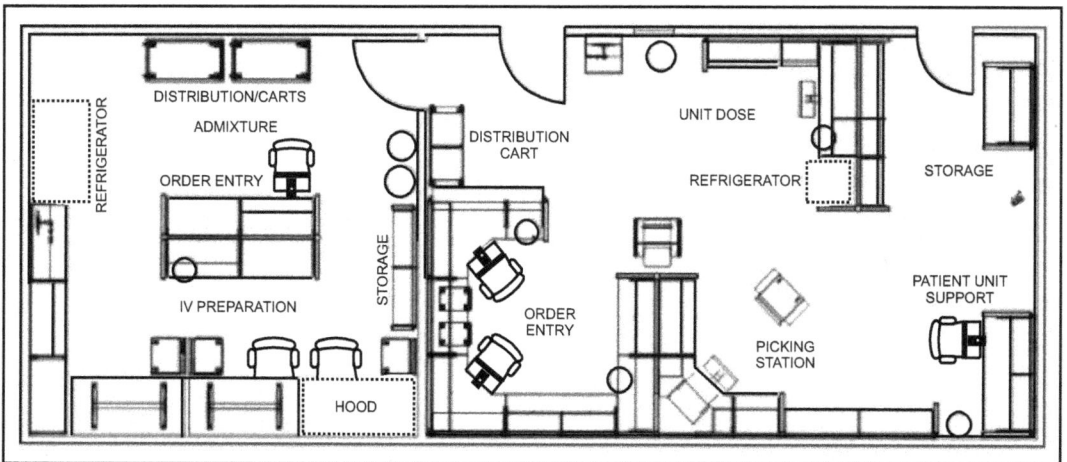

Fig. 1.3: Inpatient Pharmacies

1.10 IN-PATIENT PHARMACY

The Inpatient Pharmacy is responsible for filling orders for unit dose medications and intravenous (IV) medications for inpatients on patient units. Pharmacy packages hospital-dispensed medications in single doses—unit dose— for accuracy and efficiency of dosage administration. The single-dose packages "unit dose" are usually the most sought after medications. In the case of intravenous (IV) fluids, the pharmacy staff adds these medications to the IV fluids and delivers to the patient units. The clinical work area in the Inpatient Pharmacy has four functions to support inventory management:

- Ordering
- Receiving
- Storing
- Distribution

Ordering

Active Stores

This area provides the link to Bulk Stores for delivery and stock. This requires an administrative station with computers and printers. Electrical and data access is necessary for the equipment.

Patient Unit Support

This area may house the mainframe computer linked to automated dispensing machines for controlled substances located on the patient units. The staff monitors these inventories on a regular basis and arranges the refills accordingly.

Receiving: Supplies from Bulk Stores are for unit dose picking or IV/admixture storage.

Storing: Supplies for unit dose picking are stored in the picking stations. IVs are stored in the IV/admixture rooms.

Manufacturing

The manufacturing area provides the compounding and manufacturing of special prescriptions for inpatients, drugs that are not available commercially. This area requires a work counter, computer, storage cabinet, and sink with an area for drying glassware.

Prepackaging

In the prepackaging area, the pharmacy staff packages bulk medications into unit dose for inpatient use. Manufacturing and prepackaging may be located in a self-contained room.

Distribution

Order Entry: Order entry is the "communications hub" of the pharmacy and is often in a central or front location. In this area, the pharmacists receive and review the indented medication, and compare with the patient's medication history or profile to prevent the administration of antagonistic or duplicated drugs. All hard copies of orders are generally stored in this area.

Unit Dose Picking: The need for the retrieval of the most frequently used medications in an efficient, timesaving manner has led to the development of the unit dose picking station. This workstation provides a space of limited dimensions containing a maximum quantity of drugs and allows the pharmacist or technician to "pick" the appropriate drugs. Orders can be filled with little wasted time and motion by having high-volume or fast-moving drugs within an arm's length.

They plan the unit dose picking stations in many different configurations based on space parameters, number of drugs to be dispensed, additional functions and equipment within the station, and the number of staff using the station. Picking stations require storage space for pharmaceuticals separated by category (orals, ingestible, and topical). They also need work surfaces where they can fill and check the unit dose. Typically, there are carts for organizing and containing the stock for delivery to patient units and small mobile work surfaces, positioned where needed.

Admixture

A specific area of the pharmacy is for the function of adding medications to IV fluids prior to administration to the patient. The process of preparing Ivs is more or less a sterile preparation of parenteral products or IV admixture. The IV/admixture area requires a large refrigerator, freezer, and generally two carts — one to hold a supply of IV bags and other for delivery to the hospital. The injection of medications into IV fluids is under a horizontal or vertical airflow hood. A large work counter is needed near the hoods for checking the Ivs. Also required is a sink with an eyewash station and storage area for IV additives. IV/admixture may also have its own order entry station with computers, printers, and fax machine. Although code requirements may differ, the IV/admixture area must be the cleanest part of the department. It is usually in a closed room with positive pressure for isolation and cleanliness in preventing contamination.

Some facilities are required to utilize a Class 10,000 clean room for IV preparation that is free of contaminants and wherein the pharmacist screens out micron-sized particles. This type of clean room can effectively remove viable microbes by removing particles (less than or equal to 0.5 microns) from standing surfaces and incoming air. As the occupancy increases with increasingly more ill inpatients, IV/admixture use will increase. Ivs will infuse with more complicated, expensive, and perishable drugs such as biotech drugs, hyperactive alimentation, and the mix of several drugs in one IV.

1.11 ROLE OF HOSPITAL PHARMACIST

(i) Technical knowledge of drugs and their action

A hospital pharmacist should have thorough knowledge of pharmacology, toxicology, chemistry, route of administration, stability and other information related to drugs. A hospital pharmacist must provide information regarding thee maintenance and handling of drugs. He is always associated with the medical staff so he must be able to provide comparative information, e.g. the data of the drug actions, toxicity and assistance in proper handling of the drugs.

(ii) Ability to organize and develop pharmaceutical manufacturing facility and inventory control

A hospital pharmacist is responsible for the manufacturing and procurement of the drugs utilized in the hospital. Manufacturing within a hospital requires the pharmacist to have control over the supply, quality, equipment and raw material cost. Usually drugs are required in large quantities in big hospitals, which pharmacists may manufacture in the hospital itself or procure from outside sources. He should be able to organize proper manufacturing function by doing proper cost benefit analysis and to evaluate the relative savings that may be possible by manufacturing drugs in large quantities provided cost of labour and maintenance cost are not so high. In order to render such services the hospital pharmacist must have readily available equipments, trained personnel etc.

Chief pharmacist has to exercise his duties on inventories of drugs, which are lying at nursing stations, supply rooms and clinical units.

(iii) Administration and management ability

Hospital pharmacist should be able to plan, organize and control various functions of hospital pharmacy. The Chief pharmacist is responsible for planning, directing the pharmacy policies and to control various functions of hospital pharmacy like budgeting, stock control, maintenance of records and preparation of reports. He is responsible for interviewing, selecting and evaluating the staff members for work in pharmacy. Hospital pharmacist must maintain the legal and administrative records properly, should interact with his staff daily and must participate in development of policies relating to charges made for pharmaceutical services.

(iv) Participation in research activity

The pharmacist should have appropriate knowledge of new research and development activities in the pharmaceutical and medical field. The pharmacist must have the basic understanding of scientific methods to evaluate the research activities. The pharmacist should participate or perform research related activities regarding stabilization, therapeutic effectiveness of drugs, their preservation and usefulness of pharmaceutical preparation.

(v) Conducting teaching training programme

The hospital pharmacist can act as a channel to impart education and conducting training programmes for the nursing staff. He can provide training on various aspects like storage of drugs, dosage forms, and adequate use of the drugs and calculation of dosages. Besides, the Chief pharmacist is responsible for training of the medical staff and pharmacy students. He should keep liasioning with the medical staff to assess their knowledge.

1.12 PHARMACY AND THERAPEUTIC COMMITTEE

The pharmacy and therapeutic committee is a tool for maintaining medical staff self-government. It is responsible to the medical staff as a whole and its recommendations are subject to medical staff approval. The pharmacy and therapeutics committee is a mandatory committee and is composed of physicians, pharmacists, and other health professionals selected with the guidance of the medical staff. It serves as a line of communication or liaison between the medical staff and the pharmacy department. The committee assists in the formulation of board professional policies regarding the evaluation, selection, procurement, distribution, use, safety procedures and other matters relating to drugs in hospitals. The P and T committee evaluates the clinical use of drugs, develops policies for managing drug use and drug administration, and manage the formulary system. It is a policy-recommending body to the medical staff and the administration of the organisation on matters related to the therapeutic use of drugs.

Purposes

The primary purposes of the P and T committee are:

(i) Policy Development: The committee formulates policies regarding evaluation, selection, and therapeutic use of drugs and related devices.

(ii) Education: The committee recommends or assists in the formulation of programmes designed to meet the needs of the professional staff (physicians, nurses, pharmacists, and other health-care practitioners) for complete current knowledge on matters related to drugs and drug use.

Organisation and Operation

While the composition and operation of the P&T committee might vary among specific practice sites, the following generally will apply:

1. The P and T committee should be composed of at least the following voting members: physicians, pharmacists, nurses; administrators, quality-assurance coordinators, and others as appropriate. The size of the committee may vary depending on the scope of services provided by the organisation. A governing unit or authorized official of the organized medical staff appoints the members of the committee.
2. They appoint a chairperson from among the physician representatives. A pharmacist should be the secretary.
3. They should meet regularly, at least six times in a year, and more often when necessary.
4. The committee should invite to its meetings persons within or outside the organisation who can contribute specialized or unique knowledge, skills, and judgments.
5. The secretary prepares an agenda and supplementary materials (including minutes of the previous meeting) and submits to committee members in sufficient time before each meeting for them to review the material properly.
6. The secretary prepares the minutes of committee meetings and maintains in the permanent records of the organisation.
7. The committee presents recommendations to the medical staff or its appropriate committee for adoption or recommendation.
8. The committee should liaise with other organisational committees concerned with drug use.
9. Actions of the committee should liaise routinely with the various health care personnel involved in the care of the patient.
10. The committee should organize and operate in a manner that ensures the objectivity and credibility of its recommendations. The committee should establish a conflict of interest policy with respect to committee recommendations and actions.

1.13 FUNCTIONS AND SCOPE

The basic organisation of each health care setting and its medical staff may influence the specific functions and scope of the P&T committee.

The following committee functions to:

1. To serve in an evaluative, educational, and advisory capacity to the medical staff and organisational administration in all matters pertaining to the use of drugs (including investigational drugs);
2. To develop a formulary of drugs accepted for use in the organisation and provide for its constant revision. The selection of items to be included in the formulary is on objective evaluation of their relative therapeutic merits, safety, and cost. The committee should minimize duplication of the same basic drug type, drug entity, or drug product;
3. To establish programmes and procedures that help ensure safe and effective drug therapy;
4. To establish programs and procedures that ensure cost-effective drug therapy;
5. To establish or plan suitable educational programs for the organisation's professional staff on matters related to drug use;
6. To participate in quality-assurance activities related to distribution, administration, and use of medications;
7. To monitor and evaluate adverse drug reactions in the health care setting and to make appropriate recommendations to prevent their occurrence;
8. To initiate or direct (or both) drug use evaluation programmes and studies, review the results of such activities, and make appropriate recommendations to optimize drug use;
9. To advise the pharmacy department in the implementation of effective drug distribution and control procedures; and
10. To disseminate information on its actions and approved recommendations to all organisational health care staff.

1.14 HOSPITAL BUDGET

The budget is a short-range plan for future operations. The meaning and appropriate use of a budget must be clearly understood by those in managerial position since their participation is required in its preparation and their cooperation is essential. Prior to embarking a upon a plan, management must first define the purpose of the unit, establish policies, for its operation and the project of the hospital's growth. The hospital budget is the measurement tool to monitor the achievements of the planned objectives. Budgeting provides a means for positioning, organizing, communicating and controlling the hospital's operational progress toward the plan. The budget provides a mechanism for the evaluation of financial performance and controlling operations in accordance with the objectives, policies and plans.

1.15 PREPARATION OF BUDGET

The ten basic activities involved in traditional hospital budget planning include the following:

1. Establish institutional and departmental goals and objectives;
2. Determine the budget calendar;
3. Distribute budget instructions, input forms and hospital wide inflation rates;
4. Obtain historical data on costs and volumes by accounting periods;
5. Analyse internal and external forces that could affect historical patterns;
6. Project the volumes of activities like patient days, emergency rooms visits, admissions, surgeries;
7. Project expenses and revenues;
8. Determine the other capital needs, e.g., equipment, debt service, working capital;
9. Establish revenue and rates schedule and net of reductions from revenue required to generate sufficient cash to cover the operating costs and capital needs; and
10. Submit the budget to board and others for final approval.

1.16 INSTRUCTIONS ON HOSPITAL BUDGETING

1. Determine hospital revenue. Revenue can come from patient payments, tax dollars, donations, insurance credits. Be sure to deduct a percentage of the patient bills that will remain uncollected, the charity work expected by the hospital and the pro bono publico work it does.
2. Figure out expenses. Start with the physical facility. How much does it cost to keep up the building or buildings? What is the maintenance cost of each department, engineering, air conditioning, heat, water, other utilities? Know what equipment costs, how much must be replaced per patient day, and if any can be recycled. Include the non-medical cost of each bed in the hospital. Include advertising.
3. Know the cost of personnel, all employees and ancillary staff, including consultants, outsourced contracts, perhaps laundry or nurse staffing services. For all employees of the hospital, from janitorial to hospitalists, figure the fringe benefits the hospital must pay for each.

4. Add all medical equipment costs, ongoing and expected expansion or replacement of new diagnostic equipment.
5. Know the medical costs of each bed. Staff spends how many hours on each bed, occupied or not. Use this figure as an average to get a cost per patient year. Add to that the non-medical costs per bed. Include every possible cost that keeps that bed in the hospital. Do not forget replacement costs per annum for all patient needs.
6. Expansion
7. Is there any planning for a new wing, or the renovation of an old one? Is there any provision for expansion into a new specialty that could bring in extra revenue? Estimate that revenue when planning your budget.
8. Do not forget parking garages, lots, landscaping, grounders keeping or window washing.
9. Include all insurance for the facility and personnel.
10. Enter all categories and the cost of each. Add all taxable items and the percentage of each. You probably get reduced rates on utilities, or at least a break on the taxes on them. Enter all formulas for those. It is possible your state or your hospital system has one already available.

SUMMARY

Hospital is an integral part of medical and social organization which is to provide for the population complete health care, both curative and preventive and whose outpatient services reach out into family in its home environment. Hospitals can be classified into various categories depending upon services, cost, bed capacity or medical systems. Various government, semi government and private hospitals are there which provide ayurvedic, allopathic, homeopathic system of medicines to public.

Organizational structure is a level of management within a hospital which allows efficient management of hospital departments. Hospital departments are grouped together to promote the efficiency of facilities like administrative, informational, therapeutic dietary, diagnostic and nursing services. All these departments cover all the services which have to be provided by a hospital so that proper care of the patient can be taken.

Hospital pharmacy department under the direction of a qualified pharmacist is responsible for the procurement, storage and distribution of medications throughout the hospital. In larger hospitals, satellite pharmacies may bring pharmacist closer to patient care areas, facilitating interactions between pharmacists and patients. Pharmacist is used as a resource for medicine information and specialized medication therapy management. The pharmacy and therapeutic committee is responsible for developing policies and procedure to promote rational medicine use, which includes management of the approved medicine list or hospital formulary, ongoing drug use review, adverse drug event reporting and implementation of safe medication practices. Members of the PTC should include representatives from the medical pharmacy and nursing staffs, hospital administrators and the quality assurance coordinator.

Pharmaceuticals are an integral part of patient care thus appropriate use of the medicines in the hospital is the multidisciplinary responsibility shared by physicians, pharmacist, nurses, administrators, support personnel, and patients.

HOSPITAL FORMULARY

2.1 HOSPITAL FORMULARY

A hospital formulary is a compendium of prescribable medicines, and other information, which reflect the clinical judgment of the hospital's medical staff. The formulary is continually updated keeping in view the inference-based opinions of physicians, surgeons, diagnosticians, pharmacists, and other experts concerned with the treatment of disease. A therapeutic committee compiles the formulary.

The committee evaluates, appraises and selects from among the numerous available drugs, both generic and branded, those pharmaceuticals that will alleviate the suffering of the patients.

Drug Formulary System

The regular studies of toxicity, side effects, untoward manifestations, quality, efficiency and bioequivalence are the deciding factor in the selection of pharmaceuticals.

2.2 NEED FOR HOSPITAL FORMULARY

1. The pharmaceutical companies are increasingly manufacturing and marketing new drugs.
2. Increasing influence of advertisement, which includes scientific and unscientific drug literature
3. Increasing complexity of untoward effects of modern potent drugs: It is a sad commentary on the pharmaceutical industry that whenever they introduce a new product, they project its plus points, but protects its minus points—Side effects. The side effects sometimes are irreversible and cause incalculable damage to the patient. Old timers—medical practitioners—may be able to recall the irreversible damage caused to the auditory nerve after the prolonged use of Kanamycin. Woe betide the patients who consult doctors who are like omnivorous sharks for "FREEE SAMPLES NOT FOR SALE" but have little time to peruse the package insert inside the sample carton. The package insert of every product highlights the side effects.
4. Newer sales promotion strategies of the pharmaceutical industry.
5. The public interest in getting possible health care at the lowest possible cost.

2.3 BENEFITS OF DRUG FORMULARY SYSTEM

Therapeutic benefits

The therapeutic aspect of a formulary system provides the greatest benefit to the patient and physician because the most efficient products are listed and available.

Economic benefits
The formulary system eliminates inventory duplication and the opportunity for volume purchasing means lower charges to the patient.

Educational benefits
The educational benefit is also significant for the resident staff, nurses and medical students because many good formularies contain various prescribing tips and additional drug information of educational value.

Factors responsible for formulary system
Scientific and economic considerations that achieve appropriate, safe and cost effective drug therapy determine the formulary system.

Clinical considerations
Strength of scientific evidence and standards of practice that include, but are not limited are the guidelines of clinical decisions:
1. Assessing peer-reviewed medical literature, including, randomized clinical trials (especially drug comparison studies), pharmacoeconomic studies, and outcomes research data.
2. Employing published practice guidelines, developed by an acceptable evidence-based process.
3. Comparing the efficacy and frequency of side effects and potential drug interactions among alternative drug products
4. Assessing the likely impact of a drug compared to alternative products
5. Thorough evaluation of the benefits, risks and potential outcomes for patients; risks encompass adverse drug events (adverse drug reactions and medication errors, such as those caused by confusing product names or labels).

Economic considerations
1. Formulary system decisions on cost factors follow after a drug's safety, efficacy and therapeutic value is ascertained.
2. Evaluating drug products and therapies in terms of their impact on total health care costs.
3. Permitting financial incentives only when they promote cost management as part of the delivery of quality medical care. Financial incentives or pressures on practitioners that may interfere with the delivery of medically necessary care are unacceptable.

Guiding principles
The formulary system, when properly designed and implemented, can promote rational, clinically appropriate, safe, and cost-effective drug therapy. Following principals may serve as a guide to physicians, pharmacists and administrators in hospitals for their professional judgment:

The following principles will serve as a guide to physicians, pharmacist, nurses and administrators in hospitals and other facilities utilizing the formulary system.
1. The medical staff shall appoint a multidisciplinary pharmacy and therapeutics committee and outline its purposes, organisation, function and scope.
2. The medical staff should adopt the written policies and procedures governing the hospital formulary system. These policies and procedures

should afford guidance in all aspects dealing with drugs in the hospitals. Action of the medical staff is subject to the normal administrative approval process. These policies and procedures shall afford distribution, safe use and other matters relating to drugs, and inserted in the institution's formulary or other media available to all members of the medical staff.
3. Drugs should be included in the formulary by their nonproprietary names, even though proprietary names may be in common use in the institution.
4. The pharmacist shall be responsible for the specifications as to the quality, quantity, and source and supply of all the drugs, chemicals, biologicals and pharmaceutical preparations used in the diagnosis and treatment of patients.
5. The institutions shall make certain that its medical and nursing staff knows well about the existence of the formulary system, the procedures governing its operation, and any changes in those procedures. Copies of the formulary must be readily available and accessible at all times.
The pharmacist shall dispense the branded products as per the rules in the absence of written policies.
6. There will be a provision for the appraisal and use of drugs not included in the formulary.
7. The medical staff shall adopt written policies and procedures.
8. The hospital formulary system shall not contain any policies or procedures, which before the time of prescribing; provide the consent by the physician to the dispensing of non-proprietary drug or to the dispensing of a proprietary brand different from the brand he has prescribed.
9. Limiting the number of drug entities and drug products routinely available from the pharmacy can produce substantial patient care and financial benefits. The generic equivalents are as effective as the branded products with respect to their active components, e.g. two brands of tetracycline hydrochloride capsules, and therapeutic equivalents, two different antacid products or two different alkyl amine antihistamines. The pharmacy and therapeutic committee must set forth policies and procedures governing the dispensing of generics and therapeutic equivalents.

These policies and procedures should include the following points.
(a) The pharmacist is responsible for selecting from the available generic equivalents the medicine that doctor has prescribed.
(b) Based on pharmacologic and therapeutic considerations the prescriber prescribes the drug or generic options to the patient.
(c) The pharmacy and therapeutic committee is responsible for the products and determining those drug products and entities, which are drug's therapeutic equivalents, defined in unambiguous terms.

Content of formulary and its organisation
The primary objectives of the formulary are to provide the hospital staff with
1. Information on Pharmacy and Therapeutic Committee approved drugs.
2. Information on hospital policies and procedures governing the use of drugs
3. Basic therapeutic information about each approved item.
4. Special information about drugs such as drug dosage rules and monograms, hospital approved abbreviation.

Based on the above objectives the formulary should consist of the following three parts:

Information on hospital policies
1. Policies and procedures for drug usage and its restriction and for addition of the drug to the formulary.
2. Information on using the formulary including entries are arranged in the formulary, their information and the procedure for looking up a given drug product.
3. Pharmacy operating procedures like hours of services, outpatient prescription policies, prescription labeling and packaging practice, and patient education programme.
4. Brief description of PTC including its membership, responsibilities and operation.

Drug product information
This section comprises of the descriptive entries of each formulary item to facilitate the use of formulary.

Formulary item entry
Every entry should include the following information:
1. Generic name of the basic drug.
2. Brand names (common names).
3. Dosage forms, strength, packaging, size.
4. Formulation of combination product.
5. Route of administration, i.e. oral, parenteral, and the like.
6. Adult or pediatric dose.
7. Special instructions like how to use and store the product.
8. Cost information.

Special information
This section includes the material, which is useful to for hospital staff but varies from hospital to hospital.
1. Nutritional products list
2. List of hospital approved abbreviations
3. Tables of drug interaction
4. Metric conversion scales and tables
5. List of sugar free products
6. Rules for calculating pediatric dosages
7. Pharmacokinetic dosage and monitoring information
8. Number of items available for emergency boxes
9. Table of the sodium content of antacid
10. Poison control information.

2.4 PREPARATION OF FORMULARY

The preparation of the hospital formulary is the prime responsibility of the Pharmacy and Therapeutic Committee. The committee is free to make the necessary decisions relative to the materials to be included in the formulary and the pharmacists undertake the production aspects of the preparation. The initial step in the compilation of a formulary for any hospital irrespective of size, specialty or control is the selection of a competent Pharmacy and Therapeutic Committee. The physical appearance and structure of the formulary plays an important influence on its use but elaborate and expensive artwork is of no use, as it is meant for professional use so it should be virtually pleasing, easily readable with proper grammar, correct spelling and with neat designing.

A typical formulary will have the composition in the following manner:
1. Title page.
2. Names and titles of the members of pharmacy and therapeutic committee.
3. Contents.
4. Information on hospital policies and procedure concerning drugs.
    (a) The Pharmacy and Therapeutic Committee of hospital.
    (b) Objective and operation of formulary systems.
    (c) Hospital regulations and procedure for prescribing and dispensing drugs.
    (d) Hospital pharmacy services and procedures.
    (e) How to use the formulary.
5. Product accepted for use in hospital.

Items added and deleted from the previous addition.
    (a) Generic, brand name, cross-reference list.
    (b) Pharmacologic/therapeutic index with relative cost codes.
    (c) Descriptions of formulary drug products by pharmacologic therapeutic class.
6. Appendix
    (a) Central service equipment and supply list.
    (b) Guidelines for calculating pediatric dosage.
    (c) Schedule of standard drug administration.

Revision of formulary

Hospital formulary requires regular review and revision every year because the addition, deletion, changes in the product, removal of drugs from the market, changes in the hospital policies and procedures necessitates periodic revision. Entry of a new drug in the formulary is a complex procedure and the members are not competent enough to evaluate each therapeutic agent, thus PTC has framed certain guidelines for inclusion and deletion of drugs in the formulary. There should be definite system for revision of the formulary. One method is to attach formulary supplements sheets to the back covers of formulary books, and second method is by using different colors for the cover of each edition of the formulary, which will help reduce any confusion between current and past edition.

During preparation and revision of formulary system, cost effectiveness and cost benefit analysis methods are often used.

Distribution of the formulary

Each patient care unit like clinics and outpatient care departments such as emergency rooms should receive a copy of the formulary. Heads of the departments who are providing direct patient care, hospital administration and medical staff should get formulary free of cost. The pharmacy divisions such as in-patient and out-patient dispensing, drug information service too should get cost-free formulary. Administration should ensure that paramedical staff is familiar with the formulary and its usage.

Limitations of Hospital Formulary
1. The system may deprive the physician's right to prescribe and obtain the brand of his choice.
2. The system in many instances permits the pharmacists to purchase and dispense drugs of their own choice.
3. The system may allow purchase of inferior quality medicine where there is no staff pharmacist.
4. The systems do not minimize the cost of medicine to the patient by passing the discount or any scheme received at the time of purchase in bulk quantity by the hospital.

Legal Importance of the Formulary System

A written and signed prescription constitutes the only legal permit to fill a prescription. It is only the prescriber's prerogative to prescribe the brand or generic name. The pharmacist is only supposed to abide by the doctor's prescription. However, a pharmacist may dispense the drug, which in his professional judgment meets the therapeutic need without being liable. It is desirable for every hospital to adopt a formulary system, as it is a health practice and a good inventory control measure that provides a wide choice for the physicians to fulfill the needs of the patient. In such a system, a doctor prescribes, and the pharmacist fills the prescription. If for any reason the physician is not aware of the formulary, the pharmacist should inform him about the use of the drug from the formulary.

SUMMARY

The formulary today is a continually defined updated list of medications and related information, representing the clinical judgment of pharmacists, physicians and other experts in the diagnosis and treatment of diseases and promotion of health.

A therapeutic committee compiles the formulary. The committee evaluates, appraises and selects from among the numerous available drugs, both generic and branded, those pharmaceuticals that will alleviate the suffering of the patients.

Drug formulary system has various benefits such as therapeutic benefits (for patient and physician) economic benefits (eliminates inventory duplication) and educational benefits (additional information for staff and medical students).

The formulary system, when properly designed and implemented, can promote rational, clinically appropriate, safe, and cost-effective drug therapy. The various principles like appointing a multidisciplinary pharmacy and therapeutic committee, adopting written policies and procedures governing the hospital formulary system.

The development of formularies is based on evaluations of efficacy, safety, and cost-effectiveness of drugs. Depending on the individual formulary, it may also contain additional clinical information, such as side effects, contraindications, and doses. The primary objective of the formulary is to provide the information of PTC approved drugs, hospital policies and procedures and special information about drugs such as drug dosages rules and monograms and hospital approved abbreviations.

***

3

DRUG INFORMATION SERVICES

3.1 INTRODUCTION

In the profession of pharmacy, the unique knowledge base is the body of drug information that pharmacists use to define, monitor, and modify the drug therapy of the patients that the patient serves. Like other categories of scientific information, drug information is always changing. These changes reflect the development of new drugs, new uses for drugs, and new interpretations of existing information and include data that are used to establish and advance the practice of pharmacy. The pharmacist ought to be able to retrieve, analyze and communicate drug and professional practice information, if society were to benefit from the existence of the profession.

The effective management and the use of drug information are the most prominent features of any successful pharmacy practice. The collection, analysis, organization, indexing and hyperlinking are some of the prerequisites for better use of such information.

Drug information is the process of providing information on the safe and effective use of therapeutic and diagnostic pharmaceuticals along with the supply of accurate, current and unbiased drug information in the promotion of rational drug therapy. This service provides up to date and unbiased information regarding medicines and their use. For example, availability, price, substitutes, interactions, safety in pregnancy and lactation, side effects and their management, storage/ stability and transportation of drugs, etc.

The concept of drug information service or DIC is an attempt to document drugs by abstracting information about them. Drug information is the knowledge gathered either in from books, journals, periodicals or transmitted by oral communication.

3.2 NEED OF DRUG INFORMATION SERVICE

Generally, people have hardly any knowledge regarding proper use of medication. This lack of knowledge may become harmful as it may lead to aggravation of disease, more side effects, less compliance, and even increased cost of therapy. Various studies have shown that if patients discuss their therapy related problems and concerns with a drug expert—a pharmacist, it resulted in increased compliance and better treatment outcomes.

The DIC routinely responds to inquiries regarding appropriate therapy for specific patients:
- Adverse reactions to drugs.
- Efficacy of drugs;
- Drug interactions.
- Intravenous additive incompatibilities.
- Biopharmaceutical and pharmacokinetic parameters of drugs.
- Dosage in renal failure.
- Appropriate therapy for a disease state.
- Identification of foreign drugs.
- Information on investigational agents.
- Information on new drugs.

Objectives of DIC
- Describe the evolution of drug information.
- Define drug information and related terms.
- Describe the importance of drug information to the practice of pharmacy.
- Explain the need for drug information skills as a health care practitioner.
- Describe the essential components needed to develop drug information.
- Explain how drug information has changed and how the practice must change to meet future health care needs.

Types of DIC

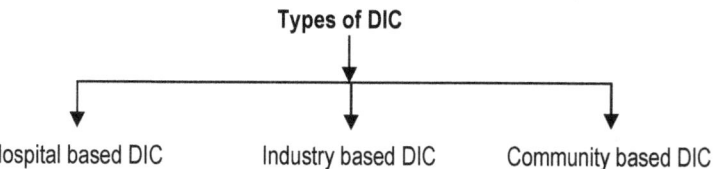

Qualification of the pharmacist to run DIC are:
1. To critically evaluate the drug literature.
2. To edit the information to facilitate decision making.
3. He should have good communication skills.
4. He should be computer literate.
5. He should be a member of PTC.
6. He should redefine his role and become an expert drug counselor from a mere drug dispenser.
7. He should have knowledge of research methodology.
8. He should be aware of the sources of information to enable him to collect secondary data.

Who Provides Information in a Hospital?

A specially trained drug information pharmacist is responsible for providing information. A pharmacist is a drug expert who can advise regarding safe and effective use of medication.
1. The proper name and indication of your medicine.
2. Benefit of taking your medicine regularly.

3. Hazards of missing frequent doses or quitting therapy against medical advice.
4. Precautions and must avoid situations with your medicine.
5. Dietary precautions.
6. Right time, right route, right dose, right frequency and right duration of taking your medicine.
7. Proper storage condition.
8. Proper disposal method.

Sources of drug information

These are those sources, which contain the original reports of scientific, technical or professional investigations. They contain recent and up to date information. Periodicals/ journals, serials, magazines, bulletins are published as issues and as volumes. They contain scientific information, research articles, review articles, book reviews.

Periodicals can be classified into:

- **Primary periodicals**
  They contain reports of original research.
- **Secondary periodicals**
  They contain that portion of original research, which is according to their needs in the condensed form.

Secondary sources

Pharmacopoeias or formularies are the books of standards and related articles with descriptions, tests and formulae for preparing the same, selected by some recognized authority. Collectively pharmacopoeias or formularies are referred as drug compendia.

Functions of DIC

Primary Functions

The primary function of a drug information centre is to respond to enquiries on therapeutic drug use. Most centers provide services to health professionals and some also offer service to the public.

1. **Drug Evaluation:** Assessment of therapeutic drugs is an important function of a drug information centre. The centre must have access to the principal medical and pharmaceutical journals. The staff should be capable of critically assessing medical literature, and information from industry and media sources. Critical analysis of published research includes an interpretation of the results in terms of relevance to local practice.
2. **Therapeutic Advice:** Many centers offer patient-related drug information as their primary activity. This requires an adequate understanding of disease states and therapy. It also requires access to appropriate resources for rapid support in situations where response time is an important factor in delivering optimum therapy. Therapeutic advice includes factors such as

efficacy, optimum dosage, interactions, adverse effects, mode of administration, effects of other disease states, and strategies to promote adherence in chronic conditions.

3. **Pharmaceutical Advice:** Most other enquiries will relate to pharmaceutical preparations generally and include issues of availability, formulation, cost, storage and stability.

4. **Education and Training:** Educational activities are important to support the quality use of drugs. Providing information to health professionals and the public is part of continuing health education. A drug information centre can also support national and regional authorities responsible for drug use programmes. Training graduates and undergraduates students are an important aspect of overall clinical training. Health care practitioners need to understand the scope and functions of drug information to utilize the services they offer.

5. **Dissemination of Information:** Drug information can be disseminated information in the form of drug monographs, bulletins and websites. Editorial skills are important for these functions. The International Society of Drug Bulletins (ISDB) runs training courses for editors and, together with WHO is preparing a manual for developing independent drug bulletins.

6. **Research:** Drug information centers should be involved in research activities including pharmacoepidemiology, e.g. drug utilization studies and pharmacovigilance. The nature of enquiries received can be used to plan educational programs within the centre or provided to organizations responsible for improving the quality of drug use. Specialists should also assess the quality and relevance of commonly used information resources.

Secondary Functions

1. **Pharmacovigilance:** Drug information centers often have a role in programmes which monitor adverse drug reactions. Enquiries about a potential adverse reaction can lead to reports of suspected reactions and research may be required to assess the likelihood that a drug has contributed to a reaction or for subsequent patient management. Some centers may serve as adverse drug reaction monitoring sites for hospitals or regions. Centers with regional responsibilities should be a member of the WHO Programme for International Drug Monitoring.

2. **Toxicology:** Most countries have one or more dedicated poisons information service. However, there may be economic or personnel advantages in combining a drug information service with a toxicology service.

Toxicology services provide information and piece of advice on the diagnosis and treatment of poisonings. Suitable information should be available to health professionals and the general public.

Personnel need to be specifically trained in toxicology. They ought to be able to respond to requests for information on the acute management of poisoning and know when to refer potentially severe cases.

Toxicology services are best located within hospitals where there is liaison with clinicians who treat patients with poisoning. This provides an opportunity for staff to enhance their clinical understanding of poisoning and its management.

A poisons information centre should also provide a public health service through educational programmes to reduce the incidence of poisoning. It should systematically collect data on the circumstances leading to poisonings and the outcome of specific cases. This can form the basis for research in the epidemiology of human toxicology.

3. Resources: Drug information centers should be organized on a cooperative model involving a multidisciplinary team, where possible, existing resources such as libraries, computers and databases should be used.

4. Personnel: The number of personnel required will depend on the range of activities offered and the hours of service. A centre should aim to provide a direct service during periods of major demand by its clients. For patient-related enquiries this is likely to be when clinic consultations occur and during peak periods for hospital functions.

The professional staff should include a full-time clinical pharmacist or a clinical pharmacologist. Clinical training and experience is essential for effective communication with clinicians. Other important attributes are computer skills, literature analysis, and editing and library management.

Management is an important component of a successful drug information centre. All pharmacists provide drug information services to some extent during dispensing and consultation services; however, a centre specializing in drug information requires coordination, monitoring and promotion.

The manager's responsibilities include:
- Establishing and maintaining a viable financial base.
- Staff recruitment and coordination.
- Training.
- Promoting the service.
- Identifying and maintaining appropriate resources.
- Data management and reporting.
- Quality assurance and improvement.
- Liaison with colleagues, professional organizations (e.g. FIP Pharmacy Information Section), networks, university departments of pharmacy practice, and government agencies
- Strategic development.

The manager of a drug information centre should have experience with service delivery as well as managerial skills. Medical and non-medical specialists may be required as additional resource personnel. As the centre expands, it may be necessary to include some of these specialists as advisers on a part-time basis. It is also necessary to have secretarial assistance and support staff for maintaining equipment and cleaning. There should be a career structure for all professional staff with the possibility of additional training and advancement. Twinning arrangements (*where two parties share experience and learn from one another*) between established centers and developing centers can facilitate the exchange of staff for education, training and sharing of experience.

Guidelines for setting up a DIC

A DIC is a valuable source of information pertaining to drugs. It is therefore the duty of hospital pharmacist to make the necessary arrangements for its proper functioning enabling it to function as a vibrant centre. The other health professionals are already overburdened and hence the pharmacy profession can well accept the challenge of setting up a drug information centre (DIC).

The following guidelines may be useful.

1. Professional and technical competence in the evaluation of critical selection and utilization of the drug literature will be a prerequisite. Information with a minimum volume of pertinent supporting documentation to permit independent, informed conclusions and decisions should be made available.
2. The knowledge of institutional and library facilities, literature utilization and library services will help in taking full advantage of all the resources available for this purpose.
3. Written and verbal communication skills, which enable to contribute effectively to intra- and inter-institutional dialogue regarding pharmaco-therapeutic information, are very important.
4. The capacity to contribute in education to all health professionals will be the duty of DIC in charge.
5. The DIC is involved directly and indirectly in patient care and acts as a monitor of its characteristics.
6. The DIC in charge should be familiar with electronics, should have basic computer literacy data processing methodology to the extent necessary for him to make use of its services to other health professionals.
7. The DIC should provide professional services to support the Pharmacy and Therapeutics Committee.

Although regional drug information services or networks are not very common, some of the goals of the regional network could be the development of a reproducible, standardized reporting system for auditing drug therapy, supplying of information to all hospitals. This facility could be the responsibility of the Government of India and have following objectives:

1. An analysis of drug information and drug therapy for critical ailments like heart disease, cancer, stroke and related diseases and provision of supply of this information to the physician.

2. A drug information abstract service to the physician in the region regarding new development in drug therapy in different diseases.
3. An analysis and evaluation of the regional utilization of drugs in the institutions served by the network and dissemination of this information to the respective medical staff.

Drug Information Bulletin

As communication of information to medical and paramedical staff is very essential, a Drug Information Centre should produce a bulletin and distribute it. The bulletin should provide new advancement in medicines, new researches, detailed analytical procedures, abstracts for new developments, etc. It forms a bridge between the information and application in clinical practice. It is the duty of the clinical pharmacist to provide information about drugs to all members of "Patient Care Team". The Bulletin should be updated with the latest developments from time to time.

Conclusion

1. Drug information is one of the essential services of health care professionals.
2. Providing drug information services is necessary for the survival of the pharmacy profession.
3. Drug Information Services help in effective and efficient drug therapy, whence a better patient care will be achieved.
4. Dissemination of information is still a problem; hence pharmacists should co-ordinate and work towards that goal.

3.3 DRUG INFORMATION CENTRE (DIC)

Drug information centre is a scientifically derived, documented and an independent body which provides information on drugs and health aspects. The centre provides unique opportunity for a pharmacist to contribute his role in health care development.

A Drug information centre comprises:

Texts and Databases

The centre should maintain its own library of commonly used resources. Additional books and other publications should be accessible in hardcopy or electronically from external sources.

Data can be extracted from textbooks, databases, data sheets, reports and scientific journals. Information from previous enquiries can also be used. An adequate literature search requires an understanding of available sources and their limitations, and training in the use of indexing terms and functions. Access to the full text of medical and pharmaceutical journals is necessary to assess the value and relevance of research.

Primary information sources provide unique data which have not been previously published. This includes the results of research studies and descriptions of unexpected clinical experience such as adverse drug reactions.

Primary, secondary, and tertiary information should be accessible and easier to apply to practice. Formats include literature reviews, databases and textbooks. The most appropriate type of information will depend on available resources and the time available for access. Many patient-related questions can be answered from basic textbooks. General questions of optimum drug use or safety will require access to primary sources.

Facilities

Basic equipment required for a centre includes:
- Furniture—desks, chairs, shelves;
- Communications —telephones, facsimile, internet access;
- Computers: including external data backup, printer;
- Software for word processing, spreadsheets, databases and presentations
- Photocopier
- Textbooks and electronic information resources.

Finance

A drug information centre should have an independent source of income and status guaranteeing its stability and objectivity. Funding from external organizations cannot be accepted unless the centre's neutrality is guaranteed. Financial support from the pharmaceutical industry or other groups which could represent a potential conflict of interest will tend to undermine a centre's reputation for independent analysis and advice.

Services should be provided free of charge to enquirers or through a contract arrangement which does not discourage appropriate use of the service to support quality healthcare. Separate charges may be made for specific reports which do not directly relate to individual patient care.

Capital equipment and management costs should be included in the budget. Sufficient expenditure to maintain up to date resources is essential for the long-term viability of the centre.

Training

Specific training is required for drug information practice. In addition to clinical knowledge and experience, drug information practitioners should be well versed in:
- Communication skills to receive and comprehend enquiries.
- Knowledge of all available resources.
- Literature searching skills.
- Capacity for critical analysis.
- Writing skills.
- Ability to summarize complex or conflicting data.

Quality Assurance

The activities of the drug information centre should be carefully documented. Standard forms or electronic databases can facilitate recording of enquiries. An effective retrieval system is essential to locate previous enquiries, monitor workload and categorize the types of enquiries received. It can also facilitate quality assurance programmes based on analysis of selected enquiries and failed deadlines. The recording process should provide secure, long-term storage and the confidentiality of enquirers should be respected.

Drug information centers have a responsibility to provide the highest possible standard of service. This will include an assessment of staff, regular review of calls taken, and answers provided besides periodic review of resources and procedures. The process should continuously identify potential improvements and document progress towards implementation.

Direct output can be monitored through peer review of enquiries. A random selection of enquiries can be regularly reviewed and feedback sought from enquirers. Where possible, the peer review process should include comments from one or more external experts, e.g. a drug information pharmacist or clinical pharmacologist.

Networking

Cooperation between drug information centers can help to optimize limited resources and enhance overall service levels. Networking can involve two or more centers, and includes regional, national and international links. Networks provide opportunities for:

- Sharing resources and experience.
- Establishing standard operating procedures.
- Quality assurance programs with external review.
- Interstice training.
- Increased awareness of practice in different locations and cultures.

Retrieval of Information

A computer is an electronic device consisting of various components like key board, CPU, VDU (Visual Display Unit), printer and mouse etc. wherein most activities follow the basic principle of Input process Cycle (IPO cycle). This can be best illustrated by an example of registration in hospitals. A person who wishes to see a senior doctor has to fill a request slip. This slip contains the relevant data, i.e., name, age, gender, etc. The operator then enters this data from the request slips into the computer. The process in this case includes examining the availability of a senior doctor and determining whether the data suits to the patient or not. As a result of this process, information is provided as output. The output may be in the form of a printed performa, if the senior doctor is available or otherwise a message may be issued by the computer turning down the request.

In hospitals, management of data is essential for effective retrieval of information. Data management involves creating; modifying, deleting and adding data in reports are shared by many doctors for further investigations as they are connected through various personal computers. Some popular database management system packages for personal computers are:

Dbase III+

FOX BASE+

Various steps involved in creating a database

Specifying the database file structure, i.e., specifying
- File name
- Field name
- Field type
- Field width

Saving the data base structure

Entering data into the files as records

Computerization of narcotics and other controlled substances may help in preventing excessive supplies and unauthorized dispensing of such drugs. The specific identification codes are given to authorized person. The drug control authorities are directly linked through computers and are able to trace quickly the erring employees. The programmes used for this purpose is DAWN (Drug Abuse Warning Network)

Role of computers in pharmacy

1. **Communication:** Computers are used within pharmacies to facilitate communication. From email to other Internet-based messaging systems, online communication allows pharmacists and other pharmacy staff to keep in contact both within their own organisation and within the professional community. Some pharmacy companies have their own Intranet systems for internal communications over the internet.

2. **Prescription Processing:** Prescription processing is invariably one of the main activities going on within a pharmacy on a day to day basis, and computers are used to make this process more reliable and efficient. Both the customer service side of pharmacy operation and the dispensing aspect are today carried out through the use of computing systems. Pharmacy computers also handle customer service activities such as sales and cash handling within the retail operation.

3. **Information:** Having access to the web via pharmacy computers is something that has enhanced the ability of pharmacists to carry out their duties to a higher standard besides giving the pharmacy staff access to the vast store of information that is available on the Internet, including those on specialist pharmacy resources; the Internet connects pharmacists to their peers on a global scale. Professional communities for pharmacists operate online, creating an atmosphere that is conducive to professional development.

4. **Database:** Various records like patient's medication history, current treatment, and financial records, etc. are maintained in computers by feeding accurate data. Data is a collection of facts. Computer works as a database manager."MEDLINE" is a database package used for such purpose. It gives the

current information of the patient regarding patient's name, age, gender; room number, weight, allergies (in past); diagnosis, and special precautions to be taken for the patient. These records such as physician's name, file, direction file, drug interaction file, etc are stored in a FILE. File contains physician's name, registration number, phone number, address. Computers store all the information (records) in FILES and make them available whenever required.

Computer databases for information about medicines, and medical treatment in general, are used within pharmacies. These database systems allow pharmacy staff to find out information about any potential conflicts or health care problems in a prescribed treatment, as well as information about the details of any particular medicine the pharmacist needs to know about. This information may include ingredients and potential effects as well as research and scientific data.

5. Error Prevention: Pharmacy computer systems can help to prevent errors in medication, potentially saving lives and generally preserving the health of patients. Along with checking medicines and combinations of medicines, these systems can check on patient information. The availability of such systems varies across the different geographical areas, but in some cases pharmacy computers are able to check on prescribed medicines with specific reference to a patient and their overall health care picture.

6. Inventory Control: Inventory control is very essential because it maintains the balance between stock in hand and excessive capital investment. Computers are used to find out the items which had attained minimum order level. It then prepares a list and purchase orders for suppliers. Generally, there are two systems for inventory control:

(i) **Periodic inventory control system:** In this system, stock levels are checked manually and the amount of inventory in hand is compared with minimum and maximum stock maintained in the computers. Computer helps in placement of orders to different suppliers after checking their terms and conditions because all the entries of stocks are present in it.

(ii) **Perpetual System:** In this system the computer tells us about the present position of all the drugs because when they are received, they are entered in the initial stocks to get the current stocks. As the drugs are delivered to various departments the quantities are subtracted accordingly. Such type of additions and subtractions from inventory balance are done with the help of database package.

7. Hospital Pharmacy and Retail Pharmacy: Computers help hospital pharmacists in recording overall patient care like maintenance of patient's record, entry of prescription, list of preparations to be manufactured; consumption of drugs, cost analysis, updating of drug information etc. for proper functioning of a hospital. Computers in a hospital pharmacy department should be linked to nursing stations, testing laboratories, registration counters; accounts and purchase section, and the like.

For a retail pharmacist, computers are of valuable assistance in the prescription processing. It includes display of computer information about patient and drug, its adverse drug reaction, caution, duplication of orders, labeling condition etc.

8. Formulary search and update: The record of approved drugs is maintained in a file. The computer system should be capable of displaying all drugs by descriptors code, therapeutic category or generic name.

9. Marketing and Distribution: Computers are used for marketing and distribution of drugs. It involves processing of orders, invoicing, maintenance of records, billing, etc.

10. Pharmaceutical Industries: Complete computerized programmes are available for drug manufacture and for quality control management. Information for the beginning of the process and for the finished product is available. Comparative evaluation is done for various products with the help of computers. Various instruments and apparatuses can be adjusted and calibrated using computers.

The concept of drug information service or DIC is an attempt to document drugs by abstracting information about them. Drug information is the knowledge either gathered from books, journals, periodicals or transmitted by oral communication.

3.4 MEDICATION ERRORS

A medication error is a preventable event that may cause or lead to inappropriate medication use while the medication is in the control of the health care professional, patient, or consumer.

Such events may be related to professional practice, health care products, producers and systems; including prescribing, order communication product labelling, packaging and nomenclature; compounding, dispensing, distribution, administration, education, monitoring, and use.

Most medication errors are considered latent. For example, when a pharmacist fills a prescription with the incorrect medication, patients realize the mistake after they have returned home and taken the first dose. Latent errors can be described as *"accidents waiting to happen"*.

The causes of these types of errors are usually identifiable and can be corrected before the error reoccurs.

1. Incomplete patient information (not knowing about patients' allergies, other medicines they are taking, previous diagnoses, and lab results for example).
2. Unavailable drug information (such as lack of up to date warnings).
3. Miscommunication of drugs orders, which can involve poor handwriting, confusion between drugs with similar names, misuse of zeroes and decimal points, confusion of metric and other dosing units, and inappropriate abbreviations.
4. Lack of appropriate labelling as a drug is prepared and repackaged into smaller units.

5. Environmental factors, such as lighting, heat, noise, and interruptions that can distract health professionals from their medical tasks.

Dispensing Errors

Dispensing errors are a consequence of misinterpretation of doctor's prescription and inaccurate calculation of doses, especially in children. Dispensing error refers to medication errors linked to the pharmacy and includes error of commission (dispensing the wrong drug or dose) and those of omission (failure to counsel on safe use of medicine). Most dispensing errors involve the dispensing of an incorrect medication, dosage strength or dosage form. Look alike and sound alike drug often cause confusion with ineligible prescriptions or verbal medication orders.

Causes for errors

A data report indicates that pharmacists perceived the following as causative factors for medication errors:
- Overload/ unusually busy day.
- No one available to double check.
- Staff shortage.
- Similar drug names.
- Illegible prescription.
- Misinterpreted prescription.

Common types of medication errors

The Institute for Safe Medication Practices (ISMP) identifies the following areas as potential causes of medication errors.
1. Failed communication: handwriting and oral communications, especially over the telephone, drugs with similar names, missing or misplaced zeroes and decimal points, confusion between metric and apothecary systems of measure, use of nonstandard abbreviations ambiguous or incomplete orders.
2. Poor drug distribution practices.
3. Workplace environmental problems increasing the job stress.
4. Complex or poorly designed technology.
5. Access to drugs by non-pharmacy personnel.
6. Dose miscalculations.
7. Lack of information to prescribers.
8. Lack of patient information.
9. Lack of patients' understanding of their therapy.

Medication error rate

Medication error rate is determined by calculating the percentage of errors. The numerator in the ratio is the total number of errors that they observe, the denominator is called opportunities for errors and includes all the doses observed and administered plus the doses ordered but not administered. The equation for calculating a medication error rate is as follows:

$$\text{Medication Error Rate} = \frac{\text{Number of Errors Observed}}{\text{Opportunities for Errors}} \times 100$$

Opportunities for Errors

Medication error rate (MER) A-medication error rate of 05 per cent

The National Coordinating Council for Medication Error Reporting and Prevention and Institute for Safe Medication Practices emphasizes that illegibility of prescriptions and medication orders has resulted in injuries to deaths of patients.

The following recommendations help to minimize errors

1. The Institute for Safe Medication Practices suggests a number of error prevention tools ranging from forcing functions to independent double-check systems. Prescription orders should include a brief notation of purpose (e.g. for cough), unless considered inappropriate by the prescriber. Notation of purpose can further assure that the proper medication is dispensed and creates an extra safety check in the process of prescribing and dispensing a medication Independent double-check systems can reduce the risk of error by way of having one person independently check another's work. When this procedure is properly carried out, the likelihood that two individuals would make the same error with the same medication for the same patient is insignificant.

2. Forcing functions and constraints they allow for designing processes to ensure that errors are virtually impossible or at least difficult to make. Examples include software programmes with forcing functions that require the entry of additional pertinent patient information before the order is completed and the medication is dispensed. Automation and computerization of medication use processes, and tasks can reduce human fallibility by limiting reliance on memory. Examples include use of technologically and clinically sound computerized drug information system.

3. All prescription orders should be written in the metric system except for therapies that use standard units such as insulin, vitamins, etc. Units should be spelled out rather than writing "U". The change to the use of the metric systems from the archaic apothecary and avoirdupois systems will help avoid misinterpretations of these abbreviations and symbols, and miscalculations when converting to metric, which is used in product labelling and package inserts.

4. Prescribers should include age, and when appropriate, weight of the patient on the prescription or medication order. The most common errors in dosage result in pediatric and geriatric populations wherein low body weight is common. The age and weight of a patient can help dispensing health care professionals in their double-check of the appropriate drug and dose.

5. The order should include drug name, exact metric weight or concentration, and dosage form. Strength should be expressed in metric amounts and concentration should be specified. Each order for a medication should be complete. The pharmacist should check with the prescriber if any information is missing or questionable.

6. A leading zero should always precede a decimal expression of less than one. A terminal or trailing zero should never be used after a decimal. Ten fold errors in drug strength and dosage have occurred with decimals due to the use of a trailing zero or the absence of a leading zero.
7. Prescribers should avoid use of abbreviations including those for drug names (e.g., MOM, HCTZ) and Latin directions for use.

A selective guide to drug information sources
Aids clinical trials information service

(http://www.actis.org/; this is the website of the US Department of Health and Human Services

Center Watch Drug Directories

(http://www.centerwatch.com/patient/drugs/drugdirectories.html)

This source calls itself "The information source for the clinical trials industry."

The following three drug directories from this site are extremely helpful
Drugs approved by the FDA

(http://www.centerwatch.com/patient/drugs/druglist.html)

This section can be searched by year and a medical specialty, such as cardiology.

Drugs Currently in Clinical Research

(http://www.centerwatch.com/patient/cwpipeline/default.asp)

According to the company, this site contains: A listing of 2,000 active drugs in Phase I – Phase III trials are profiled sometimes including NDA submissions and withdrawals. Each summary contains information about the new treatment: the branded and generic name of the new therapy, the company sponsoring the research, and the phase of the clinical trials. It can be searched by medical condition.

Clinical Trials Results Database

(http://www.centerwatch.com/patient/results/default.asp)

The information from this website dates back to May 2000 and is updated weekly. It is compiled from published materials from medical conferences, journals, and company reports. The clinical trial result summaries typically include the name and phase of the new therapy, the company sponsoring the research, a description of the trial design, and information on how well the drug has performed.

Clinical Trials.gov

(http://clinicaltrials.gov/)

ClinicalTrials.gov: this website provides patients, family members, health care professionals, and members of the public easy access to information on clinical trials for a wide range of diseases and conditions, achieved through a collaborative effort of NIH, NLM, and the FDA.

DrugTopics.com

(http://www.drugtopics.com/be_core/d/index.jsp)

The online news magazine for pharmacists

Food and Drug Administration (FDA)—main website with news and more

(http://www.fda.gov/)

This website includes news, product reports, and safety alerts for all FDA-regulated products.

FDA/Center for Drug Evaluation and Research (CDER)

(http://www.fda.gov/cder/)

According to their Web site, CDER serves as a consumer watchdog by evaluating new drugs before they are marketed. Their goal is to ensure that prescription and over the counter drugs (brand name and generic) work correctly and that their health benefits outweigh the known risks. Three sections of special interest on the site are:

New and Generic Drug Approvals

(http://www.fda.gov/cder/approval/index.htm)

This is an alphabetical listing of all prescription drugs approved during 1998 through 2001. It is updated on daily basis and contains links to labels, approval letters, and reviews.

FDA Drug Approvals List

(http://www.fda.gov/cder/da/da.htm)

This is a reverse chronological listing of all drugs approved since September 1996. It is updated on a weekly basis.

Electronic Orange Book—Approved Drug Products with Therapeutic Equivalence Evaluations

(http://www.fda.gov/cder/ob/default.htm)

Allows searching by Active Ingredient, Applicant Holder, Proprietary Name, and Application Number

FDA Enforcement Report Index

(http://www.fda.gov/opacom/Enforce.html)

It is a weekly report that contains information on actions taken in connection with agency regulatory activities.

FDA—Med Watch

(http://www.fda.gov/medwatch/safety)

This site provides FDA safety information and adverse event reporting programmes.

The Institute for Safe Medication Practices

(http://www.ismp.org/)

A non-profit organization that works closely with health care practitioners and institutions, regulatory agencies, professional organizations and the pharmaceutical industry to provide education about adverse drug events and their prevention. The Institute provides an independent review of medication errors that voluntarily submitted by practitioners to a National Medication Errors Reporting Program (MERP) operated by the United States Pharmacopeia (USP) in the USA. Information from the reports may be used by USP to impact on drug standards. All information derived from the MERP is shared with the US Food and Drug Administration (FDA) and the pharmaceutical companies whose products are mentioned in reports.

Mosby's GenRx Top 200 Most Prescribed Drugs (ranked by sales volume)

(http://www.genrx.com/genrxfree/Top_200_2000/Top_200_2000.html)

Includes information about each drug listed.

NIH Clinical Alerts and Advisories

(http://www.nlm.nih.gov/databases/alerts/clinical_alerts.html)

Clinical alerts are provided to expedite the release of findings from the NIH funded clinical trials where such release could significantly affect morbidity and mortality.

Databases for Drug and Chemical Information

Biological Abstracts (BIOSIS)

Nearly 6,000 international journals are monitored for inclusion, representing virtually every life science discipline such as agriculture, biochemistry, biotechnology; ecology, immunology, microbiology; neuroscience, pharmacology, public health, and toxicology.

ChemID and ChemIDPlus National Library of Medicine, producer

It is a chemical dictionary file for over 340,000 compounds of biomedical and regulatory interest.

EMBASE Elsevier, producer. It is an index of the biomedical literature with Depth of indexing than MEDLINE, unique Western

European journal coverage and coverage of drug research EMBASE searches available upon request to the Uva Health Sciences Librarians.

MEDLINE National Library of Medicine, producer. Available to search through the Pub Med, Ovid, and MDConsult search interfaces.

Ovid MEDLINE Search Guide (PDF)

(http://www.med.virginia.edu/hs -library/info_serv/edserv/guides/7steps.pdf)

More MEDLINE Search Tips (PDF)

(http://www.med.virginia.edu/hs -library/info_serv/edserv/guides/tips.pdf)

Pub Med Search Tutorial

(http://www.nlm.nih.gov/bsd/pubmed_tutorial/m1001.html)

PREMEDLINE National Library of Medicine, producer. The in-process" database for MEDLINE, PREMEDLINE provides basic information and abstracts before a record is indexed with MeSH heading(s) and added to MEDLINE. New records are added daily* to PREMEDLINE. After MeSH terms, publication types, GenBank accession numbers, and other indexing data are incorporated into a PREMEDLINE record; the completed citation is added to MEDLINE. Completed PREMEDLINE records are added as citations to MEDLINE on a weekly basis.

OLDMEDLINE National Library of Medicine, producer. Contains citations published in the 1958–1965 *Cumulated Index Medicus* and covers the fields of medicine, preclinical sciences, and allied health sciences. OLDMEDLINE is only available through the NLM Gateway.

MICROMEDEX Thompson Healthcare, producer. It comprises peer-reviewed full-text drug information. It consists of several databases that can be searched separately or through an integrated index. These databases allow you to search for summaries and detailed monographs for drugs, alternative medicine, toxicological managements, reproductive risks, and acute/emergency care.

Toxline National Library of Medicine, producer. This database provides toxicological, pharmacological, biochemical, and physiological effects of drugs and other chemicals.

TOXNE National Library of Medicine, producer; it Consists of a computerized collection of data and reference files on toxicology, hazardous chemicals, and related subjects. The records are derived from about 16 secondary sources that do not require royalty charges based on usage. Entering free text terms as they appear in titles, keywords, and abstracts of articles will retrieve citations. The portions of the database derived from MEDLINE, DART, and that portion of BIOSIS added since August 1985, may be searched using MeSH vocabulary. Chemical substances can be searched by entering their corresponding CAS Registry Numbers and/or synonyms.

Web of Science, *aka* **Science Citation Index** Institute for Scientific Information, producer, which provides a citation index of more than 5,700 major journals covering 164 scientific disciplines, 1,700 social sciences journals, and 1,100 arts and humanities journals; it is updated weekly. It finds papers that have cited a primary paper.

Search Guide (PDF)

(http://www.med.virginia.edu/hs -library/info_serv/edserv/guides/wos.pdf).

SUMMARY

Drug information is the process of providing information on the safe and effective use of therapeutic and diagnostic pharmaceuticals along with the supply of accurate, current and unbiased drug information in the promotion of rational drug therapy. This service provides up to date and unbiased information regarding medicines and their use e.g. availability, price, substitutes, interactions, safety in pregnancy and lactation, side effects and their management, storage/ stability and transportation of drugs, etc. Drug information is the knowledge gathered either in from books, journals, periodicals or transmitted by oral communication.

Drug information service or DIC is of three types, hospital based DIC, Industry based DIC and community based DIC. Sources of DIC include original reports of scientific, technical and professional investigations and can be classified into primary periodicals which include original research and secondary periodicals which include portion of original research according to their needs. Secondary sources include pharmacopoeias or formularies or standard books.

Functions of DIC can be divided into two i.e. primary and secondary functions. Primary functions include drug evaluation, therapeutic advice, pharmaceutical advice, education and training, dissemination of information and research whereas secondary functions include pharmacovigilance, toxicology, resources and personnel aspects.

Various guidelines are required for setting up the DIC such as, professional and technical competence in the evaluation of critical selection and utilization of the drug literature will be a prerequisite. The information with a minimum volume of pertinent supporting documentation to permit independent, informed conclusions and decisions should be made available, knowledge of institutional and library facilities, literature utilization and library services will help in taking full advantage of all the resources available for this purpose, written and verbal communication skills, which enable to contribute effectively to intra- and inter-institutional dialogue regarding pharmacotherapeutic information, are very important.

Computers are used within the pharmacy to facilitate communication, prescription processing, information database, error prevention, inventory control pharmacy, perpetual system, hospital pharmacy and retail pharmacy and marketing and distribution with pharmaceutical industries.

A medication error is preventable event that may cause or lead to inappropriate medication use while the medication is in the control of the health care professional, patient, or consumer. Dispensing errors are a consequence of misinterpretation of doctor's prescription and inaccurate calculation of doses, especially in children. Dispensing error refers to medication errors linked to the pharmacy and includes error of commission (dispensing the wrong drug or dose) and those of omission (failure to counsel on safe use of medicine). Medication error rate is determined by calculating the percentage of errors.

Medication error rate can be minimized forcing functions and constraints for designing processes to ensure that errors are virtually impossible or at least difficult to make. Examples include software programmes with forcing functions that require the entry of additional pertinent patient information before the order is completed and the medication is dispensed. Automation and computerization of medication use processes, and tasks can reduce human fallibility by limiting reliance on memory. The order should include drug name, exact metric weight or concentration, and dosage form. Strength should be expressed in metric amounts and concentration should be specified. Each order for a medication should be complete. The pharmacist should check with the prescriber if any information is missing or questionable.

✳✳✳

4

NUCLEAR PHARMACY

4.1 INTRODUCTION

Nuclear pharmacy is a developing branch of pharmacy which deals with the preparation, quality control and dispensing of radiopharmaceuticals. Like a traditional pharmacy, nuclear pharmacy also fills the prescription, processes the orders, and maintains the records of inventory and dispensing of radiopharmaceuticals.

Radiopharmaceuticals

Radiopharmaceuticals are radioactive pharmaceuticals used in nuclear medicine. These drugs are made up of two components; a radioactive isotope, and a carrier molecule: radioactive isotope can be injected safely into the body while the carrier molecule delivers the isotope to the site of treatment or examination. For example, Thallium-201 is used for cardiac stress tests. Other common nuclear components in radiopharmaceuticals include indium-111, gallium-67, iodine-123, iodine-131 and venom-133.

Radionuclide

A radionuclide is an atom with an unstable nucleus, which is a nucleus characterized by excess energy available to be imparted either to a newly created radiation particle within the nucleus or to an atomic electron. Radionuclide occurs naturally and can also be artificially produced; e.g., naturally occurring Uranium and thorium.

Mass number

It is the total number of protons and neutrons in the nucleus. Due to the variation in the number of neutrons, the atoms of particular elements can have different mass numbers.

Isotopes

The nuclides having the same atomic number but different mass numbers are called isotopes and they vary in the number of neutrons in the nucleus. There are three isotopes of hydrogen, $_1H$, ^2_1H, ^3_1H.

Units of radioactivity

The fundamental unit of radioactivity is "curie" (IC). It is defined as the amount of radioactive substance which undergoes disintegration at the rate of 3.7×10^{10} per second and this amount 01 gm of radium which undergoes 03.7×10^{10} disintegration per second. Consequently subunits of curie like mili curie and micro curie. They are the amounts of radioactive material wherein the number of disintegrations per second are 03.7×10^7 and 03.7×10^4 respectively.

4.2 CLASSIFICATION OF ISOTOPES

Generally isotopes can be categorized as given below:

1. **Stable isotope:** Stable isotopes are chemical isotopes that may or may not be radioactive, but if radioactive, have half-life too long to be measured.

2. **Unstable isotopes/radioactive isotopes:** Whenever a radioactive isotope decays, it undergoes radioactive decay, and emits γ ray(s) and/or subatomic particles. These particles constitute ionizing radiation.

   (i) **α-particles:** α-particles consist of two protons and two neutrons bound together into a particle identical to a helium nucleus. They are heavy and positively charged. They are least penetrating; their range is fraction of mm of body tissues. They are not used in pharmaceutical preparations.

   (ii) **β-particles:** β-particles are high energy, high speed electrons or positrons emitted by certain types of radioactive nuclei such as potassium-40. The β-particles emitted are a form of ionizing radiation also known as β-rays. The production of β-particles is termed β-decay. β-particles can be used to treat health conditions such as eye and bone cancer, and are also used as tracers. Strontium-90 is the material most commonly used to produce β-particles.

   (iii) **γ-radiation** is a packet of electromagnetic energy—a photon. γ-Photons are the most energetic photons in the electromagnetic spectrum. γ-photons have no mass and no electrical charge and high electromagnetic energy gives them excellent penetrating power through human tissues. Penetration power of γ-rays is 10,000 times more than α- particles and 100 times more than β-particles.

3. **Radioactive Half Life:** Half-life may be defined as the time required for any radioactive isotope to decay to one half of the original value at any given point of time. It is denoted by $t_{1/2}$. Half-life of radio pharmaceuticals must be taken into consideration while calculating the dose and rate of decay of radio pharmaceuticals.

Radioactive nuclei involve release of α, β and γ- rays depending upon the degree of instability of their nuclei. This process of disintegration of radioactive nuclei is a continuous process and due to spontaneous decay, the activity of any radioactive sample diminishes with time. The rate of radioactive decay is constant and characteristic for each individual radionuclide. The exponential decay curve is described mathematically by the equation:

$$N = N_o e^{-\lambda t}$$

The half-life period is related to the disintegration constant by the equation:

$$T_{1/2} = 0.693/\lambda$$

N is the number of atoms at elapsed time t
No is the number of atoms when t = 0
Λ is the disintegration constant characteristic of each individual radionuclide

4.3 RADIOPHARMACEUTICAL PREPARATION

A radiopharmaceutical preparation is a medicinal product in a ready-to-use form suitable for human use that contains a radionuclide. The radionuclide is integral to the medicinal application of the preparation, making it appropriate for one or more diagnostic or therapeutic applications. Some particulate radiopharmaceuticals achieve site-specific localization of radioactivity in the body. These specialized dosage forms permit imaging of the principal organs of the reticuloendothelial system (liver, spleen, and bone marrow) with radio labelled colloidal particles, the cardiac blood pool with radio labelled red blood cells, and lung perfusion with albumin aggregates.

Radioisotopes may be used internally or externally. If the radioisotopes are used externally or as implants in sealed capsules in a tissue, the dose could be terminated by removal of the sources. If they are given internally as unsealed source, the dose cannot be stopped by removal of the source. The total dose in therapeutic applications may be calculated on the basis of effective half-life of the isotope, concentration of the isotope and the type and energy of radiation emitted.

Preparation of radiopharmaceutical include following steps

1. **Radionuclide generator:** A system in which a daughter radionuclide (short half-life) is separated by elution or by other means from a parent radionuclide (long half-life) and later used for production of a radiopharmaceutical preparation.
2. **Radiopharmaceutical precursor:** A radionuclide produced for the radiolabelling process with a resultant radiopharmaceutical preparation.

Kit for radiopharmaceutical preparation

In general, a kit is a vial containing the non-radionuclide components of a radiopharmaceutical preparation, usually in the form of a sterilized, validated product whereto the appropriate radionuclide is added or in which the appropriate radionuclide is diluted before medical use. In most cases the kit is a multidisc vial and production of the radiopharmaceutical preparation may require additional steps such as boiling, heating, filtration and buffering. Radiopharmaceutical preparations derived from kits are normally intended for use within 12 hours of preparation.

Therapeutic Radiopharmaceuticals

Therapeutic radiopharmaceuticals are radio labelled molecules designed to deliver therapeutic doses of ionizing radiation to specific diseased sites. Therapeutic applications of radiopharmaceuticals have emerged from the concept that certain radionuclide possessing particulate emission such as α and β-radiations or low-energy low-range electrons (Auger electrons) possess the ability to destroy diseased tissues.

4.4 PRODUCTION OF RADIOPHARMACEUTICAL

Production of a radiopharmaceutical involves two processes:
1. The production of the radionuclide on which the pharmaceutical is based.
2. The preparation and packaging of the complete radiopharmaceutical.
3. Radionuclide used in radiopharmaceuticals are mostly radioactive isotopes of elements with atomic numbers less than that of bismuth, that is, they are radioactive isotopes of elements that also have one or more stable isotopes. These are dichotomized into two classes:
4. Those with fewer neutrons in the nucleus to those required for stability are known as neutron-deficient and tend to be most easily produced using a proton accelerator such as a medical cyclotron.
5. Those with excess neutrons in the nucleus to those required for stability are known as proton-deficient, and tend to be most easily produced in a nuclear reactor.

4.5 METHODS OF PRODUCTION OF ARTIFICIAL RADIONUCLIDES

1. Cyclotron produced radionuclide

The cyclotron and similar particle accelerators can be used only with charged particles such as electrons, protons and deuterons. This is because; the operation of such machines depends upon the interaction of magnetic and electrostatic fields with the charge of particles undergoing acceleration. A beam of charged particles is produced by accelerating ions around a widening circle using magnetic field for control and electric current for acceleration. Various separation techniques are available to separate the product from target. It is required that chemical forms of the target and the product must be different to effect separation. It includes production of position emitting isotope such as C, N, O and F. Cyclotron yield is dependent upon number of target atoms, energy of particles, decay of product after it is formed, length of irradiation and isotope enrichment of target.

2. Pile produced isotope

Most of the radioactive materials produced for the use in industry, academic research and medicines are produced in a nuclear pile (nuclear reactor). Uranium fission reaction produces a large supply of neutrons. Only neutrons of uranium atoms undergoing fission are used to sustain the reaction. The remaining neutrons are used either to produce plutonium or interact with specific substances, which have been inserted into the pile, the latter process being known as neutron activation. Production of ^{133}Xe, ^{99}Mo and ^{131}I is carried out by this method. These isotopes are produced by the nuclear power industry as waste products. Once they have been purified adequately, they are perfectly suitable for human use.

3. Thermal neutron reactor produced radioisotope

Radioisotopes used in nuclear medicine are by and large synthetic. For thermal neutron reactor produced radioisotopes, the reactor is a source of thermal neutrons. It causes increase of atomic weight by one and no change in atomic number. Same element is therefore present, e.g. ^{98}Mo after reaction produces ^{99}Mo. Reactor yield is dependent upon neutron flux in the reactor, nuclear capture cross section, number of target atoms, isotope enrichment of target, decay of product after it is formed and length of irradiation. The product of a reaction or other reactions may be described in terms of specific activity, i.e. radioactivity per unit mass of the element present. Efficient separation requires that chemical forms of element in the target and the product must be different.

The radio nuclides so produced are used in radiopharmaceuticals in the form of proper dosage forms. The physical form of radiopharmaceutical depends upon the type of study or characteristics of the organ. They can be in the form of gases, gases in solution, liquids, true solutions, colloidal solutions or suspensions, macro-aggregates, microspheres, emulsions, freeze dried solids and capsules.

4.6 PREPARATION OF RADIOISOTOPES IN LABORATORY

Preparation of radio isotopes in the laboratory should include the following special rooms:

1. **Dispensary:** Preparation of radioactive isotopes involves aseptic techniques; hence a well-designed and well-equipped aseptic laboratory is the primary requirement for their preparation.
2. **Counting room:** The counting room is a separate small laboratory and it should be far away from hot laboratory because sources of high activity can increase the background radiation in the counting room. It should have adequate ventilation, easily cleaned, non-absorbing surfaces and a liquid scintillation counter.
3. **Basic Radioisotope Work Areas**
    (a) **Fume Hood:** Routine use of a working fume hood will minimize the intake of radioactive materials. Plan to use the hood to avoid inhalation exposures. Use the fume hood for work with large activities (hundreds of micro curies to mill curie activities).
    (b) **Hot Sink:** Designate a sink to wash contaminated glassware.
    (c) **Hot Bench:** The hot-bench should be used for low activities, (on the order of micro curies or less).
    (d) **Sample Preparation area:** Designate an area on the bench for preparing samples for counting. Decontaminate the area frequently to avoid contaminating your counting equipment.

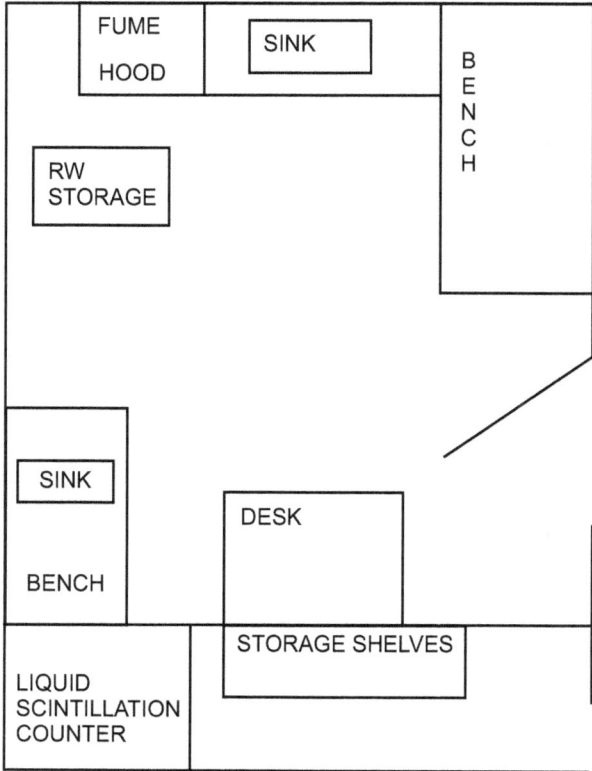

Fig. 4.1: Radioactive Isotope Laboratory

1. **Label containers:** Conspicuously label all radioactive materials and samples. Include the radioisotope, its activity, the date on which the activity was assayed, and its chemical form.
2. **Spill trays:** Use spill trays under any vessel or piece equipment which may leak, burst, or spill radioactive liquid.
3. **Contamination control:** Cover the bench and other work areas with absorbent coverings to confine contamination. Place a tray under the radioactive waste container.
4. **Store:** Radiopharmaceuticals should be kept in well-closed containers and stored in an area assigned for the purpose. The storage conditions should be such that the maximum radiation dose-rate to which persons may be exposed is reduced to an acceptable level.
5. **Annexed:** it is an area which includes changing, washing and monitoring facilities. It is called inactive area leading to the dispensing of the laboratory.

6. **Housekeeping:**
   - Clearly distinguish contaminated areas from uncontaminated areas.
   - Mark and label contaminated areas and items.
   - Minimize the build-up of contamination.
7. **Security:** All areas of the department in which radioactive materials are stored should be locked at all times except under the direct supervision of laboratory personnel.

Aseptic laboratory is an important area to be considered for dispensing isotopes. It should include following:

(a) Radioactive work areas should be defined by radioactive warning tape that displays the radiation warning symbol.
(b) All the surfaces should be smooth, non-porous and heat resistant.
(c) Flooring should be easily removable, e.g. waxed linoleum is very common.
(d) Each worker should be allocated proper floor space to minimize radiation hazard from the neighbouring worker.
(e) Laboratory coats must be worn.
(f) Radioactive work areas and waste trays ought to be covered with appropriate absorbent bench top covering. The absorbent side should face up.
(g) The covering should be changed at least once a week. Replace contaminated covering immediately.
(h) All waste must be retained in special receptacles.

Radiation dosimeter is an important parameter to be considered. Therefore, there need to be two separate areas.

Exposure dose: It refers to the quantity of harmful radiation in the ambience of area or the amount of radiation available with target material. The unit measurement for such radiation dosage is roentgen 'r'.

Absorbed dose: Roentgen Equivalent Man (REM) is commonly used to determine the doses received by those working with radioisotopes.

Dose in REM = Dose in RAD × Quality factor × Distribution factor

Where, RAD is the unit of absorbed dose.

4.7 THERAPEUTIC APPLICATION OF RADIOPHARMACEUTICALS

Radiopharmaceuticals are used in treatment of:

1. **Hyperthyroidism:** ^{131}I-iodine is used extensively for the treatment of hyperthyroidism. Upon oral administration of the radionuclide, approximately 60 per cent of the radioactivity is taken up by the overactive gland. The principal disadvantage of the radio-iodine therapy is the high

incidence of early and late hyperthyroidism, making it necessary to monitor patients adequately after treatment.

2. **Intracavitary Therapy:** Direct intracavitary administration is a means of delivering radiopharmaceuticals in high concentration to tumors that are spread out over the serosal linings of cavities and tumors cells present in malignant effusions. In order to minimize leakage of the radionuclide from the cavity, it is usually given in the form of a radionuclide. Intracavitary therapy is applied to the peritoneal, pleural and pericardial cavities as well as cystic brain tumors and to the spinal canal.

3. **Colloidal:** ^{198}Au was formerly the most widely used agent, but the radionuclide emits unwanted γ-radiation, leading to unnecessary exposure of non-target tissue within the patient and of other personnel. The agents of choice are now ^{32}P and ^{90}Y radiocollids, with perhaps radiolabel antibodies having a wider role to apply in the future.

4. **Bone tumour:** Bone metastases are a common finding in patients suffering from cancers of the prostate, breast and lungs, and in these patients control of bone pain is a significant clinical problem. In patients with breast and prostate carcinoma, bony metastases are usually multiple and in these, systemic administration of a therapeutic radiopharmaceutical provides the opportunity of a more specific and less toxic method of treating disseminated diseases. Several β-emitting radionuclide are used in the treatment of bone metastases. For example, ^{32}P and ^{89}Sr are commonly used.

5. **Neuroendocrine tumour:** With the development of new radiopharmaceuticals there is a tendency to apply nuclear medicine therapy for malignancies of higher incidence (lymphoma, prostate) than have been treated for many years (thyroid cancer, neuroendocrine tumors). One of the most important areas of current development in radionuclide cancer therapy is the immunotherapeutic use of new or already available radiopharmaceuticals in preclinical or phase I studies and to a lesser degree in phase II trials. Radio immunotherapy is showing important advances in the treatment of medullary thyroid carcinoma, malignant lymphomas and brain tumors with potential extension to neuroblastoma therapy. ^{131}I-metaiodobenzylguanidine (^{131}I-MIBG) has been used in the treatment of neuroblastoma, carcinoid tumors and medullary carcinoma. More recent development includes the use of ^{131}MIBG as a first line treatment in high risk neuroblastoma patients and the use of agents in combination with

chemotherapy and whole body irradiation for the treatment of neuroblastoma.

6. **Thyroid carcinoma:** Radioiodine has been used commonly for the treatment of differentiated thyroid carcinoma, a tumour which metastases to the bone, lungs and other soft tissues. It is slow growing and prognosis is relatively good, allowing long term follow up of treated patients. Repeating radionuclide imaging with radioiodine can assess response to therapy and ^{131}I may be required in advanced or resistant cases.

7. **Myleoproliferative diseases:** ^{32}P has been used for more than 50 years in the treatment of various hematological disorders. ^{32}P is selectively concentrated by rapidly proliferating tissue and bone after intravenous injection. In this way, a significant dose is delivered to the bone marrow and results in growth retardation of haemopoeitic cell lines. The primary application of ^{32}P-Phosphate is its role in the treatment of polycythemia rubric Vera, in which there is an abnormal increase in the number of red cells in the circulation. Treatment with radioactive phosphorous or chemotherapy results in significant increase in life expectancy.

4.8 DIAGNOSTIC APPLICATIONS

In recent years, scanning techniques have developed rapidly and are now among the most useful tools in diagnostic medicines. By means of scanning, tissues and organs can be visualized and such visualization facilitates the detection of abnormalities in their function.

Radioactive materials are administered to the individual and distribution of the radioactive material in the body is measured by using imaging techniques.

1. **Cardiovascular imaging:** Radiopharmaceuticals are useful in cardiac imaging as agents that provide information of regional myocardial blood perfusion. They are administered to provide information at peak cardiac output. The study involves stressing the patient with exercise on a treadmill or giving an intravenous injection of dipyridamole. An injection of thallium chloride or technetium-99m (^{99m}Tc) labeled methoxy isobutyl isonitrile is then given and imaging is carried out. Tc sodium pyrophosphate injection is primarily a skeletal imaging agent has been used as a cardiac imaging agent as an adjunct to the diagnosis of acute myocardial infarction.

2. **Bone imaging:** This method is widely used in the diagnosis of benign and malignant, primary and metastatic bone tumors. It is also useful in the study of patients with suspected fracture, arthritis, metabolic bone diseases,

vascular necrosis, bone infarcts and bone healing. Bone imaging radiopharmaceuticals consist of diagnosis (primary single photon emitters) and therapeutic agents. The therapeutic radiopharmaceuticals are utilized on the basis of their particulate emission (primarily β) and are treated differently than the single photon bone imaging agents. Tc-99 citrate is a promising agent for localizing and showing the extent of bone infection that help the surgeon to determine areas of debridement before surgery.

3. **Lung imaging:** The main purpose of the lung imaging is the diagnosis of pulmonary emboli and to evaluate pulmonary perfusion and pulmonary ventilation and to assess pulmonary function prior to pneumonectomy. The agent used is ^{99m}Tc macro-aggregated albumin. Radioembolization is used in diagnosis imaging of the lungs and for therapy of hepatic tumors.

4. **Renal imaging:** This is used to determine renal function, renal vascular flow and renal morphology. These are also used for evaluation of renal transplant patients for complication such as obstruction, infarction, leakage, tubular necrosis and rejection. ^{99}Tc-diethylenetriaminepantaacetic acid (^{99}Tc-DTPA) and ^{131}I-ibdohippurate are commonly used radiopharmaceuticals.

5. **Spleen imaging:** Radiopharmaceuticals are used for spleen imaging for various purposes. Spleen imaging is performed using ^{99m}Tc-denatured erythrocytes. After a blood sample is withdrawn from the patients the erythrocytes are labeled with ^{99m}Tc *in vitro*. The labelled cells are then denatured by heating at 49.5^{0}C for 15 mins following reinjection into the patient. The cells are then taken up by the spleen. Imaging with ^{99m}Tc-denatured erythrocytes is used to detect spleen nucleus.

6. **Brain imaging:** Brian imaging is performed using radiopharmaceuticals by single photon emission computed tomography (SPECT) and positron emission tomography (PET). SPECT and PET radiopharmaceuticals are classified according to blood-brain-barrier (BBB) permeability, cerebral perfusion and metabolism receptor-binding and antigen-antibody binding. The blood-brain-barrier SPECT agents, such as ^{99m}Tc-DTPA, ^{291}Ti and ^{67}GA-citrate are excluded by normal brain cells, but enter into tumour cells because of altered BBB. Imaging of brain tumors requires a disrupted BBB; however it is intact in the early stages of brain tumour growth, when diagnosis is most critical. Relative to normal brain, brain tumor cells frequently over express peptide receptors, such as the receptor for epidermal growth factor (EGF). Peptide radiopharmaceuticals such as radio labelled EGF could be used to image early brain tumors.

7. **Imaging of inflammatory lesions:** Scintigraphic imaging of infection and inflammation is a powerful diagnostic tool in the management of patients with infectious of inflammatory diseases. Many radiopharmaceuticals have been introduced for the scintigraphic demonstration of infectious and inflammatory lesions and some of them are currently in clinical use. They can be dichotomized into two major categories according to their specificity. Specific radiopharmaceuticals include *in vitro* labelled leukocytes, radiolabelled monoclonal antibodies and receptor specific small proteins and peptides. Non-specific radiopharmaceuticals include radiolabelled nanocolloids, liposomes, macromolecules such as human immunoglobulin, dextran and human serum albumin, various small molecules and ions. Nowadays, a few radiopharmaceuticals are available that could replace radiolabelled leukocytes, such as ^{67}Ga-citrate, ^{99m}Tc-IgG and ^{99m}Tc-labeled antigranulocyte antibody preparations. Furthermore, various agents labelled with ^{99m}Tc are currently developed for this application.
8. **Gastrointestinal imaging:** Latex particles coated with either amino or carboxyl groups can be efficiently labelled with ^{99m}Tc and used in the studies of gastrointestinal function.

4.9 PERMISSIBLE RADIATION DOSE LEVEL

Permissible radiation dose is the dose of radiation which should not cause appreciable body harm to an individual at anytime during his life. Their main aim is to prevent harmful effects on gonads and blood forming organs. Permissible dose for any age above 18 years is:

Maximum permissible dose = 5 (N − 18)

N = Age of person in years

This ensures that the dose to the gonads is not more than 60 REMs by the age of 30.

Following considerations are important to ensure the exposure below the maximum permissible levels:

Dose rate (from the isotopes being used): Dose rate is measured using suitable radiation detectors. It is the rate of delivery of energy from a radionuclide.

For β-emitters: various formulae are used to calculate the dose rate.

Dose rate at 100 mm = 3100 × Ci (rads/hr)

Ci = Source strength in curies

Dose at surface of solution = S × E (rads/hr)

Where S = Specific activity of isotopes in micro curies/ml
E = Mean energy/disintegration

For γ emitters

D = $0.5Ci \times E/d^2$

Where D = Dose rate in rads/hr
Ci = Source strength in curies
E = Total energy of γ-radiation in MeV per transformation
d = Distance from the source in meters

This formula is generally used if the distance is larger than the size of the source.

Dose received (by the operator): There are various methods which are used to measure the dose received by the personal handling these radioisotopes.

1. **Film badges:** These badges contain a small strip of photographic paper which is clipped on to the breast pocket. The darkening of the film depends upon the amount of energy absorbed. The film is then developed after a week/month and results are compared with standard dose of radiation.

2. **Pocket Ionization chambers (dosimeters):** These dosimeters are quartz fibre electroscopes and they are always charged before use. Ionization caused by the radiation cause the charge to leak away and the fibre gradually moves back. Its image is then viewed by lenses. Whenever it exceeds the preset dose rate, there is an audible alarm which sounds immediately. Hence these instruments give immediate indication of dose received particularly in case of hazardous operations.

4.10 RADIATION HAZARDS AND THEIR PREVENTION

Direct radiation effect: It results from ionization or excitation within a biologically functional molecule and probably will abolish its biological functions. In this, protein molecules get aggregated which leads to loss of solubility and some degree of fragmentation. DNA, RNA and polysaccharides exhibit fragmentation and some cross linking occurs which abolishes the biological activity as it prevents the uncoiling of closely coiled structure and forms immobile configuration.

Indirect radiation effects: Damage caused by indirect radiation effects is due to radiolysis of intracellular water which comprises about 80 per cent of most cells and of any extra cellular water which may be present. For example, action on water molecules leads to the production of free radicals. This hydrogen peroxide is a powerful oxidizing agent and the free radicals OH and HO_2 are responsible for radiation damage.

Effect on rate of cell division: All cells are prone to radiation damage but the extent of damage varies because any defect that arises in imperfect replication of cells and would be multiplied at each cell division. More the rate of cell division, greater will be the observed damage.

Effect on skin: Persons receiving x-rays for prolonged period showed damaging effects on skin like loss of hair, dryness, brittleness. Even a short time exposure of intense radiation is responsible for erythema.

Genetic effects: Radiations can damage the chromosomes and increase the frequency of gene mutation. Damage to genetic makeup is cumulative and irreparable. These mutations are always inherited from one generation to the next, and are very harmful. Hence, it is essential to avoid or minimize radiation during the first 30 years of life.

Effect on human body: Effect of radiation and absorbed radioactive material on the entire body depends on the proportion irradiated. It becomes most severe if the whole body gets exposed and least if only a small mass of tissue such as hands or feet is exposed.

Short term effects: When human body gets exposed to a dose of 25 REM, it may cause transient change in WBC count, nausea whereas the dose of about 100 REMs may lead to diarrhoea, vomiting and 400 REM is a median lethal dose (LD). This may lead to death within 30 days.

Long-term effects: Long-term effects are observed after an exposure over long periods. They may appear within few months or even after 50 years. These effects include permanent skin damage, bone necrosis, leukemia, cataract, anemia.

SUMMARY

Nuclear pharmacy is a developing branch of pharmacy which deals with the preparation, quality control and dispensing of radiopharmaceuticals. The basic functions and responsibilities of nuclear pharmacist are the same as those for others who practice pharmacy. The nuclear pharmacist is an expert in a specific class of drugs but also remain current on all medications employed in the treatment of diseases especially those whose effectiveness or toxicity may be monitored by nuclear medicines studies.

Radiopharmaceuticals are radioactive pharmaceuticals used in nuclear medicine. These drugs are made up of two components; a radioactive isotope, and a carrier molecule: radioactive isotope can be injected safely into the body while the carrier molecule delivers the isotope to the site of treatment or examination. Radiopharmaceuticals can be used for therapeutic and diagnostic applications. Radionuclide can be prepared by artificial method e.g. cyclotron produced radionuclide, pile produced isotope, thermal neutron reactor produced radioisotope.

Radioisotopes can be produced in the laboratory. Radiopharmaceuticals have various therapeutic application e.g in the treatment of hyperthyroidism (^{131}I-Iodine), bone tumour (^{32}P and ^{89}Sr), intracavity therapy for the treatment of cavities and tumor cells in spinal canal, neuroendocrine carcinoma (^{131}I-MIBG) and myleo-proliferative diseases (^{32}P). Radiopharmaceuticals have various applications e.g. cardiovascular imaging, bone imaging, lung imaging, renal imaging, spleen imaging, brain imaging, imaging of inflammatory lesions and gastrointestinal imaging. Radiopharmaceuticals can produce a variety of radiation hazards i.e. effect on the rate of cell division, effect on skin, human body, direct radiation effect, indirect radiation effect, short term and long term effects.

✸✸✸

CENTRAL STERILE SUPPLY MANAGEMENT

5.1 INTRODUCTION

Sterilization means the complete removal of micro-organisms from materials. This can be achieved by physical or chemical methods, e.g. by any physical agent such as heat, ultraviolet light, x-rays, supersonic waves, or by mechanical methods such as filtration through materials which hold back micro-organisms, shaking with glass beads, grinding, etc. or by antiseptic solutions.

The Sterile Processing Department provides that service within the hospital in which medical/surgical supplies and equipment—both sterile and non-sterile—are cleaned, prepared, processed, stored, and issued for patient care.

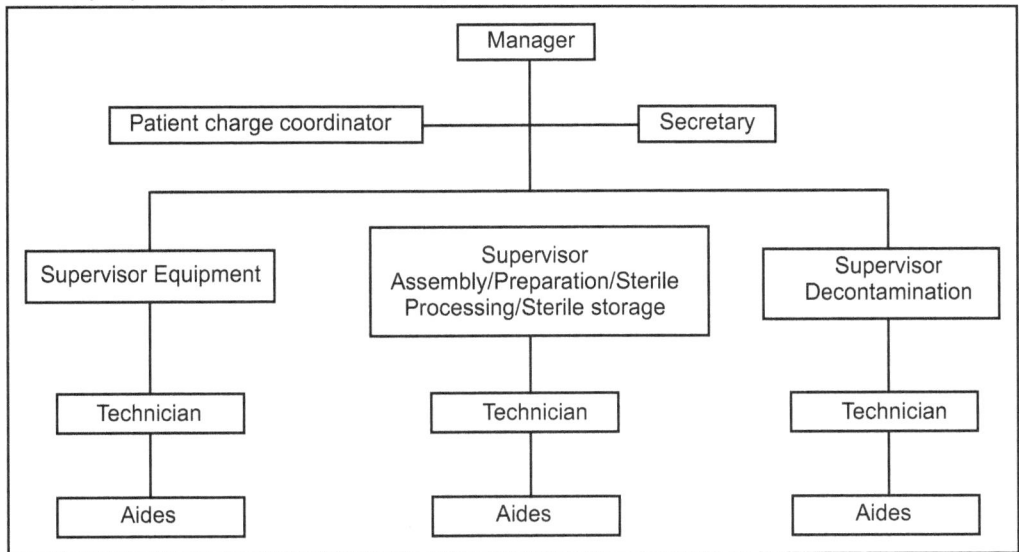

Fig. 5.1 : Organizational Structures for Sterile Supply Department

5.2 OBJECTIVES OF CENTRAL STERILE SUPPLY DEPARTMENT (CSSD)

The objective of Central Service is to provide the health care facility with services in the areas of supply processing and distribution. The distribution area is responsible for the delivery of supplies to designated customers. Sterile and non-sterile items must be separated and placed in defined and separate storage areas.

Objectives of central sterile supply department (CSSD)

The objectives of central service include the following:

1. Provide inventoried supplies and equipment to customer areas.
2. Promote better patient care by providing prompt, accurate service.
3. Provide supplies of sterile linen packs, basins, instruments, trays, and other sterile items.
4. Maintain an accurate record of the effectiveness of the cleaning, disinfecting, and sterilizing processes.
5. Strive for uniformity and simplicity in the trays and sets that the department provides.
6. Maintain an adequate inventory of supplies and equipment.
7. Monitor and enforce controls necessary to prevent cross-infection according to infection control policies.
8. Establish and maintain sterile processing and distribution standards.
9. Operate efficiently to reduce overhead expense.
10. Stay abreast of developments in the field and to implement changes as needed to stay current with new regulations and recommended practices.
11. Review current practice for possible improvements in quality or services provided.
12. Provide consulting services to other departments in all areas of sterile processing and distribution, including in-service education programmes, review of policies and procedures, and implementation of new processes.

5.3 FUNCTIONS OF CENTRAL STERILE SUPPLY DEPARTMENT (CSSD)

Sterile Processing Departments are typically divided into four major areas to accomplish the functions of decontamination, assembly and sterile processing, sterile storage, and distribution.

1. **Decontamination area:** In the decontamination area, reusable equipment, instruments, and supplies are cleaned and decontaminated by means of manual or mechanical cleaning processes and chemical disinfection.
2. **Assembly and packaging area:** Clean items are received in the assembly and packaging area from the decontamination area and are then assembled and prepared for issue, storage, or further processing (like sterilization).
3. **Sterile storage area:** After assembly or sterilization, items are transferred to the sterile storage area until it is time for them to be issued.
4. **Distribution area:** Several major functions are carried out in the distribution area: case cart preparation and delivery, exchange cart inventory, replenishment and delivery, telephone-order and requisition-order filling and, sometimes, patient care equipment delivery.

5.4 TYPES OF MATERIALS
5.4.1 Materials for Containers
1. **Glass**
   - Lime soda glass, Neutral glass
   - Lead free glass, Silicon treated glass
   - Boro-silicate glass, Sulphured containers
2. **Plastics**
   - Polyethylene (Polythene), Polyvinyl chloride (PVC)
   - Polycarbonate, Polypropylene
   - Polystyrene, Polyamides (Nylon)
   - Polytetrafluoro (PTFE)
3. **Thermosetting types**
   - Phenol-formaldehyde, Urea-formaldehyde
   - Melamine formaldehyde

5.4.2 Materials for Closures
1. **Natural rubber**
   - Smoked sheet, Pale creep
2. **Synthetic rubbers**
   - Butyl rubber, Nitrile rubber
   - Silicon rubber, Chloroprene rubber (Neoprene)

5.5 OBJECTIVES OF STERILIZATION
- It should not affect the contents.
- It should be easy to clean and maintain.
- It should be strong enough to withstand the changes of temperature and pressure.
- It should protect the contaminants from harmful light radiations.

Table 5.1 : List of materials sterilized by different methods

Materials		Methods of Sterilization /Preferred Methods
Injections	**Intravenous infusions** (a) Isotonic solution of sodium chloride/Glucose (b) Blood products and Plasma substitutes, e.g. Dextran and degraded gelatin	Filtration sterilization Terminal sterilization (a) Autoclaving for thermo stables (b) Radiation for thermolabile

Materials		Methods of Sterilization /Preferred Methods
Non-injectable sterile fluids	Non-injectable waters	Filtration sterilization/Terminally sterilization by autoclaving
Instruments and equipments	Syringes (glass) Syringes(glass),dismantled, disposable Needles (all metal, disposable)	Dry heat using γ-radiation
	Metal instruments	Dry heat
Ophthalmic preparations	Eye drops, eye lotions	Thermostables by autoclaving at 121°C for 15 minutes Thermolabile by filtration sterilization
	Eye ointments	Dry heat sterilization at 160°C for 02 hrs
Dressings		Any combination of dry heat, ethylene oxide and gamma radiation
Miscellaneous	Dry bulk drugs, porcelain	Dry heat sterilization
	Food products	Radiation sterilization or gaseous sterilization
	Culture medium	Gaseous sterilization

5.6 PACKAGING PROCESS

Instruments and other items that are prepared for sterilization must be so packaged that their sterility can be maintained up to the point of use. The packaging material selected must also permit the device to be removed aseptically.

Types of Packaging
- Textiles
- Nonwovens
- Pouch packaging
- Rigid container system

5.7 PACKAGING CONCEPT FOR STERILE PRODUCTS

Depending on use, storage and transportation, a sterile product should be packaged in one or more packaging layers:

5.7.1 Primary Packaging containing the Product

The primary packaging prevents recontamination of the product after sterilization. In a dust free storage or in case of immediate use of the materials, the primary packaging maintains sterility during storage and transport. Examples of primary packaging: 02 layers of paper, 02 layers of non-woven sheets, single or double laminated film pouch, paper bag or container with adequate filter(s).

5.7.2 Secondary Packaging

It may offer extra protection against dust and gives extra mechanical protection, making handling easier.

5.7.3 Transport Packaging

A transport package is used for external transporting of sterile goods in their primary and secondary packaging.

5.8 NEED OF PACKING OF STERILE GOODS

At the end of a correct sterilization process, products inside the sterilizer chamber are sterile. The air in the room where the sterilizer is installed contains dust particles, which may carry microorganisms. So when taking out the load from the sterilizer, it will soon be contaminated again. In addition, usually sterile goods are stored for quite some time before they are used, and where they are transported through the hospital to the place they are to be used. It thus is obvious, that, when not protected, the goods will definitely be contaminated by the time they are used. The goods must be put in a packaging to prevent recontamination after sterilization. At the same time the packaging should be suitable for sterilizing the goods it contains. Moreover, the packaging protects the contents against damage during handling and transport.

5.9 STERILIZATION METHODS

The various methods of sterilization are:

Physical:
1. Thermal (Heat) methods
2. Radiation method
3. Filtration method

Chemical Method
1. Gaseous method

1. Heat Sterilization

Heat sterilization is the most widely used and reliable method of sterilization, involving destruction of enzymes and other essential cell constituents. The process is more effective in hydrated state where under conditions of high humidity, hydrolysis and denaturation occur, thus lower heat input is required. Under dry state, oxidative changes take place, and higher heat input is required.

This method of sterilization can be applied only to the thermostable products, but it can be used for moisture-sensitive materials for which dry heat (160–180°C) sterilization, and for moisture-resistant materials for which moist heat (121-134°C) sterilization is used. The efficiency with which heat is able to inactivate microorganisms depends upon the degree of heat, the exposure time and the presence of water. The action of heat will be due to induction of lethal chemical events mediated through the action of water and oxygen. In the presence of water much lower temperature time exposures are required to kill microbes than in the absence of water. In this processes both dry and moist heat are used for sterilization.

Dry Heat Sterilization

Examples of Dry heat sterilization are:
- Incineration
- Red heat
- Flaming
- Hot air oven

It employs higher temperatures in the range of 160–180°C with an exposures time for 02 hours, depending upon the temperature employed. The benefit of dry heat includes good penetrability and non-corrosive nature, which makes it applicable for sterilizing glassware and metal surgical instruments. It is also used for sterilizing non-aqueous thermostable liquids and thermostable powders.

Hot-air Oven

Dry heat sterilization is usually carried out in a hot air oven, which consists of the following:
- An insulated chamber surrounded by an outer case containing electric heaters.
- A fan
- Shelves
- Thermocouples
- Temperature sensor
- Door locking controls.

Operation

1. Articles to be sterilized are first wrapped or enclosed in containers of cardboard, paper or aluminum.
2. Then, the materials are arranged to ensure uninterrupted airflow.
3. Oven may be pre-heated for materials with poor heat conductivity.
4. Temperature is allowed to fall to 40°C, prior to removal of sterilized material.

Moist Heat Sterilization

Moist heat may be used in three forms to achieve microbial inactivation.
- Dry saturated steam—Autoclaving
- Boiling water/ steam at atmospheric pressure
- Hot water below boiling point

Moist heat sterilization involves the use of steam in the range of 121–134°C. Steam under pressure is used to generate high temperature needed for sterilization. For efficient heat transfer, steam must flush the air out of the autoclave chamber. This method of sterilization works well for many metal and glass items but is not acceptable for rubber, plastics, and equipment that would be damaged by high temperatures. Autoclaves should be tested periodically with biological indicators like cultures of *Bacillus stearothermophilus* to ensure proper function.

Autoclaves, or steam sterilizers essentially consist of following:

1. A cylindrical or rectangular chamber, with capacities ranging from 400–800 liters.
2. Water heating system or steam generating system.
3. Steam outlet and inlet valves.
4. Doors—single or double — with locking mechanism.
5. Thermometer or temperature gauge.
6. Pressure gauges.

Operation

For porous loads (dressings) sterilizers are generally operated at a minimum temperature of 134°C, and 121°C for bottled fluids. The stages of operation of autoclaves include air removal, steam admission and sterilization cycle (includes heating up, holding/exposure, and cooling stages).

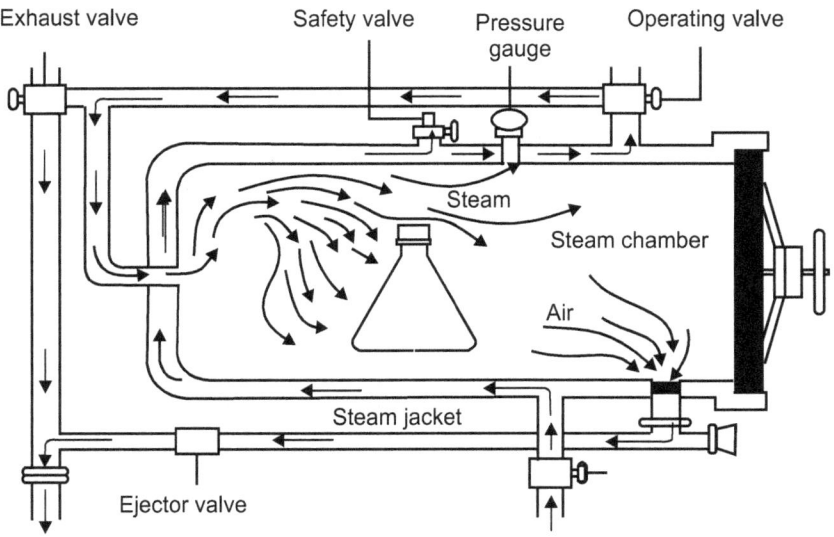

Fig. 5.2 : An Autoclave

2. Radiation Sterilization

Many types of radiations are used for sterilization like electromagnetic radiation, e.g. gamma rays and UV light; particulate radiation e.g. accelerated electrons. The major target for these radiations is microbial DNA. Radiation sterilization with high energy gamma rays or accelerated electrons has proven to be a useful method for industrial sterilization of heat sensitive products.

Radiation sterilization is generally applied to articles in the dry state: including surgical instruments, sutures, prostheses; unit dose ointments, plastic syringes and dry pharmaceutical products.

γ-ray Sterilizer

Gamma rays for sterilization are usually derived from cobalt-60 source, the isotope is held as pellets packed in metal rods, each rod carefully arranged within the source and containing 20 Kc of activity. This source is housed within a reinforced concrete building with 02 m thick walls. Articles being sterilized are passed through the irradiation chamber on a conveyor belt and move around the raised source.

3. Filtration Sterilization

Filtration process does not destroy but removes the microorganisms. It is used for both the clarification and sterilization of liquids and gases as it is capable of preventing the passage of both viable and non viable particles. Sterilizing grade filters are used in the treatment of heat sensitive injections and ophthalmic solutions and biological products. Membrane filters are used for sterility testing.

Application of filtration for sterilization of gases: HEPA (High efficiency particulate air) filters can remove up to 99.97% of particles >0.3 micrometer in diameter. Air is first passed before filtration to remove larger particles and then passed through HEPA filters. The performance of HEPA filter is monitored by pressure differential and airflow rate measurements.

There are two types of filters used in filtration sterilization.

(a) **Depth filters:** Consist of fibrous or granular materials so packed as to form twisted channels of minute dimensions. They are made of diatomaceous earth, unglazed porcelain filter, sintered glass or asbestos.

(b) **Membrane filters:** These are porous membranes about 0.1 mm thick, made of cellulose acetate, cellulose nitrate, polycarbonate, and polyvinylidene fluoride, or some other synthetic material. The membranes are supported on a frame and held in special holders. Fluids are made to transverse membranes by positive or negative pressure or by centrifugation.

Ultraviolet Irradiation: The optimum wavelength for UV sterilization is 260 nm. A mercury lamp giving peak emission at 254 nm is the suitable source of UV light in this region.

Gaseous Sterilization

The chemically reactive gases such as formaldehyde, (methanol, H.CHO) and ethylene oxide $(CH_2)_2O$ possess biocide activity. Ethylene oxide is a colorless, odourless, and flammable gas. The mechanism of antimicrobial action of the two gases is assumed to be through alkylations of sulphydryl, amino, hydroxyl and carboxyl groups on proteins and amino groups of nucleic acids.

5.10 SUPPLY OF STERILE MATERIALS

As sterile material has to pass through many hands, it becomes very important to provide special packaging to remove the contents without contamination. The desirable characteristics of packaging materials in which the material is supplied should:

1. Be compatible with the process of sterilization.
2. Offer complete storage protection to the material.
3. Maintain sterility until time to use, and*
4. Be durable and provide and ease of opening to avoid explosions due to pressure differences.

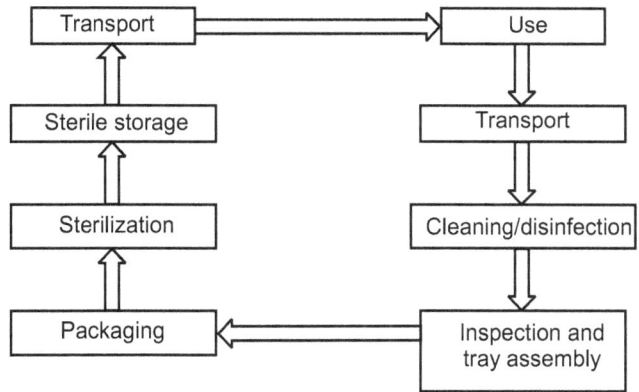

Fig. 5.3 : The Sterile Supply cycle

Some packages or stoppers tear/open uncontrollably, which on removal may cause explosions due to uncontrollable release of pressure. This coating eliminates rupturing of fibre or film.

SUMMARY

The Sterile Processing Department provides service within the hospital in which medical/surgical supplies and equipment—both sterile and non-sterile—are cleaned, prepared, processed, stored, and issued for patient care. Objectives of the central sterile supply department includes providing inventoried supplies and equipment to customer areas, promote better patient care by providing prompt, accurate service, to provide supplies of sterile linen packs, basins, instruments, trays, and other sterile items, providing consulting services to other departments in all areas of sterile processing and distribution, including in-service education programms, review of policies and procedures, and implementation of new processes.

Functions of this department are typically divided into four major areas i.e. (i) decontamination area (manual, chemical and mechanical cleaning), (ii) assembly and packaging area (assembly and further processing), (iii) sterile storage area and (iv) distribution area (major function).

Sterilization is very important and it should not affect contents. Sterilization can be done by physical methods (thermal method, radiation method and filtration method), e.g. dry heat using γ-radiation for syringes (glass) and needles (all metals and disposable) whereas dry heat for metal instruments, autoclaving at 121°C for 15 min for thermostable eye drops and eye lotions and filtration sterilization for thermolablile eye drops and eye lotions. Dry heat sterilization at 1600C for 2 hours is used for eye ointments.

Instruments and other items that are prepared for sterilization must be so packaged that their sterility can be maintained up to the point of use. As sterile material has to pass through many hands, it becomes very important to provide a special packaging to remove the contents without contamination. The packaging material selected must also permit the device to be removed aseptically.

DRUG STORE MANAGEMENT AND INVENTORY CONTROL

6.1 DRUG STORE MANAGEMENT

A drug store is defined as a sub-organization in the hospital where material, drugs are held in abeyance, till the time they are inspected, approved and stocked. A store should maintain the regular flow of material and proper storage conditions.

Objectives

The main objectives of drug store management are:
- To preserve, stock, procure, supply drugs of all types.
- To store drugs required in research work.
- To maintain records of receipt and issue of drugs.
- To supply drugs to consuming department.

Racks are used for storing material and closed bins for costly items.

Layout: It must be located on the ground floor, close to the pharmacy in an area of about 600-1000 sq. Ft. It must have 2 entries, one for receiving and another for issuing of materials. Racks are used for storing material and closed bins for costly items.

Products and drugs are identified on the basis of special codes.

F, S, N: Fast moving, Slow moving, Non-moving.

H, M, L: Heavy, Medium, Light material.

Thus the fast moving materials are placed near the exit while the non-moving away from the exit. Heavy items are placed at the base and the light items on the top of the racks.

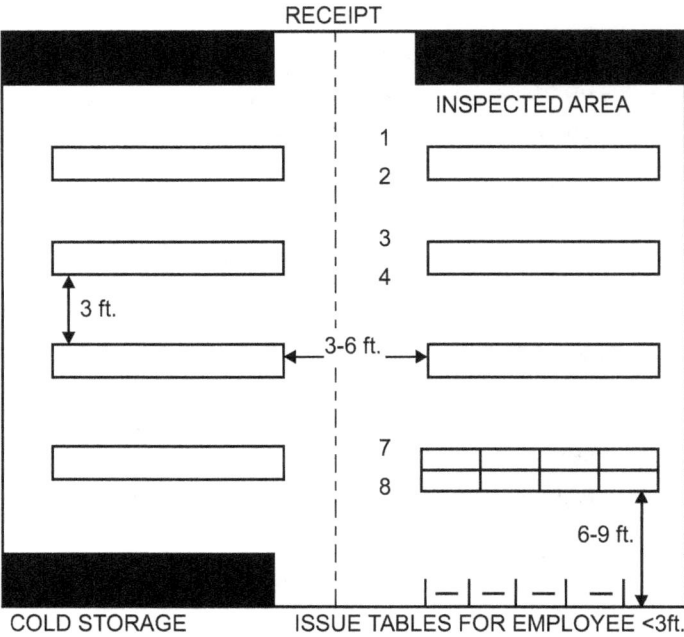

Fig. 6.1 : Layout of a drug store

Types of material stocked

- Capsules, tablets, liquid dosage forms and injection etc.
- Alcohol and alcohol containing preparations.
- Poisons are stored in separate closed rack labeled as poison.
- Narcotics and psychotropic substances are stored under lock and key.
- Vaccines and other thermolabile drugs are required to be stored at cold stores 2°C-10°C. Antibiotics, vitamins, liver preparations etc should be stored at cool temperatures (15°C-20°C).
- To avoid pilferage costly drugs and prescribed schedule x drugs should be stored separately under lock and key.
- Biological, antibiotics are stored properly in refrigerator.
- Large bulk items on bottom.

Storage conditions:

Drugs stores are used to store all kind of material like capsules, tablets, liquid dosage, injections, antibiotics, biological, narcotics & psychotropic drugs and poisons.

(i) Cold storage – 2-8°C.
(ii) Cool temperature – 8-25°C.
(iii) Room temperature (RT)--temperature prevailing in working area.
(iv) Warm – 30-40°C.
(v) Excessive heat – above 40°C.

6.2 STORAGE AT COOL TEMPERATURE

LIST A

These are the drugs that require storage at 2-8°C. These includes sera, vaccines, whole human blood, normal human plasma, thrombin, thromboplastin, cobra and viper in solution, oxytocin and vasopressin, insulin preparations, posterior pituitary injection, human gamma globulin injection etc.

LIST B

These are the drugs that require storage at 8-25°C. It includes antibiotics, arsenicals, blood preparations, hormone preparations, vitamin preparation and other.

All drugs should be stored according to conditions described on the label. When specified on the label, controls for humidity, light, etc. should be maintained. Temperatures should be controlled and monitored using calibrated monitoring devices and records of temperature and alarms should be maintained. Monitoring is conducted at points representing the extremes of the temperature range based on temperature mapping.

Refrigerators and freezers used to store drugs should:
- Be well maintained,
- Be equipped with alarms,
- Be free from frost buildup,
- When combined, be a two door unit with separate freezer compartment and door,
- Allow for adequate air distribution and orderly storage within the chamber. Storage practices and loading configurations should not lead to the obstruction of air distribution,
- Have sensors for continuous monitoring and alarms located at the points representing the temperature extremes.

Written procedures should be available describing the actions to be taken in the event of temperature excursions outside the labeled storage conditions. All excursions outside the labeled storage conditions must be appropriately investigated and the disposition of the stock in question must be evidence-based.

6.3 PURCHASING

Purchasing is a basic function in materials management department. Professional expertise is required to be exercised to obtain the materials of proper quality and in proper quantity.

6.3.1 Methods of Purchasing

Purchasing is basically of two types:
1. De-centralized.
2. Centralized.

De-Centralized:

The user department is responsible for purchasing. The system has got one advantage; the user knows exactly, as to what is required to be purchased, but this advantage also disappears, if proper specifications of the items to be purchased are not laid down.

Centralized:

When one person or department makes purchases of all the supplies required for a hospital, it is called centralized purchasing. This method has got certain distinct advantages, as given below and should be adopted as far as possible:

1. The technical manpower (medical and nursing) should be relieved of the responsibility of purchasing.
2. The purchase officer to be specialized in his job, which will result in more efficient purchasing, better control on inventories and overall savings to the hospital.

Group Purchasing:

The hospital may go a step further in centralized purchasing and a number of hospitals may group themselves and resort to what is known as group purchasing, which can further result in saving to the hospitals by pooling the resources at reduced direct and indirect material costs. This system is being followed by central government health scheme hospitals and employee's state insurance scheme hospitals.

An efficient purchasing system can be developed in the hospitals by considering the following functions of purchasing:

1. Right quality.
2. Right price.
3. Right quantity or inventory management.
4. Right time.

6.3.2 Inventory

Inventories are generally classified as

1. Official inventory
2. Unofficial inventory

Official inventory is the inventory, which is brought into a storage space or unit, counted and controlled until it is disposed to a using department.

Unofficial inventory includes those supplies that have been expended and dispensed to the various departments and units where they are stored until used. Unofficial inventory exists in all supply consumer departments such as nursing units, laboratories, cost rooms, maintenance department, and special care units.

The inventories in the hospital are generally located in the following categories of materials.
- Surgical stores
- Medical and drugs stores
- General stores
- Linen stores
- Dietary stores
- Stationery stores
- Engineering And Maintenance Stores

6.3.3 Inventory and its Functions

1. To provide maximum supply service consistent with maximum efficiency and optimum inventory investment.
2. Permits to meet new demand
3. Allow continuous and smooth production system

6.3.4 Inventory Control

Inventory control is a tool available to modern management to decide the level of inventory that can be economically maintained. Inventory control is to find the optimum between the procurement and carrying cost to keep the total cost at the minimum. Inventory control is basically a scientific term which indicates when to order and how much to order. To attain various objectives, inventory control must,

1. Determine items to be stocked
2. Determine when and how much to replenish
3. Keep suitable records
4. Weed out obsolete items.

Some of the criteria for inventory control used are,
- Time and extent of probable use
- Obsolescence
- Storage costs
- Shrinkage
- Transportation costs
- Investment costs
- Cost to purchase
- Quantity price differential
- Market conditions and price trends
- Time required for delivery
- Availability of a substitute
- Cash flow
- Alternative investment potential.

6.3.5 Objectives of Inventory Control

1. To minimize the cost of ordering and holding inventory which is often the largest single investment of the hospital.
2. To maintain acceptable levels of patient care services by minimizing stock outs.
3. To reconcile the potential conflict between these objectives. Inventory control policies and techniques therefore to aim to optimize stock levels viz-a-viz patient care requirements.
4. To reduce financial investment in the inventories: the capital required to carry inventories costs money and holding unduly large amount of inventory leads to blockage of scarce capital.
5. To facilitate hospital operation: hospital functioning depends on the supply of various items for day-to-day operation. The disruption of supply will lead to disruption of schedule services leading to loss of productivity and decreased utilization.
6. To avoid losses from inventory obsolescence.
7. To improve patient care services.
8. Smooth and uninterrupted supply of the item in a hospital will lead to efficient and better patient care.

6.3.6 Need for Inventory Control

Materials constitute nearly 30 to 60 per cent of the total expenditure of an organization. The entire system and sub-system of the hospital are dependent on the materials and without materials availability the patient care function of the hospital will come to a grinding halt. Hence it is of great importance that materials of right quality are supplied to all users in right quantity at the right time and place.

Inventory control is one of the important elements in materials management and an effective measure for containing cost of materials. Its modus operandi is:

1. Inventory analysis
2. Inventory cost
3. Inventory control system

Inventory analysis

The three levels of analysis for effective control over inventories are:
- Overall analysis
- Category analysis
- Individual item analysis

The management should fix targets for each category of items according to various conditions lead time, nature of item etc.

Individual item analysis includes selective control of the items deserving attention leads to better control. Some of the important individual item analysis are,

1. ABC analysis
2. VED analysis
3. SDE analysis
4. HML analysis
5. FSN analysis

ABC analysis: This technique, popularly called *always better control* or the *alphabetical approach* has universal applications in many areas. This technique is most commonly used for inventory control and it is based on the cost criteria. The annual consumption analysis of any organization would indicate that a vital few items (10%) account for a substantial portion (70%) of total consumption value; and these items are called 'a' items, which need careful attention of the manager. Similarly, the one which account only for 10% of the consumption value are called 'c' items. The items that are between the top and bottom are called the 'b' category items, these are moderate cost and needs middle level supervision.

VED analysis: The items are classified into vital, essential, and desirable items. The analysis helps management in deciding the safety stock of the vital items, which are critical for the function of the organization.

SDE Analysis: The items of the inventory are categorized into scarce, difficult, and easily available items depending upon the availability of the items. It focuses attention of managers on the scarce and difficult items, which helps in proper control of inventory to prevent stock out situation.

HML Analysis: The items of inventory are classified into high, medium, and low cost items according to unit cost of the items. It helps management in concentrating on costly items. The basis HML analysis is the unit cost of the items/unit of inventory.

FSN Analysis: FSN analysis includes the quantity and rate of consumption of items to classify item as fast moving (f), slow moving (s) and non moving (n) items. This analysis helps in deciding the stocks, distribution and handling methods.

Use of ABC and VED Analysis: The findings of ABC and VED analysis can be coupled and regroup to evolve a priority system of management of stores.

Inventory cost

After the inventory analysis two basic problems of inventory control need to be considered.

(a) cost of materials itself.
(b) the cost associated with keeping the materials in stock (inventory carrying costs).
(c) the cost associated with the placement of a purchase order (ordering costs).

Inventory carrying costs: This cost includes:

Cost of obsolescence and deterioration: Obsolescence and deterioration of material and equipment while in inventory and these costs are part of inventory carrying.

Ordering cost

It is also called the inventory acquisition cost or replenishment cost. It is the cost incurred in placing an order.

These three cost factors help in determining the economic order quantity.

$$EOQ = \sqrt{\frac{2 \times A \times S}{IC}}$$

EOQ : Economic order quantity
A : Annual usage of the item
I : Annual inventory carrying cost
C : Unit cost of the item

Lead time: The lead time comprises (a) internal lead time-time taken in completing the formalities for placing the order, and (b) External lead time, i.e. the time taken from placing an order to the receipt of material.

Buffer stock

Buffer stock can be calculated using the formula:

Buffer stock: Buffer stock is the quantity of stores set apart as a safeguard against the variations in demand and procurement period. This quantity of items can be used only at the time of emergency for unforeseen demands. It is calculated by multiplying the differences between maximum and average consumption rate per day multiplied with the lead time for the item.

Buffer stock: (maximum consumption rate/day average-consumption rate/day) x Lead time

- Lead time
- Stock out cost

Computers and Inventory Control

Computers are being used in materials management and particularly for inventory control.

6.4 INVENTORY CONTROL OPERATION

The operation of an inventory control system takes place through a channelized flow of information, connected with inventory control, among the various departments of an organization.

6.4.1 Causes of Inventory Imbalance

1. Failure to review and revise, as necessary, inventory policies on a regular basis.
2. Failure of the system to react to rapid change in usage or to accurately forecast future needs and requirements.
3. Failure to give the cooperation and assistance of using departments and to properly determine their needs and direction of operation.

6.4.2 Purchase Order (PO)

Purchase order is a commercial document issued by a buyer to a seller, indicating types, quantities, and agreed prices for products or services the seller will provide to the buyer.

6.5 PROCUREMENT

The procurement system is a major determinant of availability of essential drugs and other medical supplies. The key principles of good procurement include:
1. Procurement by generic name (drugs).
2. Limitation of procurement to the essential drugs list or standard list of medical supplies.
3. Procurement in bulk.
4. Competitive procurement.

6.5.1 Procurement Procedures

The different steps involved in the purchase of goods are known as purchase procedure. Purchase procedure comprises the following steps:

1. **Determination of material requirement:** The material to be purchased for a particular period is well planned for the purpose of their regular and continuous use. The purchase department requests the various user departments to send their requirement on a proper requisition form in which the items, its specifications, quantity to be purchased and approximate costs are mentioned.

2. **Determination of purchase budget:** An approximate purchase budget of the company is prepared out of which every user department is allocated the funds for the purchase of their items. If allocated surplus funds are present then the purchase for that department will be affected. In case of urgency the purchase will be done by diverting the funds from other departments.

3. **Sources of supply:** The pharmacy and therapeutic committee sets adequate standards for the purchase of quality drugs. Procurement of stores is generally done by the following sources:

- **Directorate general supplies and disposals (DGS&D):** There are six depots of this organization at different places in India. The material purchased by these organizations is subjected to various tests at the testing units in Chennai and Mumbai. It runs on no profit-no loss basis.
- **Direct purchase from vendor:** The vendor's premises must be visited by a responsible officer of the hospital to find out if the vendor possesses the required capabilities to manufacture the items being offered to the hospital.
- **Competitive bidding: Discount:** The vendors may offer discounts on large quantity of materials to be purchased and also on prompt payment of bills.
- Emergency drugs from local market
- **Receipt of acknowledgement:** After placing the order to the supplier by sending a copy of the purchase order, the supplier in turn sends acknowledgement of the order that he is able to supply the goods with terms and conditions mentioned in the purchase order.
- **Receipt of drugs:** Preferably the same person is responsible for reviewing the stocks, date of expiry, description, quantity, batch number.

6.6 DISTRIBUTION OF DRUGS

Drugs should be supplied in the original packing of manufacturers. Name and quantity of the drug should be properly labeled. The Chief pharmacist should visit wards to check if drugs are properly stored under special storage conditions like cold storage, cool temperature and at room temperature. The drugs are then distributed as:

(i) Supply/ indent of drugs to various wards/emergency/operation theatres/departments of the hospital and college through hospital issue counter.

(ii) Delivery of drugs to the respective nursing stations under the direct supervision of pharmacist.

(iii) Issue of drugs to the OPD drugs distribution center and injection room.

(iv) Drug information to the nursing staff, Para-medical staff and technicians.

SUMMARY

The main function of the drug store is to preserve, stock, procure and supply and distribute the drugs of all types. It should be at the ground floor, close to pharmacy and the materials like narcotics, vaccines, and biological products apart from the common solid/liquid drugs are stocked under the proper storage conditions. Depending upon the storage conditions, the drugs are categorized into List A and List B type drugs. Material can be purchased by a centralized and decentralized method and to obtain the cost-effective material in the right quantity from reliable suppliers of high quality products who ensures timely delivery and by achieving the lowest possible total cost.

Inventory provides maximum supply service, consistent with maximum efficiency and optimum inventory investment and to minimize the cost of ordering and holding inventory which is often the largest single investment of the hospital. To maintain an in-stock position of wanted items and to dispose of unwanted items, it is necessary to establish adequate controls over inventory on order and inventory in stock. The economical balance of the inventory should be maintained by its control which finds the optimum level between the procurement and carrying cost to keep the total cost at the minimum. The tools and techniques which maintain inventory control are analysis, cost ordering system of the inventory.

Purchase of the materials should be properly planned before the order is placed as well planned purchases affect the price, delivery and availability of products for sale. Procurement and right source determines the cost effectiveness of the inventory thus quantity of the material required, purchase budget and supplier should be identified. Proper guidelines and norms should be followed during the purchase of the material. Thus the as per demand to particular departments drug store fulfills the requirement and chief pharmacist is responsible to check the wards whether the drugs are properly stored under special storage conditions like cold storage, cool temperature and at room temperature.

THE PRESCRIPTION

7.1 INTRODUCTION

A prescription is a written direction from a doctor to a pharmacist for the preparation of medicaments in a suitable form for administration to a patient.

Traditionally, a prescription commences with the letter R_x which signifies Latin *"ecipe"* which means "take". Thereafter is the body of the prescription with details of the medicine, their quantities and the manner in which they are to be supplied, i.e. whether mixture, tablets, pills, injection, powder and ointment.

In addition to medicines, a prescription may contain other item or appliances required by the patients for their treatment, e.g. wound dressings, elastic hosiery, blood glucose monitoring equipments, needles and syringes and nutritionally complete feeds. After this the doctor signs the prescription, affixes his stamp mentioning his registration number, and hands it over to the patient.

7.2 INFORMATION REQUIRED ON PRESCRIPTION

A prescription is a three in one document:
- a clinical document;
- a legal document; and
- an invoice.

Law may require some information on the prescription and some of the information is required to ensure the patient is given correct information. The dispenser will also have to take payment for the medicine from the patient or send the prescription to the appropriate body for them to pay; hence it is also an invoice.

Other information
1. Name of the patient,
2. Address of the patient;
3. Age;
4. Gender;
5. Pulse rate;
6. Blood pressure—both diastolic and systolic;
7. Any pathologic test undergone by the patient;
8. X-ray and or ultrasound.
9. Thereafter, he directs the patient to the pharmacy.

All the prescriptions should be dispensed within the 06 months of the date on the prescription except for the certain types of controlled drugs, which are dispensed within 28 days.

How and when to take the medicine

Patients ask this question from the doctor till he/she is satisfied. Doctor has to answer this question. Answering this question is embarrassing for the doctor; asking the question is equally awkward for the patient.

In the bygone days a doctor would add *b.i.d* (twice in a day) *t.i.d* (thrice in a day) or *q.i.d* (four times in a day) after each medicament.

All prescribing doctors faced this dilemma in the days past. No more of it now. In late 1980s or early 1990s a set of doctors devised a new method: easy for the patient and convenient for the prescribers. This is prevalent currently:

O_____x_____O = twice a day
O_____x = once a day
o_____O_____O = thrice a day

O . . . means tablet/capsule/powder. . .

O on the left denotes morning while O on the right is evening. In the centre signifies afternoon.

× **Means no dose required/to be taken.**

Liquid/syrup/fluid

Every liquid syrup or fluid has a container cover fitted on the metallic cover of the bottle. This container bears a circular mark in its middle, which means 05 ml, i.e. one teaspoonful. Above the middle circular mark is the upper/outer mark; in fact, this is the end of the container: it means 10 ml, i.e. two spoonfuls/one table spoonful.

SOS

Depending upon the disease, doctors sometimes prescribe a medicine on SOS basis.

SOS —a Latin word— stands for *Si Opaes Sit*. SOS medicines are prescribed for emergent situations. SOS medicine is to be taken if and when required. Not otherwise.

Metered dose

These are available as inhalers. Such inhalers are propelled by hand-held device to transmit required ingredient to the affected site. A propellant used in an inhaler ought to be:

- a liquefied gas.
- have adequate solvent properties.
- have minimal toxicity.
- have appropriate density.
- be chemically stable.
- be compatible with other medicines.
- be acceptable to the patient.
- be non-inflammable.

In sinusitis patients have a tendency to use nasal drops because they can exceed the dose for immediate relief from the discomfort of breathing, little realizing that excessive dose of nasal drops can aggravate their situation to *Medica mentosa*. Therefore, be cautious.

Have confidence in your doctor, and never exceed the prescribed dose.

Direction should be as specific as possible. Ideally, the amount to be used and the number of times a day that it should be taken should be stated. Vague direction- in particular "Take as directed" should be avoided. In such situations the pharmacist will have to ensure that the patient is clear about how to use or make their medication. The direction for use will include the dose and dosage regimen but the prescriber may include additional information about the product. This can include how to use (e.g. in the eye, in the ear, on the scalp), why they are using it (e.g. for pain, for sleeping). The prescriber may also indicate a maximum amount that should be taken, particularly if the medicine is dosed on a 'when required' basis.

Name and address of the patient

This identifies the patient who is to receive the medicine. The name of the patient should be given in full, including at least. The age of the patient should also be mentioned to enable the pharmacist to check the dose of the medicine, particularly if the person is very young or very old.

Length of the treatment

The length of the treatment may be stated on the prescription or it may be possible to calculate the length of the time from the amount prescribed and dosage regimen.

Prescriber's signature

This is usually a legal requirement of prescription.

Total amount to be supplied

This refers to the total amount of the medicine to be supplied to the patient. This can be expressed as a number of units (e.g. 21 tablets, 12 suppositories), as a volume (e.g. 100 ml of mixture, 5 ml of eye drops) or as a weight (e.g. 30 g of cream) or as a single pack size or multiple thereof (e.g. 1 tube of ointment, 2 inhalers). It may mean that the person dispensing the prescription may have to calculate the total amount if the prescriber states a dosage regimen for the preparation and a number of days of treatment (e.g. one to be taken three times a day for 28 days).

The following are some general guidelines when reviewing prescriptions:
- ➤ Patient name should be given in full, including atleast the full first and last names. Initials alone are not acceptable. If necessary, rewrite the patient's name in full above the name on the prescription and verify the spelling of the patient's name when it is not legible.
- ➤ Patient address is required for the patient records. In most states, the address is required for all prescriptions.

- Pre-printed prescriptions often contain a space for the patient's birth date. If this space is not filled in, then this information should be requested. The patient birth date is helpful for third-party billing and for distinguishing among patients with the same name. Knowing the patient's age also helps the pharmacist evaluate the appropriateness of the drug, the quantity, and the dose form prescribed, thus minimising medication errors.
- The date the physician wrote the prescription should be provided. For pharmacy records, the date when the prescription is received should be written on the prescription as well. If no date is written on the prescription, then the date the prescription is brought into the pharmacy should be recorded and noted as such.
- Drugs may be listed on a prescription using a brand or generic name. A given drug (i.e., one with a particular generic name) may be marketed under various brand names. For example, Prinivil and Zestril are two brand names under which the generic drug Lisinipril is marketed. A generic name is one that is often less expensive than brand name drugs and often substituted. Such substitutions can be made, of course, only if generic drug and thee brand name drug are bioequivalent. If the prescription for a brand name is filled with a generic equivalent, then the name, strength and manufacturer of the generic substitution must be written on the medication container label.
- The **Signa** or directions for use, from the prescription must be placed on the label produced for the medication. The medication container label should read exactly as indicated on the prescription.
- If the refill blank on the prescription is left blank, then there can be no refill for the prescription. The words *no refill* should appear on the medication label and an indication of *no refill* will be entered into the patient's record.
- If refills are required, then prescriptions should generally be refilled 1 or 2 days before the patient's supply run out.
- Pharmacy technician must ask the patient about allergies to medication or food, as well as about past adverse drug reactions, when receiving each and every prescription. An allergy is a hypersensitivity to a specific substance that is manifested in a physiological disorder. Common allergic reactions include sweating, rashes, swelling and difficulty in breathing. In extreme cases, allergic reaction can lead to shock, coma or death. An adverse drug reaction is any negative consequence to any individual from taking a particular drug. If the patient indicates that he or she does not have any allergies, the notation NKA, or *no known allergies,* should be made on the back of the prescription from and on the patient profile. If the patient indicates that he or she does have an allergy, then the allergy should be entered into the patient profile. Inquiring about allergies every time a patient comes to the pharmacy with a prescription for an antibiotic is a good practice.

Antibiotics are the most common medication allergy and allergies can begin at any age. A patient could have safely taken antibiotics several times and becomes allergic to it on a subsequent occasion. Thus confirming and updating the patient's allergies in the profile is important. Some patients may think of stomach upset as an allergy. However, an upset stomach is a side effect, not an allergy. Therefore the patient should describe the allergy before entering the description into the profile.

7.3 HANDLING OF THE PRESCRIPTION

The dispensing of prescriptions requires a logical and very thorough approach in order to ensure the patient gets the right product in the right form, at the right dose with the right advice. It is imperative that the pharmacist conducts a thorough check of the prescription to ensure that it is complete and clinically acceptable. The product should then be assembled and labelled in a manner that ensure the product and all the information is accurate and that it is professional in appearance. All stages involved in the dispensing process should be covered b standard operating procedure.

The stages involved in dispensing a prescription are:
1. Receiving the prescription
2. Clinical and legal checking of the prescription
3. Assembly of the product and labelling
4. Accuracy checking the product against the prescription
5. Delivery of the product to the patient with the appropriate advice about the product.

1. Receiving the prescription: It is important at this stage that the person receiving the prescription has checked the patient details so that:
- The appropriateness of the prescription for that patient can be assessed.
- Any required records can be completely corrected.
- The product can be labelled for that patient.
- If necessary the prescription can be delivered to the correct patient at the correct address.
- The patient can be contacted, if necessary, even after the medicine has been dispensed and supplied to the patient.

2. Clinical and legal checking of the prescription: This is an essential role of the pharmacist to ensure that the prescription is legally complete and clinically correct for the patient. The pharmacist should check that all the information required to select and dispense the right product is available on the prescription. If information is not present the pharmacist should ascertain this information and information and the prescription in might have to be sent back to then prescriber or the prescriber cannot be contacted, the pharmacist can add information relating to the dose, strength and quantity to be supplied. The pharmacist should also check that the prescription is appropriate for the patient and that it will be of benefit and not cause the patient harm.

3. Assembly of the product and labelling: This stage involves producing a label for the product, selecting the product from where it is stored in the pharmacy and doing any assembly work and putting the label onto the product. Assembly work can range from picking a patient pack from a shelf to making the product from ingredients. Accuracy at this stage of the assembly process is paramount in that the patient gets the product ordered in the prescription. The dispenser needs to take great care in selecting the products because many drugs have similar names or they may be in container in a similar appearance. At this stage of the process the dispenser to make records, either for legal purposes such as completion of a controlled drugs register or as good practice, such as adding information to a patient medication records.

4. Accuracy checking the product against the prescription: The final accuracy check is present to ensure that there has not been an error in the dispensing process. It is an important stage in minimizing risk to the patient. The person involved in carrying out this check needs to work in a structured and methodical manner to have the best work done.

5. Delivery of the product to the patient with the appropriate advice about the product: The final stage is to hand the product to the patient. This stage can be done by the pharmacist or can be delegated by other member of staff. It is important that whoever gives the medicine to the patient ensures the patient has all the advice they need. The pharmacist must be confident that the patient can take or use their medication correctly. Once the prescription has been handed to the patient, the prescription form will be filled or sent to the appropriate place so that the pharmacy receives the payment.

7.4 PATIENT MEDICATION PROFILE

The patient medication profile is one of the major advantages of the unit dose system. The medication profile gives pharmacy personnel the opportunity to actively participate in monitoring patient care. The form used for the profile is designed locally and may vary from one hospital to another, but the information contained on the form should be similar. The patient medication profile is divided into six sections:

1. Patient Information: This identifies the patient and should include information such as name, age, sex, weight, social security number, ward, and bed number.

2. Allergy Information: It is important to know of any allergies the patient has to allow the pharmacy to make sure the patient is not being given medication to which he is allergic. The physician should have checked this before ordering the medication, but this allows for one more safety check.

3. Diagnosis and Pre-existing Conditions: This allows the pharmacy to check for medications which may be contraindicated (could cause harm to patient because of an ailment currently being treated, a different ailment, or other drugs the patient is taking) for the diagnosed condition. This also allows the pharmacy to make sure that any pre-existing conditions are receiving treatment. An example might be a patient in for surgery who also has high blood pressure for which he is taking medication. With the pharmacy aware of this condition, the physician can be notified if he forgot to continue the medication.

4. Scheduled Medications: This portion of the profile is a major safety check for the patient. With all medications listed, the pharmacy is now able to check for drug interactions. The medications identified on this part of the form are those ordered by the physician. Scheduled medications are those that are prescribed to be given at definite intervals.

5. Non-scheduled/Nonrecurring Medications: A non-scheduled/non recurring medication is one that is ordered for a one-time administration or for porn (as needed) medications. These medications do not have a specific time-span between doses. STAT and now doses also indicate non-recurring medications.

6. Floor stock/Ward stock Medication: These are medications that are already on the wards in accordance with the local SOP. They are handled by the bulk drug order section of the p

7.5 FILLING PRESCRIPTIONS

Prescription Verification

The prescription received is a bonafide one and the person received it from is entitled to have it filled by pharmacy. The simplest and best way is to ask for an ID card and verify the expiration date on the ID card. Study the prescription carefully and make sure that the drug prescribed is reasonable, that its amount or dosage is realistic in consideration of the patient's age, and that the quantity of the medication is practical. A prescription calling for 1,000 tetracycline tablets or a pint of paregoric, for example, warrants further inquiry.

If, in the process of verification, there is a discrepancy, an ambiguity, or an incompatibility, or for any reason find it is necessary to consult the prescriber, never allow the patient to suspect that anything is amiss. You should never fill a prescription you do not completely understand or that you feel is incorrect. What appears to be an overdose may be the desired dose for a specific patient, but the prescriber will appreciate being called for verification.

When you are sure you understand the prescription and are satisfied that it is in all respects correct, you should give its filling your undivided attention. Most mistakes are made when the person filling the prescription is either interrupted while doing so or is trying to accomplish more than one task at a time.

During the process of filling a prescription, the label on the containers used in filling the prescription should be verified at least three times. Initially, the label should be read when the container is taken from the shelf. Then it should be read again when the contents are removed from the container. And finally, the container's label should be read before it is returned to the shelf. By following these three verification steps for each prescription you fill, you will reduce the possibility of making a prescription error.

Prescription Labelling: Proper labelling of a prescription is as important as filling it correctly. It is reasonable to assume that if a great deal of accuracy is necessary to properly compound a prescription, it is just as important that the patient take the correct amount of medication in the right manner to receive its maximum benefits. Improperly written or misunderstood directions on a prescription label can be disastrous. Make sure all labels are typed clearly and their directions translated into simple layman's language. Keep in mind that the prescription label serves two purposes. First and most important, it gives the patient directions pertaining to the medication; second, in case of misuse or error, it is the quickest means by which the contents of the prescription container, the person who wrote the prescription, and the person who filled it can be traced.

Consequently, the following information should always be on the label:

- The name and phone number of the dispensing facility: A serialized number that corresponds with the number on the prescription form.
- The date the prescription is filled.
- The patient's name: The directions to the patient, transcribed accurately from the prescription, in clear, concise layman's language.
- The prescriber's name and rate or rank: The initials of the compounder. Authorized refills, if any.
- The expiration date, if applicable.
- Name, strength, and quantity of medication dispensed

Note: Pharmaceutical preparations should be identified and labelled with the generic name. However, trade or brand names may be used if the trade or brand name is actually on the container. Other information that may need to be attached to the prescription container are labels reading "Shake Well Before Using" or "For External Use Only."

"Poison" labels should be omitted when a preparation is intended for external use, as many physicians prefer the "For External Use Only" labels. After the prescription is labelled, check the ingredients again by some systematic method to ensure accuracy. As an added precaution and to aid expeditious identification of drugs in case of undesirable effects, note the manufacturer and the lot number of the proprietary drug dispensed on the prescription form. This procedure, however, does not apply to medications consisting of a mixture of several ingredients. The initials or the code of the person filling the prescription must also be written on the prescription form.

Prescriptions that have been filled must be maintained in one of several separate files: **Schedule II and III narcotics** — Prescriptions containing narcotics are numbered consecutively, preceded by the letter "N" and filed separately.

Alcohol: These prescriptions are numbered consecutively, preceded by the letter "A" and filed separately.

Schedule III (no narcotic), IV and V drugs: These prescriptions are part of and are numbered in the same manner as the general files; however, they are maintained separately.

General files: All other prescriptions are numbered consecutively and filed together.

7.6 MEDICATION ERRORS

Medication errors are considered to be one of the many types of medical errors. Like medical errors, medication errors have no specific definition, because the possible causes can be endless; however medication errors can generally be described as a medical error in which the source of error of harm includes a drug. An estimated 1.7% of all prescriptions dispensed in a community hospital contain a medication error. The results of the medication errors cannot be measured easily. The medication errors further increases the additional hospitalizations, admissions to long-term care and continuation of disease.

7.6.1 Causes of Medication Errors

(i) Physiological Causes of Medication Errors
(ii) Social Causes of Medication Errors

(i) Physiological Causes of Medication Errors: Each patient has a unique response to medication can highlight the importance of medication safety. Each person is genetically unique and the speed at which a person can remove medications from the body varies extremely. For example, G6PD (glucose-6-phosphate dehydrogenise) is an enzyme that helps to remove medication from the body. A lack of G6PD is the most common human enzyme deficiency. A patient with enzyme deficiency, taking a mediation that depends upon the enzyme to be removed from the body, could come to serious harm or even death.

(ii) Social Causes of Medication Errors: Patients in the outpatient setting can also contribute to medication errors through incorrect administration. As a result, the medication does not work well, does not work at all, or may cause harm. Social causes of medication errors include failure to follow medication therapy instructions because of cost, noncompliance, failure to take therapy as the physician instructs, or misunderstanding instructions (language barriers). Patients can thus contribute to medication errors by doing the following:

- Forgetting to take a dose or doses
- Taking too many doses
- Dosing at wrong time
- Not getting a prescription filled or refilled in a timely manner
- Not following directions on dose administration
- Terminating the drug regimen too early

Such social causes may result in an adverse drug reaction or a sub therapeutic or toxic dose. For example, over 50 per cent of patients on necessary long-term medication are no longer taking medication after 1 year. Any of these circumstances could result in lasting harm or death depending upon the drug or the disease being treated.

7.6.2 Categories of Medication Errors

An exact listing of the medication errors is difficult to create, because the possible causes of medication error can often be too numerous to count. However, categorizing errors into types or groups often aids in the identification and prevention of possible causes. Classic examples of medication errors are grouped into the following major categories:

- **Omission error**: An omission error occurs when a dose is not given. An omission occurs when the next dose is due, but the previous dose was not administered.
- **Wrong dose error**: It occurs when a dose is either above or below the correct dose by more than 5 per cent.
- **Extra dose error**: It occurs when a patient receives more doses than prescribed by the physician.
- **Wrong dose form error**: It occurs when any dose form or formulation is given to the patient that is not the accepted interpretation of the physician order. For example, a drug given by mouth for a drug ordered as an intramuscular injection, a capsule formulation dispensed instead of a tablet, or an immediate-release drug dispensed instead of a controlled-release drug.
- **Wrong time error**: It occurs when any drug is given 30 minutes or more before or after it was prescribed, up to the time of the next dose. This is a common error in the hospital and nursing home.

Another way of categorizing medication errors is to define them by what causes the failure of the desired results. The purpose of defining errors in this way is to clearly identify what the error was, where the error took place, and through closer examination to determine a specific cause. Medication errors can be categorized within three basic definitions of failure:

- **Human failure:** Failures that occurs at an individual level. An example of this type of error would include pulling a medication bottle from the shelf based on memory, without cross-referencing the bottle label with the shelf label and the medication order/prescription. Human errors also include those made by the patient such as non-compliance to prescribed drug therapy.
- **Technical error:** Failures that result from location or equipment. An example of this type of failure would include the incorrect reconstitution of medication because of a malfunction of sterile-water dispenser or failure to properly operate automated equipment.
- **Organizational errors:** Failures because of organizational rules, policies or procedures. An example of this type of failure would include a policy or rule requiring preparing or admixing parenteral drugs such as cancer chemotherapy in an inappropriate setting.

Other medication errors due to handlers and prepares of medication. Three of the most common causes are as follows:

> **Assumption error:** It occurs when an essential piece of information cannot be verified; therefore an assumption is made. An example of assumption errors includes errors such as a pharmacy technician making a prescription while misreading an abbreviation.

> **Selection error:** It occurs when two or more options exist, and the wrong option is chosen. An example of a selection error— a pharmacy technician might fill a prescription mistakenly using a look-alike or sound-alike drug instead of the prescribed drug.

> **Capture error:** It occurs when focus on a task is diverted elsewhere and therefore the distraction captures the person's attention, preventing the person from detecting the error or causing an error to be made. An example of capture error might be taking a phone call in the middle of filling a prescription order and as a result dispensing the wrong number of tablets.

7.6.3 Prevention of Medication Errors

Safety of the patient and prevention of medication errors can be avoided by employing the following measures:

> The correct patient is being given the medication and other associated medications are correct.
> The correct drug is dispensed.
> The correct dose is prepared, whether for a child or adult, to maintain a correct body concentration or blood level.
> The correct route of administration is indicated.
> The appropriate dose form is prepared (e.g. a tablet would not be dispensed for administration by nasogastric tube and antibiotic capsules would not be appropriate for administration to an infant.
> The correct administration times and the correct conditions for administration (e.g. medications that must be taken with or without food) are indicated.

SUMMARY

Prescription is an order for medication which is dispensed to or for a patient. The prescription order is a part of the professional relationship among the prescriber, the pharmacist and the patient. It is the responsibility of all to handle the prescription in a correct manner to avoid any harmful occurrence. The physician should prescribe proper medications including all information regarding the patient and directions on the prescription while the pharmacist should dispense the right medicines with no near expiry date and the patient should take those as per the directions.

Patient medication profiles are necessary to maintain so that the pharmacists can monitor inpatient medication therapy. It contains the data on the patient's current and recent pharmaceutical therapy, allergies, diagnosis etc and it allows the pharmacist to review the medication that a patient is taking before dispensing the first dose and with each new medication orders.

A medication error is any preventable event occurring in the medication-use process, including prescribing, transcribing, dispensing, using and monitoring, that results in inappropriate medication use or patient harm. Several measures can be followed to prevent the errors but pharmacists should ensure that right patient is receiving the "right drug in a right dose". Pharmacists and other health care professionals involved in the medication use process must work together to develop a system approaching medication error reduction and improving the safety of the patients.

DRUG DISTRIBUTION SERVICES

8.1 INTRODUCTION

The medication distribution system requires an in-depth examination of activities with an obligation to efficiency, economy, and safety pursuant to the distribution of medications. The sequence of events begins with the purchase and follows a logical pattern to the point of consumption by the patient.

The managerial aspects of a medication distribution system must interface with many pharmacy functions. It is difficult to remove purchasing, inventory control, pricing, receiving, storage, quality control, and similar functions from those involved in the actual distribution of medications to patients. On the other hand, the clinical aspects of a medication system extend beyond the distribution of a medication to a patient and include activities related to the action of medications on the patient.

8.2 IN-PATIENT DRUG DISTRIBUTION SERVICES

An inpatient is "admitted" to the hospital and stays in the hospital till he recovers or is discharged by the doctor. The patient's stay in the hospital can extend from overnight to an indeterminate time, as in the case of coma patients.

Treatment provided in this fashion is called inpatient care by an in-patient pharmacy, which is a multifunction department of storage, dispensing, manufacturing of IV fluids, and parenteral.

There are four systems for inpatient drug distribution:

8.2.1 Floor or Ward Stock System

It is a system of distribution that consists of an individual storage area on each nursing unit where drugs are stored prior to preparation and administration by the nurse. The medications are usually unsecured in this system and the role of pharmacy is primarily distributional. Drug products which require special control are often omitted from floor stock, and are sent to the nursing unit upon receipt of a prescription order for the individual patient. All containers used for floor stock must meet specific labelling requirements.

Advantages:
- Ready availability of most drugs for the in-patients.
- Fewer inpatient prescription orders.
- Minimized return of medication.
- Reduced pharmacy personnel requirements.

Disadvantages:
- Increased incidences of medication errors as a result of review by the pharmacist of each individual patient medication order.
- Financial loss due to misappropriation of medication by hospital personnel and the administration of medication to patients without initiating charges.
- Increased drug inventory in the institution.
- Increased cost of loss due to obsolescence and deterioration.
- Limited capacity for proper storage facilities on the nursing units in many hospitals.
- Increased danger of unnoticed drug deterioration jeopardizing patient safety.
- Consumption of nursing manpower in the preparation of medication doses and in conducting other medication-related activities.

8.2.2 Individual Prescription Order System

Individual Prescription Order System is an antiquated system of medication distribution that consists of patient specific container with 02–05 days supply of drugs delivered to and stored on nursing units. Within this system, drug orders are transcribed by the nurse and reviewed by a pharmacist although no patient information is available to the pharmacist.

Disadvantages:
- Increased incidence for medication errors due to the lack of checks in the distribution of medication doses and inefficiencies in the procedures.
- Consumption of excessive nursing manpower in the preparation of medication doses and in conducting other medication-related activities.
- Increased potential for drug loss due to waste, obsolescence, and deterioration.

8.2.3 Combination of the Above Mentioned Systems

This is the most common method of medication distribution. In this system most drugs are dispensed on an individual prescription basis. In this system nursing personnel spend a great amount of time preparing individual doses, reconstituting injectable medications, and ordering floor stock.

The system lacks adequate checks of the dosages prepared and the accuracy of charting of medication administration is often less than desirable.

8.2.4 Unit Dose System (UDS)

Unit Dose System (UDS) is a system of distribution coordinated by the pharmacy that dispenses medication orders to be administered, not prepared by the nurse. Although the UDS may differ in form, depending on the specific needs resources, and characteristics of each institution, four elements are common to all:

1. Medications are contained in, and administered from, single unit or unit dose packages.

2. Medications are dispensed in ready to administer form to the extent possible.
3. For most medications, not more than a 24-hour supply of doses is provided to or available at the patient-care area at any time.
4. A patient medication profile is concurrently maintained in the pharmacy for each patient.

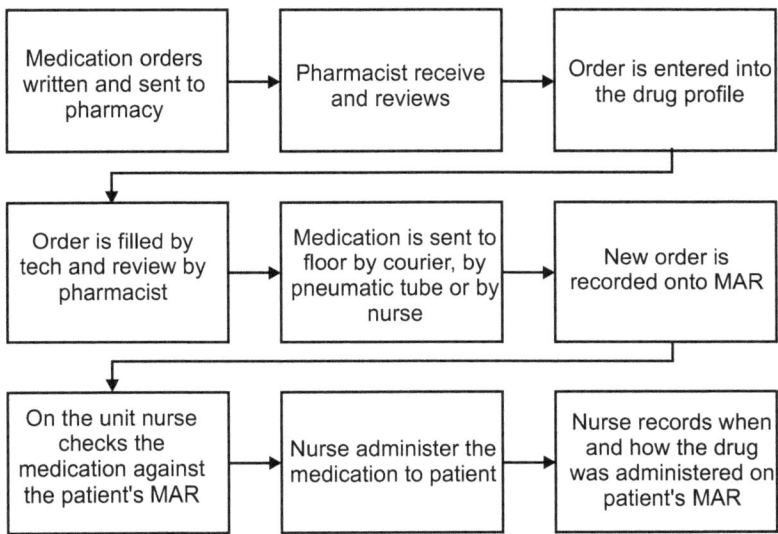

Fig. 8.1 : Unit Dose Drug Fulfillment Process

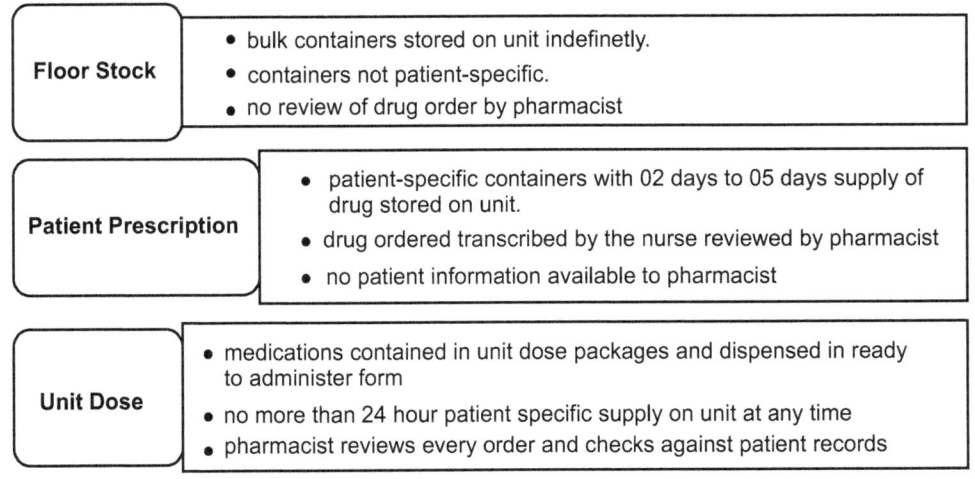

Fig. 8.2 : Comparisons of key features of Drug Distribution System

8.3 TYPES OF UDS

Unit Dose (UD) Package is a package that contains the ordered amount of a drug in a dosage form ready for administration to a particular patient by the prescribed route at a prescribed time.

Single-Unit Package is one which contains one pharmaceutical dosage form.

There are three major types of UDS

1. **Centralized UD Program:** Drugs are dispensed from the central pharmacy to the inpatient ward, this system is applicable in smaller units.
2. **Decentralized UDS:** The doses are prepared in two or more "satellite" pharmacies located in or near the patient care areas of the hospital:
3. **A combination of the two systems:** This utilizes one of two approaches:
   (a) The pharmacists are decentralized while the doses are prepared in a central location.
   (b) Satellite pharmacies are operated for limited periods of time when pharmacies are not open.

Advantages of UDS

- Safer for the patient.
- More efficient and economical for the organization.
- A more effective method of utilizing professional resources.
- A reduction in the incidence of medication errors.
- A decrease in the total cost of medication-related activities.
- A more efficient usage of pharmacy and nursing personnel allowing for more direct patient-care involvement by pharmacists and nurses.
- Improved overall drug control and drug use monitoring.
- More accurate patient billings for drugs.
- The elimination or minimization of drug credits.
- Greater control by the pharmacist over pharmacy workload patterns and staff scheduling.
- A reduction in the size of drug inventories located in patient-care areas.
- Greater adaptability to computerized and automated procedures.

8.4 UNIT DOSE PROCESS

8.4.1 Physician's Medication Order

Medications should be given only on the *prescription* of a qualified doctor. Allowable exceptions to this rule should be put in written form immediately and the prescriber should countersign the nurse's or pharmacist's signed record of these orders within 48 hours. Only a pharmacist or registered nurse should accept such orders. Provision should be made to place physician's orders in the patient's chart, and a method for sending this information to the pharmacy should be developed. Prescribers should specify the date and time medication orders are written.

(A) Medication orders should be written legibly in ink and should include:
   (i) Patient's name and location (ward, room No, and bed No).
   (ii) Medication generic name.
   (iii) Dosage, frequency and route of administration.
   (iv) Signature of the physician.
   (v) Date and hour the order was written.

(B) Any abbreviations used in medication orders should be agreed to and jointly adopted by the medical, nursing, pharmacy, and medical records staff . . . **Do Not Abbreviate** . . . is the new practice nowadays.

(C) Before dispensing the drug

The pharmacist must receive the physician's original order or a direct copy of the order except in emergency situations. This permits the pharmacist to:
   (i) Resolve questions or problems with drug orders before the drug is dispensed and administered.
   (ii) Eliminate errors which may arise when drug orders are transcribed into another form for use by the pharmacy.

(D) Any questions arising from a medication order

After receiving the medication order, the pharmacist clarifies any discrepancies with the prescriber. After the order is reviewed and deemed appropriate for the patient, the medication is entered into a medication profile in the pharmacy information system. The medication profile is the primary record used by the pharmacist to document patient medications.

(E) Order's Time limits and changes

Medication orders should be reviewed automatically when the patient goes to the delivery room, operating theatre, or a different service. In addition, a method to protect patients from indefinite, open-ended drug orders must be provided. This may be accomplished through one or more of the following:
   (a) Routine monitoring of patients' drug therapy by a pharmacist;
   (b) Drug class-specific, automatic stop order policies covering those drug orders not specifying a number of doses or duration of therapy;
   (c) Automatic cancellation of all drug orders after a predetermined time interval unless rewritten by the prescriber.

Whatever the method used, it must protect the patient, and provide for a timely notification (48 hours) to the prescriber that the order will be stopped before such action takes place.

(F) Before the drug is entered into the dispensing system the pharmacist must review and interpret every medication order and resolve any problems or uncertainties. He must be satisfied that each questionable medication order is, in fact, acceptable. This may occur through:
   (a) Study of the patient's medical record.
   (b) Research of the professional literature.
   (c) Discussion with the prescriber or other medical, nursing, or pharmacy staff.

It is advisable for the pharmacist to document actions related to a questionable medication order on the pharmacy's patient medication profile form or other pharmacy document. Once the order has been approved, it is entered into the patient's medication profile.

(G) Special orders such as stat, emergency, non-formulary drugs, investigational drugs, restricted use drugs, or controlled substances, should be processed according to specific written procedures meeting all applicable regulations and requirements.

(H) A schedule of standard drug administration times must be developed by the pharmacy, nursing, and medical staffs, through the P&T committee. The nurse should notify the pharmacist whenever it is necessary to deviate from the standard medication schedule.

(I) A mechanism to continually inform the pharmacy of patient admissions, discharges, and transfers should be established.

8.5 METHODS OF SENDING THE PHYSICIAN'S ORDERS TO THE PHARMACY

1. **Self-copying order forms:** This method provides the pharmacist with a duplicate copy of the order and does not require special equipment. There are two basic formats:
   (a) Orders for medications included among treatment orders.
   (b) Medication orders separated from other treatment orders on the order form.

2. **Electromechanical:** Copying machines or similar devices may be used to produce a duplicate copy of the physician's order.

3. **Computerized:** Computer systems, in which the physician enters orders into a computer which then stores and prints out the orders in the pharmacy or elsewhere.

8.6 PATIENT MEDICATION PROFILE

Patient medication profile is an essential item to be maintained in the pharmacy for all in-patients and those outpatients routinely receiving care at the institution, and updated.

The patient medication profile may be a written copy or computer maintained. It must be reviewed by the pharmacist before dispensing the patient's drug(s), and it serves many purposes such as:

(a) Enables the pharmacist to become familiar with the patient's total drug regimen, enabling him to detect quickly potential interactions, unintended dosage changes, drug duplications and overlapping therapies, and drugs contraindicated because of patient allergies or other reasons.

(b) It is required in UDS for the individual medication doses to be scheduled, prepared, distributed, and administered on a timely basis.

(c) It may be useful for retrospective drug use review studies

Patient profile format may vary from hospital to another hospital. It should include:
- Patient's full name, date hospitalized, age, sex, weight, hospital ID number, and provisional diagnosis or reason for admission.
- Laboratory test results.
- Other medical data relevant to the patient's drug therapy.
- Sensitivities, allergies, and other significant contraindications.
- Drug products dispensed, dates of original orders, strengths, dosage forms, quantities, dosage frequency or directions, and automatic stop dates.
- Intravenous therapy data.
- Blood products administered.
- Initials of the pharmacist or technician transcribing and verifying the transcription of the medication order.
- Number of doses or amounts dispensed.
- Items relevant or related to the patient's drug therapy not provided by the pharmacy.

After each physician order, the nurse's Medication administration record (MAR) is updated on the nursing unit. An MAR is a record of all current medications prescribed for each patient. The record contains information on the drugs, administration times and directions for use. Prior to giving the new medicine to the patient, the nurse cross-checks the MAR against the patient order to ensure that it is appropriate. After patient administration, the nurse initials the MAR to denote that the drug was given and at what time.

Pharmacy medication profiles and the nursing MARs are linked within each institution's computerized medication system. In completely computerized record keeping systems, the MARs is electronic and is updated instantaneously with each new order entered in the pharmacy medication profile. For some systems hard copy of each MAR is also maintained and any changes in the patient medications are updated manually on the nursing unit.

8.7 INSTRUCTION LABELS

The pharmacist is responsible for labelling medication containers. Labels and medication containers should:
1. Any container to be used outside the institution should bear its name, address, and phone number.
2. The metric system should be given prominence on all labels when both metric and apothecary measurement units are given.
3. The names of all therapeutically active ingredients should be indicated in compound mixtures.
4. Labels for medications should indicate the total amount of drugs.
5. Drugs and chemicals in forms intended for dilution or reconstitution should carry appropriate directions.
6. The expiry date of the contents, and proper storage conditions, should be clearly indicated.
7. For parenteral medications, route of administration should be indicated—IM or IV.

8. Labels for large volume sterile solutions should permit visual inspection of the container contents.
9. Digits, letters, unofficial synonyms, and abbreviations should not be used to identify medications, with the exception of approved letter or number codes for investigational drugs, or drugs being used in blended clinical studies.
10. Containers presenting difficulty in labelling, such as small tubes should be labelled with no less than the prescription serial number, name of drug, strength, and name of the patient. The container should then be placed in a larger carton bearing a label with all necessary information.
11. The label should conform to all applicable local laws and regulations.
12. Medication labels of stock containers and repackaged or prepackaged drugs should carry codes to identify the source and lot number of medication.
13. Drug strengths, volumes, and Amount dispensed should be indicated.

8.8 MEDICATION DELIVERY TO PATIENTS

Table 8.1: Medication delivery from Pharmacy to Patient Care unit

Medication category	Delivery/Storage method
Stable scheduled medications	A 24 hr supply is kept in a patient-specific bin on the medication cart in the unit
Unstable scheduled medications	Automatic delivery of medications to the unit 1 hr before administration time
Scheduled IV/TPN solutions	Automatic delivery of medications to the unit before administration time
PRN medications	A limited supply is kept in a patient-specific bin on the medication cart.
Controlled medications	A limited patient-specific supply is secured in an automated dispensing cabinet or in a medication cart
Emergency medications	Emergency drug kits are located on units and replaced by the pharmacy in response to a request from the unit
Investigational medications	Per investigational drug protocol

8.9 CHARGING POLICY

1. Breakeven point pricing

The break-even point is the level at which total sales are equal to total costs i.e. no profit no loss. Break-even analysis is a critical tool for the administration to understand the relationship between prices, volume, and costs. The pharmacist has to ascertain the fixed and indirect expenses including expenses of hospital administration, maintenance, housekeeping etc. This knowledge affects decisions about cost structure, pricing strategy.

2. Cost plus pricing

Desired income from drugs/Cost of prescription drugs × 100 = per cent above cost to be charged for prescription.

Easy to: Calculate minimal information, to administer, and to be sure about escalation to justify in all fairness to the hospital and patients.

3. Fee concept

It is the professional fee which charges the patient of all operating, overhead and compensatory expenses but not the actual cost of drug and container.

4. Computerized pricing

This system is fair and provides computerized online pharmacy pricing. The computer program has the following information:
- Patient number
- Dose factor
- Total number of doses dispensed
- Drug identification number

5. Profit feature

In this, profit is calculated into price to the patient in following ways:
- A fixed fee per prescription.
- Addition of predetermined percentage of the break-even point figure.

6. A per diem drug charge

The basic per diem charge covers drug purchasing and inventory control, department management, drug information services; dose preparation, drug order interpretation, drug therapy monitoring, and helps the pharmacists to be answerable to nurses and physicians. This system provides quality pharmaceutical services and enables hospital to reduce administrative and accounting cost.

8.10 DISPENSING OF DRUGS TO AMBULATORY PATIENTS

After the registration, consultation with the doctor, and finally receiving the prescription, the patient goes to the pharmacist to obtain the medicines.

1. While dispensing a prescription, pharmacist should take every precaution to eliminate errors. The prescription should be received without raising any doubt in the mind of the patient.
2. If pharmacist needs any clarification about the prescription, he should contact the physician without the knowledge of the patient.
3. Pharmacist checks the ingredients and collects the materials for compounding and dispensing.
4. The compounded prescription is filled in a counter and labelled with detailed instructions including name, gender, age, registration number for use and storage.
5. The pharmacist shall maintain a register for the purpose of accounting. Mixtures like ointments, lotions, and powders are not recorded while records of costly drugs like injections; antibiotics etc. are maintained and are issued to poor patients only on special drug form.

6. Prescription is given back to the patient so that the same can be produced by him during his next visit.
7. Prescription relating to schedule G, H and X drugs to be written and dealt with the provision of Drugs and Cosmetics (Amendments) Act 1972. The emergency cases of the hospital may be issued medicines immediately.

The ambulatory care pharmacy in modern hospitals is located in an area that facilitates the services provided for ambulatory patients. The role of the pharmacist working in such area is very important and includes the following:
- Reviewing all prescriptions for, clinical appropriateness of the choice of drug and its dosage, route of administration, and duration of therapy.
- Monitoring of the patient's medication profile for indications of drug abuse, misuse or noncompliance.
- Maintaining a professional communication with the prescribers and nurses working in ambulatory area to achieve together the quality patient's care required.
- Supervising all activities and personnel involved in drug dispensing to ensure the quality of services provided.
- Providing drug consultation for individual patient.
- Participating in patient education programs.
- Participating in DUE concerning ambulatory area.
- Communicating with the IV area for the preparation of all injectable drugs to be administered to ambulatory and personal care patients, except in emergencies.

8.11 OUTPATIENT DISPENSING

An outpatient is a patient who visits a hospital, clinic, or associated facility for diagnosis or treatment. The patient with minor and common illness visits OPD (Outpatient department) for physician's consultation and post examining the patient, the physician prescribes medicines to the patient who goes to the pharmacy to collect the prescribed medicines where the pharmacist after proper examination carries out the compounding of medicines. The medication is well packed into required containers and is properly labeled directing the precautions, dose and route of administration of the medication. Pharmacist also calculates the price of dispensed prescription and hands it over to patient.

Outpatients load is divided into three categories by the hospitals:

1. Ambulatory care is a personal health care consultation, treatment or intervention using advanced medical technology or procedures delivered on an outpatient basis where the patient's stay at the hospital or clinic and the discharge, occurs on the same calendar day. Ambulatory care is given to persons who are able to ambulate or walk about. Many medical investigations and treatments for acute illness and preventive health care can be performed on an ambulatory basis, including minor surgical and medical procedures, most types of dental services, dermatology services, and many types of diagnostic procedures. Other types of ambulatory care services include emergency visits, rehabilitation visits, and in some cases telephone consultations.

2. **Tertiary outpatient** is a direct referral from a primary or secondary health professional, in a facility that has personnel and facilities for advanced medical investigation and treatment, such as a tertiary referral hospital. Examples of tertiary care services are cancer management, neurosurgery, cardiac surgery, plastic surgery, treatment for severe burns, advanced neonatology services, palliative, and other complex medical and surgical interventions.

3. **Primary care** is the medical care a patient receives upon first contact with the health care system, before referral elsewhere within the system. All physicians and most pediatricians and internists are in primary care. The aims of primary care are to provide the patient with a broad spectrum of care, both preventive and curative, over a period of time and to coordinate all of the care the patient receives.

8.12 LOCATION AND LAYOUT OF OUTPATIENT DISPENSING

There is no set rule regarding the location of outpatient dispensing area; however, it should be close to the central registration and outpatient department so that patients or attendants do not find any difficulty to locate.

In an outpatient pharmacy, dispensing workflow is as follows

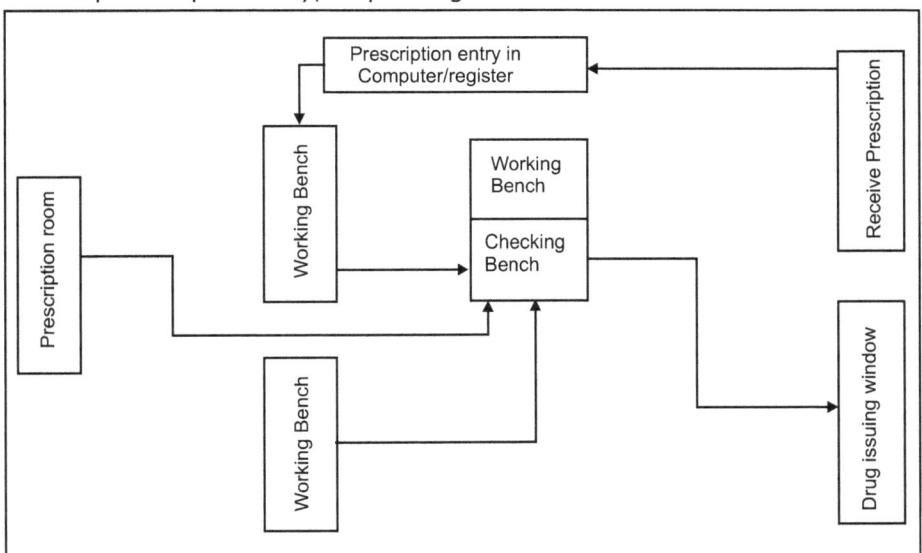

Fig. 8.3: Prescription dispensing workflow in pharmacy

- Prescription taken in from patient.
- Prescription item typed into computer to generate label.
- One set of labels and prescription is taken away by one dispenser to pick medications.
- The dispenser finishes picking all the medication and takes them to a checking point.
- Medications checked.
- Medication handed to patient.

8.13 EMERGENCY MEDICATION SUPPLIES

There should be a system to supply emergency drugs when the pharmacist is off the premises or when there is insufficient time to reach the pharmacy. Emergency drugs should include only such medicines whose prompt use is immediately required. The emergency drug supply should not be a source for normal "SOS (Si Opus Sit)" or "prn (Pro Re Nata)" drug orders. The medications included should be primarily for the treatment of cardiac arrest, circulatory collapse, allergic reactions; convulsions, and bronchospasm. The Pharmaceutical and Therapeutics committee should specify the drugs and supplies to be included in emergency stocks lest their non-availability create an awkward situation. Emergency drug supplies should be inspected by pharmacy personnel on a routine basis to determine if contents have become outdated and are maintained at adequate levels. Emergency kits should have a seal which should indicate when they were opened.

8.14 DISPENSING OF CONTROLLED DRUGS

Controlled drugs are classified in the order of their abuse risk and placed in Schedules by the Federal Drug Enforcement Administration (DEA). The drugs with the highest abuse potential are placed in Schedule I, and those with the lowest abuse potential are in Schedule V. These schedules are commonly shown as C-I, C-II, C-III, C-IV, and C-V. Some examples of drugs in these Schedules are as follows:

- **Schedule I** — drugs with a high abuse risk are heroin, marijuana, LSD, PCP, and crack cocaine.
- **Schedule II** — These drugs can cause severe psychological or physical dependence. Schedule II drugs include certain narcotic, stimulant, and depressant drugs such as morphine, cocaine, Oxycodone, methylphenidate, and dextroamphetamine.
- **Schedule III, IV, or V** — Schedule III, IV, or V drugs include those containing smaller amounts of certain narcotic and non-narcotic drugs, anti-anxiety drugs, tranquilizers; sedatives, stimulants, and non-narcotic analgesics. Some examples are acetaminophen with codeine paregoric, hydrocodone with acetaminophen, diazepam, Alprazolam, propoxyphene, and Pentazocine.

A prescription for a controlled substance must be dated and signed on the date of issue. The prescription must include the patient's full name and address, and the practitioner's full name, address and registration number. The prescription must also include:

1. drug name
2. strength
3. dosage form
4. quantity prescribed
5. directions for use
6. number of refills (if any) authorized

8.14.1 Labelling

The pharmacist dispensing a prescription containing a controlled substance shall affix to the container a label showing the date of dispensing; the pharmacy name and address; serial number of the prescription; full name of the patient; name of the prescribing practitioner; directions for use; and cautionary statements, contained in the prescription order or required by law.

8.15 RESPONSIBILITIES OF A PHARMACIST IN DRUG DISPENSING
1. Preparation, compounding could be done by a pharmacist or technician under supervision of another senior pharmacist.
2. A pharmacist should ensure that the prescriptions are written on the appropriate prescription form and countersigned by the physician.
3. The pharmacist will check the prescription for printed patient's information (Name, hospital number, age and telephone number), allergies if available.
4. The pharmacist has to be sure about the information required on the prescription.
   - Prescription should be absolutely legible.
   - Diagnosis.
   - Generic name of the drug, drug strength and concentration, dose, frequency and duration of therapy.
   - Date of writing the prescription.
   - All prescription should be written in English.
   - Metric system should be used.
   - Only approved abbreviation is to be used.
   - Desirable is that situations such as pregnancy, breastfeeding, renal failure is written on the prescription to allow drug monitoring or safety and dose accuracy.
6. The prescription is filled and initiated by a pharmacist or a pharmacy technician, and cross-checked by another pharmacist.
7. All medicines in each prescription should be entered in the computer.
8. The label should be compatible with good labelling standard (refer to the pharmacy policy and procedure for labelling).

8.16 VALID PRESCRIPTION AND DISPENSING REQUIREMENTS
1. A prescription for a controlled substance may only be issued by a physician, dentist, pediatrician, mid-level practitioner, or other registered practitioner authorized to prescribe controlled substances by the jurisdiction in which the practitioner is licensed to practice. The practitioner is liable for ensuring that the prescription conforms to all requirements of the law and regulations.
2. A prescription for a controlled substance must be issued for a legitimate medical purpose by a practitioner acting in the usual course of professional practice. A prescription for a controlled substance must be signed on the date of issue. A prescription may not be issued to obtain controlled substances for supplying the individual practitioner for the purpose of general dispensing to patients.
3. A pharmacist is required to exercise sound professional judgement when making a determination about the legitimacy of a controlled substance prescription. The law does not require a pharmacist to dispense a prescription of doubtful, questionable, or suspicious origin. A pharmacist who deliberately ignores the norms for issuing controlled drugs is liable and may be prosecuted along with the issuing practitioner.
4. The delivery of narcotic drugs from pharmacy to the wards and nursing stations must be carried through authorized persons.

5. Charges for controlled substances depend on policy of hospital.
6. While administering a dose, if the patient refuses or doctor cancels any dose, it is the duty of the nurse to cause the demise of the drug and record "Refused by the patient" or "Cancelled by the doctor". Nurses should maintain such records and inform to the pharmacy.

8.17 RECORD KEEPING

Any pharmacy practitioner shall maintain complete and accurate records of each controlled substance received, distributed, dispensed or disposed/contaminated. Records required shall be maintained at the location where the drug is received, distributed or dispensed, and be available for inspection by authorized persons for at least 05 years from the date of such record. A complete and accurate biennial physical inventory of all schedule II, III, IV and V controlled substances on hand shall be made in conformance with all applicable laws.
 (a) Records of schedule II controlled substances, other than prescription orders, shall be maintained separately from all other records.
 (b) Records of schedule III, IV and V controlled substances shall be maintained either separately or in such form that the information required is readily retrievable from the registrant's ordinary records.

8.17.1 Records in drug distribution system

The pharmacist must establish and maintain adequate record keeping systems. Various records must be retained by the pharmacy because of governmental regulations and are necessary for sound management of the pharmacy department. Records must be retained for the length of time prescribed under law.

It is essential that the pharmacist study the laws to become familiar with their requirements for permits, tax stamps, storage of alcohol and controlled substances, records, and reports. Among the records needed in the drug distribution and control system are
 (a) Controlled substances inventory and dispensing records.
 (b) Records of medication orders and their processing.
 (c) Manufacturing and packaging production records.
 (d) Pharmacy workload records.
 (e) Purchase and inventory records.
 (f) Records of equipment maintenance.
 (g) Records of results and actions taken in quality-assurance and drug audit programs.

8.18 PHARMACY SERVICE WHEN THE PHARMACY IS CLOSED

Hospitals provide services to patients 24 hours a day; hence, the services of a pharmacist should be available at all times. Where around the clock operation of the pharmacy is not feasible, a pharmacist should be available on an "on call" basis. The use of "night cabinets" and drug dispensing by non-pharmacists should be minimized and eliminated wherever possible. Drugs must not be dispensed to outpatients or hospital staff by anyone other than a pharmacist while the pharmacy is open. If it is necessary for nurses to obtain drugs when the pharmacy is closed and the pharmacist is unavailable, written procedures covering this practice should be developed.

In such a situation only limited supply of the drugs needed in emergent situations is availed; the drugs should be in proper single dose packages and a log should be kept of all doses removed. This log must contain the date and time the drugs were taken, a complete description of the drug product(s), name of the (authorized) nurse involved, and the patient's name. When no pharmacist is available, emergency room patients should receive drugs packaged as per the rules recommended in the emergency room "formulary".

8.19 AUTOMATED MEDICINE STORAGE AND DISTRIBUTION DEVICES AND PRESCRIPTION-FILLING SYSTEMS

Medicines may be stored in and dispensed from automated storage and distribution devices in patient care areas, which are particularly helpful in urgent care situations and facilities without 24-hour pharmacy services. The use of such devices for controlled substances can facilitate audits.

Automated medicine storage and distribution devices can reduce the rate of medication errors and increase the efficiency of drug administration. They also may free the pharmacist for clinical services.

Automated medicine storage and distribution systems should be fully integrated with the health care institution's medication-use process to provide medicines in unit dose or single unit-of-use packages in ready-to-use form, make medicines available only near the time of administration, create an individualized patient medication profile, allow for pharmacist review of medication orders before dispensing, ensure proper storage conditions, prevent access by unauthorized personnel, allow access in emergencies, and meet applicable regulations and standards.

Automated prescription-filling systems can reduce the pharmacy staff time required for the direct and indirect activities related to the filling of prescriptions. These activities include receiving, order entry, filling, inspection, packaging, dispensing, telephone calls, and inventory management.

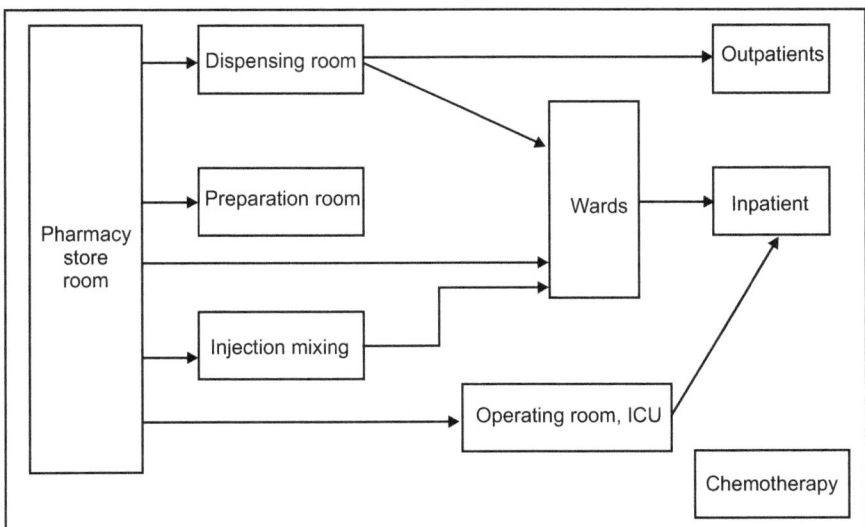

Fig. 8.4 Distribution of medicines from the pharmacy to the patients in the hospital

SUMMARY

Drug distribution service is the vital part of hospital organisation. The hospital pharmacist working with other professionals accepted responsibility to purchase or prepare drug products approved for use by the PTC. These products are then distributed by the pharmacist so they are available to the nurse to administer to the patient as prescribed by the physician.

Drug distribution services is classified in two types — in-patient drug distribution system and out-patient drug distribution service. In in-patient drug distribution system there are four systems for drug distribution; floor or ward stock system, individual prescription order system and combination of the above two mentioned systems and unit dose system in which medication are contained in and administered from single unit or unit dose packages. Unit dose system is the most favoured and has several advantages over the other systems.

Medications should be given only on the prescription of a qualified doctor and medication order should include patient's name and location, medication generic name, dose regimen and date and hour the order was written. Physician's order can be sent to the pharmacy by self-copying order forms, electromechanical and computerized system. Patient medication profile is an essential item to be maintained in the pharmacy for all in-patients and those out-patients routinely receiving care at the institution and updated. Dispensing to the ambulatory patients is very critical as pharmacist should take care of every precaution to eliminate the errors. The ambulatory care pharmacy in modern hospitals is located in an area that facilitates the services provided for the ambulatory patients.

Outpatient dispensing is divided into three categories by the hospitals, e.g. ambulatory care in which medical care is provided to those who can ambulate or walk about whereas in tertiary outpatient, a direct referral from primary and secondary health professional to advanced medical treatment. In primary care, patient receives first contact with health care system. Controlled drug are classified into Schedule I, II, III, IV and V depending on the abuse risk, those with the lowest abuse potential are in Schedule V.

Pharmacist is responsible for preparation, compounding of the drugs. Any pharmacy, practitioner shall maintain complete and accurate records of each controlled substance received, distributed, dispensed or disposed/contaminated. Records required shall be maintained at the location where the drug is received, distributed or dispensed, and be available for inspection by authorized persons for at least 05 years from the date of such record.

MANUFACTURING UNIT HOSPITAL

9.1 INTRODUCTION

Hospitals, in the present scenario are becoming self dependent by manufacturing the medicines within the premises which proves to be cost effective both for the hospital and the patients. Hospitals emphasize the manufacturing of daily required medicines rather than to buy from outsourced suppliers which shows a huge variation in price. Sterile medications like parenteral and non sterile products like emulsions, suspensions and semisolids are manufactured in the hospital.

9.2 POLICY MAKING OF MANUFACTURABLE ITEMS

1. *Medicines to be manufactured*: Hospital should manufacture those medicines whose consumption rate is on the higher side in a particular hospital. It should be taken into consideration that the manufacturing in hospital meets the regular demand.
2. *Manufacturing requirement*: It should be determined each time by calculating the consumption rate for each item by comparing it with the previous records.
3. *Material requirement and procurement*: Material required for medicine, packaging and other should be calculated and procured after identifying the right vendor who can provide the material at proper price, good quality and should be capable of supplying it regularly.
4. *Production control*: There should be proper production planning and control as planning initiates action while control is an adjusting process, providing corrective measures for planned development. Production control regulates the orderly requirement of materials in the manufacturing process from the beginning to the end.
5. *Good Manufacturing practice* (**GMP**): Good manufacturing practices should be followed for manufacturing in both sterile and non sterile products.
6. *Quality*: It should be the main priority in the policy as the manufacturing deals with the public healthcare. Quality should be maintained at each step i.e.,
   (a) By sorting the right vendors who provide the quality material.
   (b) Inspecting the raw material before its use.
   (c) Implementing the GMPs in production and packaging.
   (d) By employing the qualified and technically competent staff.

7. **Cost of operation:** Operating cost includes both direct costs which is labour, cost of material and in direct cost like maintenance of building, insurance policies, space maintenance etc.
8. **Staffing:** Inexpedient number of staff disturbs the manufacturing programmes. The production section should always be supervised by technically competent and legally qualified personals that will guide and support the technical and non-technical staff.

9.3 PARAMETERS FOR BUYING THE HOSPITAL MEDICINES

1. **Quality:** The quality of the purchased item and the quality that the hospital could have made it on its own are compared. If there is possibility of a very wide variation from outsourcing, quality consideration plays a key role in making a make-or-buy decision. A wide variation in quality results in own manufacturing by the hospital.
2. **Quantity:** This decision is taken when the supplies are likely to be too large to interest an outsider. Items which are required on daily routine can be manufactured in the hospital and corresponding large inventory can be maintained to meet production needs.
3. **Cost consideration:** The comparison between the cost of buying and cost of own manufacturing is the main criterion for making or buying the products.
4. **Supply assurance:** Hospital manufacturing assures supply vis-à-vis supply from outside.

9.4 DEMAND AND COSTING

Demand estimation or demand forecast is the process of forming judgment about the quantities of product or services that will be demanded by customers in the future. Such forecast of demand is very useful for planning and control of activities in production, procurement, marketing, personnel.

Following parameters affect the decision of manufacturing in hospital:

1. **Quality**: Quality of purchased drug and manufactured drug is compared. If quality of manufactured drugs is better than decision of manufacturing the drugs in hospital is taken. In case of LVP the hospitals manufacture because outside manufacturing may compromise the quality of LVP.
2. **Quantity:** Drugs which are used in large quantities are manufactured in hospital after deciding break even-point.
3. **Cost:** Here we compare cost of buying from outside with the cost of manufacturing in the hospital.
4. **Service:** Manufacturing in hospital assures regular supply of medicine at proper time.

9.5 ESTIMATION OF DEMAND

The production of sterile and non-sterile pharmaceutical products in hospital is related to requirements of the hospital in a given period of time. A correct estimation of future demand is necessary. There are three methods of demand estimation.

1. **Judgement method:** These are the judgements of the clinical and pharmacy staff based on their experience about quantity of drug required for hospital.
2. **On the basis of past history:** With the help of past records the requirements of drugs for future is determined.
3. **Casual method:** For example, the demand of whole blood is related to admissions in the casualty/ emergency wards; demand for antibiotics is related to the number of patients with infectious diseases.

9.6 PERSONAL REQUIREMENTS

1. Each person responsible for supervising the manufacture, processing, packing, or holding of a drug product should have the education, training, and experience, or any combination thereof, to perform assigned functions in a manner to provide assurance that the drug product has the safety, identity, strength, quality, and purity that it purports or is represented to possess.
2. Personnel engaged in the manufacture, processing, packing, or holding of a drug product should wear clean clothes commensurate with the duties they perform. Protective apparel, such as head, face, hand, and arm coverings, should be worn as necessary to protect drug products from contamination.
3. Changing and washing should follow a written procedure designed to minimize contamination of clean area clothing or carry-through of contaminants to the clean areas.
4. Personnel should practice good sanitation and health habits.
5. Only personnel authorized by supervisory personnel should have access to the buildings and facilities designated as limited-access areas.
6. There should be an adequate number of qualified personnel to perform and supervise the manufacture, processing, packing, or holding of each drug product.
7. An air shower is also used for personal to remove any loose shreds.
8. Movements within the room should be minimal, and entry and exit be restricted during operations.
9. Wristwatches, make-up and jewellery should not be worn in clean areas.

9.7 STERILE MANUFACTURING

Sterile products are very critical and sensitive in nature, a very high degree of precautions, prevention and preparations are needed. Dampness, dirt and darkness are to be avoided to ensure aseptic conditions in all areas. There shall be strict compliance in the prescribed standards especially in the matter of supply of water,

air, active materials and in the maintenance of hygienic environment. Sterile products include parenteral and sterile ophthalmic preparations. The special equipment required for manufacturing sterile products includes components:
- Washing machines.
- Steam sterilizers (autoclave).
- Dry heat sterilizers (hot air oven).
- Membrane filter assemblies.
- Manufacturing vessels.
- Blenders.
- Ampoule filling machines.
- Powder filling machines.
- Sealing and labeling machines.
- Vacuum testing chambers.
- Inspection machines.
- Lyophilizes.
- Pressure vessels.
- Suitable and fully integrated washing sterilizing filling lines may be provided, depending upon the type and volume of activity.

9.8 FACILITIES AND REQUIREMENTS

9.8.1 Environmental Control

Effective environmental control, both physical and biologic is essential but the level achievable is related to the characteristics of the facility. Further rigid standards from plant to plant and from geographic location to another are not appropriate. Allowance also must be made for variation in control associated with the seasonal conditions. The standards of environmental control vary depending on the area involved and type of product being prepared. Unquestionably, the entire area used for the preparation of a product prepared aseptically must be maintained under the rigid control that the existing technology permits. If the product is to be terminally sterilized, somewhat less rigid biologic control of the compounding and filling areas may be acceptable. However, rigid standard of cleanliness must be maintained. High standards of cleanliness, excluding daily use of disinfecting procedures are usually acceptable for the cleanup and packaging areas.

9.8.2 Traffic Control

Carefully designed arrangement to control and minimize traffic, particularly 'in' and 'out' of the aseptic areas is essential. Access by personnel to the aseptic corridor and aseptic compound and filling rooms should be only possible through an airlock. Pass-through openings and double ended sterilizers are provided to permit controlled passage of supplies from non-aseptic to aseptic area. Persons should be permitted to enter aseptic areas only after following rigidly prescribed procedures for removing daily clothing, washing their hands and putting on gowns, hats, shoes, facemasks, gloves and other prescribed attire. Once the workers entered the aseptic area, they are not permitted to move in and out of the area without lab gown; personnel assigned to cleaning and packaging should be restricted to these areas. Unauthorized personnel should never be permitted to enter the aseptic area.

9.8.3 Housekeeping

All equipment and the surrounding work area must be cleaned thoroughly at the end of the working day. No contaminating residues from the concluded process may remain. The ceiling, walls, and other structural surfaces must be cleaned with a frequency which is most appropriate. All cleaning equipments should be selected for its effectiveness and freedom from lint-producing tendencies. It should be reserved for use in the aseptic areas only.

9.8.4 Surface Disinfection

All surfaces should be disinfected, at least in the aseptic areas. An effective liquid disinfectant should be sprayed or wiped on all surfaces. Irradiation from ultraviolet lamps that are located provide adequate radiation intensity on the maximum extent of surfaces in a room and that are maintained free from dust and films further reduces the viable micro-organisms present on the surface and in the air. Ultraviolet rays may be particularly useful to irradiate the inside exposed surfaces of the processing tanks, surfaces under hoods. The surface of the conveyor belts and the similar confined surfaces those are otherwise, difficult to render aseptic. However, they cannot reach unexposed surfaces such as pipe connections to tanks, the undersides of conveyors and the inside of containers. The UV lamps must be kept clean and care must be taken to check for a decrease in effective emission, a natural occurrence due to a change in the glass structure with aging.

9.8.5 Air Control

In aseptic area, air must be exchanged at frequent intervals. Fresh outside or recycled air must first be filtered to remove gross particulate matter. A spun glass, cloth, or shredded polyethylene filter may be used for this preliminary cleaning operation. At a time, more than one pre-filter may be used in series, the first one is quite large and the next somewhat smaller pore size to provide a gradation of particle size removal from heavily contaminated air. To remove finer debris down to the submicron range, including micro-organism, a high efficiency particulate air (HEPA) filter is used. The HEPA filter has been defined as at least 99.97 per cent efficient in removing particles of 0.3um size and larger and composed of glass fibers and filters or electrostatic precipitators may be employed. Air passing though these units can be considered virtually free from foreign matter. Another air cleaning system washes the air with a disinfectant and controls the humidity at the same time.

Blowers should be installed in the air ventilation system upstream to the filters, so that all the dirt producing devices are ahead of the filter. The clean air is normally distributed to the regulated areas by means of metal ducts. Since it is practically impossible to keep these ducts as clean as required, it is normally preferred to install

HEPA filters at spots where the clean air enters the controlled room. Alternatively, the ducts may be replaced with a room usually above the production area, into which clean air is blown and then distributed through opening into each of the process rooms. The entire plenum can be kept clean and aseptic.

The clean and aseptic air is distributed in such a manner that it flows into the maximum security room at the greatest volume flow rate, thereby producing a positive pressure in these areas. This prevents unclean air from rushing into the aseptic area though cracks, temporarily opened doors or other openings. The pressure is reduced successively so that the air follows from the maximum security area to other less critical areas for return to the filtration system. At the intake end of the system, fresh air usually about 02 per cent is continually introduced for the comfort and needs of the personnel. The air is usually conditioned with respect to the temperature and humidity for the comfort of the personnel and sometimes to meet the special requirements of a product.

9.8.6 Horizontal Laminar Flow Hood Vertical Laminar Flow Hood

A relatively new air control system, based on laminar flow principle, has greatly improved the potential for environmental control of aseptic areas. Currently, it is the only means available for achieving a class 100 clean room. A class 100 clean room is defined as a room in which the particle count in the air is not more than 100 per cubic feet of 0.5um and lager in size. The air filtered through HEPA filter is blown evenly out of the entire back or top of the work bench or entire side or from ceiling of a room. The air flow must be uniform in velocity and direction throughout any given cross-section of the area, being exhausted from the opposite side. The air velocity employed should be 100 k 20 ft/min. Contamination is controlled because it is swept away with the airflow.

9.9 STERILE PRODUCT AREAS

9.9.1 Clean- up Area

- Free from dust, fibers and micro-organisms.
- Constructed in such a way that should withstand moisture, steam and detergent
- Ceiling and walls be coated with material to prevent accumulation of dust and micro-organisms.
- Exhaust fans are fitted to remove heat and humidity.
- The area should be kept clean to avoid contamination to aseptic area.
- The containers and closures are washed and dried in this area.

9.9.2 Preparation Area

- The ingredients are mixed and preparation is done for filling.
- Strict precaution be taken to prevent contamination from outside.
- Cabinets and counters.
- Ceiling and walls : sealed and painted.

9.9.3 Aseptic Area

- Walls, floors and ceiling should be impervious, non-shedding, non-flaking and non-cracking so that they can be easily washed and disinfected.
- Doors should be made of non-shedding material like Aluminum or Steel material. Wooden doors should not be used. Doors should open towards the higher-pressure area so that they close automatically due to air pressure.
- Storage tanks, mixing tanks containing compounded products should be kept outside the aseptic area.

9.9.4 Quarantine Area

- After filling, sealing and sterilization the products or batch is kept in this area.
- The random samples are chosen and given for analysis to QC department.
- The batch is sent to packing after issuing satisfactory reports of analysis from QC.
- If any problem is observed in above analysis the decision is to be taken for reprocessing.

9.9.5 Labelling and Packaging Area

- Batch numbering and overprinting of labels takes place.
- Packing is done to protect the product from external environment.
- The ideal packing is that which protects the product during transportation, storage, shipping and handling.
- The labelled container should be packed in cardboard or plastic containers.
- Ampoules should be packed in partitioned boxes.

9.10 MANUFACTURING PROCESS FOR STERILE PRODUCTS

9.10.1 Equipments Cleaning

Equipments should be cleaned thoroughly after disassembling with a stiff brush using an effective detergent. The equipments are then washed with distilled water and sometimes dichromate solution is used for glassware, rubber tubing followed by rinsing with distilled water.

Washed containers should be sterilized immediately before use. Sterilized containers, if not used within established given time, should be rinsed with distilled or filtered purified water and re-sterilized. Components, bulk-product containers, equipment and any other articles required in a clean area where aseptic work is in progress should be sterilized and passed into the area through double-ended sterilizers sealed into the wall.

9.10.2 Preparation of Solution

Manufacture of sterile products should be carried out only in areas under defined conditions. Various ingredients of formulations are collected at one place where compounding is to be done.

9.10.3 Filtration Membrane

(a) Solutions for Large Volume parenteral should be filtered through a non-fibre releasing, sterilizing grade cartridge/membrane filter of nominal pore size of 0.22 μ for aseptic filling whereas 0.45 μ porosity should be used for terminally sterilized products.

(b) A second filtration using another 0.22 μ sterilizing grade cartridge / membrane filter should be performed immediately prior to filling. Process specifications should indicate the maximum time during which a filtration system may be used with a view to precluding microbial build-up to levels that may affect the microbiological quality of the Large Volume Parenteral.

The contents of all vessels and containers used in manufacture and storage during the various manufacturing stages should be conspicuously labelled with the name of the product, batch number, batch size and stage of manufacture.

9.10.4 Filling of Product

Each lot of finished product should be filled in one continuous operation. In each case, where one batch is filled in using more than one operation, each lot should be tested separately for sterility and held separately till sterility test results are known. Special care should be exercised while filling products in powder form so as not to contaminate the environment during transfer of powder to filling machine-hopper.

Form-Fill-Seal units are specially built automated machines in which through one continuous operation, containers are formed from thermoplastic granules, filled and then sealed.

Blow, fill-seal units are machines in which containers are molded/ blown (pre-formed) in separate clean rooms, by non-continuous operations. Form-Fill-Seal/Blow, Fill-Seal machines used for the manufacture of products for terminal sterilization.

9.10.5 Sterilization

Before any sterilization process is adopted, its suitability for the product and its efficacy in achieving the desired sterilizing conditions in all parts of each type of load pattern to be processed should be demonstrated by physical measurements and by biological indicators. Sterilization is done by various methods depending upon the nature of preparation.

- **In case of drugs:** Autoclaving at 115°C for 30 minutes.
- **Thermolabile drugs:** Filtration through bacteria proof filters.
- **Oily vehicles:** Dry heat method.
- Ionizing radiation, but not with ultraviolet radiation unless the process is thoroughly validated.
- **Gaseous method:** By ethylene oxide or other suitable gaseous sterilizing agents.

All the sterilization processes should be appropriately validated. The validity of the process should be verified at regular intervals, but at least annually. Whenever significant modifications have been made to the equipment and product, records should be maintained.

9.11 STERILITY TESTING

A sterility test may be defined as a test that critically assesses whether a sterilized product is free from contaminating micro-organisms.

9.11.1 Membrane Filtration and Direct Transfer

The membrane filtration method requires the test article to first pass through a size exclusion membrane capable of retaining micro-organisms. The concept is that the micro-organisms will collect on the surface of a 0.45 micron pore size filter. This filter is segmented and transferred to appropriate media. The test media are Fluid thioglycollate medium (FTM) and Soybean casein digest medium (SCDM). FTM is selected based upon its ability to support the growth of anaerobic and aerobic micro-organisms. SCDM is selected based upon its ability to support a wide range of aerobic bacteria and fungi (i.e. yeasts and molds). The incubation period is 14 days. The majority of biological samples are tested using the immersion method. However, for test articles with large volumes in which the entire contents must be tested or if there is a substance within the test article that is known or determined to be bacteriostatic or fungistatic the membrane filtration method may be required.

Advantages

(i) It can accommodate large volume samples (up to 500 ml).

(ii) If the test article contains substances that inhibit the growth of micro-organisms, rinsing the filter membrane with a suitable rinse agent can remove all or most of these inhibitory substances.

Disadvantage

This method consumes a large volume of final product during B and F testing, especially in the case of final container testing.

9.11.2 Direct Inoculation

In the Direct Inoculation (the immersion) method the test articles are inoculated directly into tubes or bottles that contain an appropriate medium and are incubated for a period of 14 days.

Advantages

(i) This method provides a means of sterility testing for materials that cannot be easily filtered.

(ii) This method consumes less product volume during the conduct of the bacteriostatic and fungi stasis (B and F) testing

Disadvantage

Disadvantage of this method is the volume constraint. Also, inherently bacteriostatic or fungistatic components cannot be removed or adequately neutralized.

9.11.3 Pyrogens Testing

Pyrogens are the by-products of micro-organisms mainly of bacteria, molds and viruses.

This test consists of measuring the rise in body temperature evoked in rabbits by the injection of a sterile solution of the substance being examined.

During the processing these pyrogens may come from water, active constituent or the excipients or from the equipments. Chemically, these pyrogens are lipid substances associated with carrier usually polysaccharides or may be proteins. Parenteral solutions are officially tested for the presence of pyrogens by a biological test in which "FEVER" response of rabbits is used as criterion.

9.11.4 Test Animals

Healthy mature rabbits each weighing not less than 01.5 kg are used and the animals should not lose body mass when kept on a constant diet for not less than one week. Rabbits are not used repeatedly in the same test unless a long resting period is taken. Animals should be excluded which have been used for a previous test that was decided as pyrogenic. Record the rectal temperature four times at 02 hr intervals for 01-03 days prior to test. House the animals individually during the period in an area free from disturbance likely to excite them and exercise particular care to avoid disturbances on the day of the test. Keep the temperature in an area of performing test uniform between 20°C and 27°C and preferably maintain constant humidity for at least 48 hrs before the test.

9.11.5 Procedure

Thermometer is inserted into rectum of the test animal to a constant depth in the range of 60-90 mm and temperature is recorded after a sufficient period of time. The food is withheld from the test animals beginning several hours before the first temperature recording and until the test is completed. Temperature of the test animals is determined three times at 01 hr interval before the sample is injected. When the second and third temperature readings show little difference, the later is taken as the control temperature. Animals whose second and third temperatures are not in accord or exceed 39.8°C should not be used even if these two values are similar. The sample is warmed at 37°C before injection and administered intravenously through an ear vein within 15 minutes after the third temperature is recorded. Hypotonic solutions other than water may be made isotonic by the addition of pyrogens free sodium chloride before the test. Temperatures are recorded three times at 01 hr interval after injection. The difference between the control temperature and the highest temperature is taken to be rise in body temperature.

9.11.6 Interpretation of Results

The test is carried out on a group of three rabbits. If two of the three rabbits show an individual rise of 0.6°C or more above the respective control temperature, the test should be considered as positive. If only one animal shows a temperature rise of 0.6°C or more, or if the sum of the temperature rises of the three animals exceeds 01.4°C, repeat the test on a group of five other rabbits. The test should be considered positive, if two or more of the five rabbits show an individual temperature rise of 0.6°C. When the pyrogens test is positive, the sample is considered to be rejected.

9.11.7 Detection of Particulate Matter

Particles are significant because they may enter a product and contaminate it physically or, by acting as vehicle for micro-organisms, biologically. The air supply systems are characterized by special parameters (temperature, humidity, positive pressure—differential pressure relative to adjacent rooms of lower air cleanliness, velocity, air changes per hour) which may influence the particulate matter. The efficacy of protection measures in the clean room is verified by the content of airborne particles. Particles in the entry air are retained by HEPA filters and particles in the clean room are removed by laminar air stream. HEPA filter are able of retaining of at least 99.97 per cent of particulates greater than 0.3 micron in diameter. The regular integrity testing of the HEPA filter is absolutely necessary.

9.12 CLARITY TESTING

Particulate matter can be detected in parenteral product by two methods, including visual inspection and electronic particulate counting.

9.12.1 Visual Methods

In visual inspection, each injectable is inspected visually against white and black backgrounds. The white background aids in diction of dark colored particles. The light or reflective particles will appear against the black back ground. Some visual-enhancing aids can increase the efficiency. A magnifying lens at 02.5 × magnification set at the eye level facilitates the inspection. Microscopic examination enhances detection of particulate matter in injectables. Visual inspection gives the qualitative estimation of the particulate matter. Acceptance Standards is that each container checked must not contain any visible particulate matter.

9.12.2 Automated Visual Inspection

The automatic systems are also called as the electron particles counter. The electronic particles counter evaluates the particles in injectables automatically. However, this method requires destruction of the ampoule/container for the particle examination.

Electronic particles counting may be based on any one of the following principles:
- Change in electrical resistance
- Light blockages principle
- Light scattering

9.13 NON-STERILE MANUFACTURING

Hospitals interested in manufacturing of drugs are required to take a license and follow the rules framed in schedule M. Part I of schedule; Schedule M deals with good manufacturing practices while part II concerned with the requirements of plant and equipment, building used for manufacturing, processing, packaging, labelling and testing. The non sterile pharmaceutical products include oral liquids, and topical products.

9.13.1 Specific requirements for manufacturing of non sterile products are:

1. The premises and equipment should be designed, constructed and maintained to suit the manufacturing of oral liquids. The layout and design of the manufacturing area should strive to minimize the risk of cross-contamination and mix-ups.
2. Manufacturing area should have entry through double door airlock facility. It should be fly proof by use of fly catcher and/or air curtain.
3. The air to this manufacturing area should be filtered through at least 20 μ air filters and be air-conditioned. The area should be ventilated.
4. Temperature and relative humidity should be controlled, monitored and recorded where relevant, to ensure compliance with materials and product requirements.
5. The area should be fitted with an exhaust system of suitable capacity to effectively remove vapours, fumes, smoke, floating dust particles.
6. The equipment used should be designed and maintained to prevent the product from being accidentally contaminated with any foreign matter or lubricant.
7. Stainless steel or any other appropriate material should be used for parts of equipments coming in direct contact with the products. The use of glass apparatus should be minimal.
8. Water used in compounding should be Purified Water IP.
9. The production area should be cleaned and sanitized at the end of every production process.
10. Powders, wherever used, should be suitably sieved before use.
11. In case of oral liquids care should be taken to maintain the homogeneity of emulsion by use of appropriate emulsifier and suspensions by use of appropriate stirrer during filling. Mixing and filling processes should be specified and monitored. Special care should be taken at the beginning of the filling process, after stoppage due to any interruption and at the end of the process to ensure that the product is uniformly homogenous during the filling process. The primary packaging area should have an air supply which is filtered through 05 micron filters. The temperature of the area should not exceed 30°C when the bulk product is not immediately packed, the maximum period of storage and storage conditions should be specified in the Master Formula. The maximum period of storage time of a product in the bulk stage should be validated.
12. A separate packing section may be provided for primary packaging of the product.

9.13.2 Requirement of equipment for external preparations are recommended for the manufacture of external preparations, i.e. ointments, emulsion, lotions, solutions, pastes, creams, dusting powders and such identical products used for external applications whichever is applicable

(a) Mixing and storage tanks (stainless steel),

(b) Jacketed Kettle (steam, gas or electrically heated),

(c) Mixer (electrically operated)

(d) Planetary mixer

(e) A colloid mill or a suitable emulsifier.

(f) A triple roller mill or an ointment mill.

(g) Liquid filling equipment (electrically operated).

(h) Jar or tube filling equipment (electrically operated)

Area

(a) A minimum area of thirty square meters for basic installation of ten square meters for Ancillary area is recommended.

(b) Areas for formulations meant for external use and internal use should be separately provided to avoid mix-up.

9.13.3 The following equipments are commended for the manufacture of oral/internal use preparations, i.e. syrups, elixirs, emulsions and suspensions, whichever is applicable.

(a) Mixing and storage tanks (stainless steel),

(b) Jacketed Kettle / Stainless steel tank (steam, gas or electrically heated).

(c) Portable stirrer (electrically operated)

(d) A colloid mill or suitable emulsifier (electrically operated)

(e) Suitable filtration equipment (electrically operated)

(f) Semi-automatic/automatic bottle filling machine

(g) Pilfer proof cap sealing machine.

(h) Water distillation unit or deionizer

(i) Clarity testing inspection units.

Area: A minimum area of thirty square meters for basic installation and ten square meters for Ancillary area is recommended.

9.14 BULK COMPOUNDING FORMULA RECORD

The Bulk Compounding Form (Master Formula Card) is the official recipe for a particular product compounded in the pharmacy. The Master Formula Card contains specific information on the preparation, packaging, and labelling of a product. Master formula means a set of instructions outlining in detail the materials, equipment and procedure to produce a specific quantity of a product. The manufacture of sterile products is subject to special requirements in order to minimize risks of microbiological contamination, and of particulate and pyrogens contamination. The Master formula Card should be prepared and endorsed by the competent technical staff, i.e. head of production and quality control. The master formula should include:

1. The name of the product together with product reference code relating to its specifications.
2. The patent or proprietary name of the product along with the generic name, a description of the dosage form, strength, composition of the product and batch size.
3. Name, quantity, and reference number of all the starting materials to be used. Mention should be made of any substance that may disappear in the course of processing.
4. A statement of the expected final yield with the acceptable limits, and of relevant intermediate yields, where applicable.
5. A statement of the processing location and the principal equipment to be used.
6. The methods, or reference to the methods, to be used for preparing the critical equipments including cleaning, assembling, calibrating, and sterilizing.
7. Detailed stepwise processing instructions and the time taken for each step.
8. The instructions for in-process control with their limits.
9. The requirements for storage conditions of the products, including the container, labelling and special storage conditions where applicable.
10. Any special precautions to be observed.
11. Packing details and specimen labels.

9.15 PRODUCTION PLANNING AND CONTROL (PPC)

Production planning and control involve generally the organization and planning of manufacturing process. Especially, it consists of the planning of routing, scheduling, dispatching inspection; and coordination, control of materials, methods machines; tools and operating times. The ultimate objective is the organization of the supply and movement of materials and labour, machines utilization and related activities to bring about the desired manufacturing results in terms of quality, quantity, time and place. Production planning and control can facilitate the small hospital in the following ways:

1. **Optimum Utilization of Capacity:** With the help of Production Planning and Control [PPC] the hospital can schedule its tasks and production runs and thereby ensure that his productive capacity does not remain idle and there is no undue queuing up of tasks via proper allocation of tasks to the production facilities. No order goes unattended and no machine remains idle.

2. ***Inventory control:*** Proper PPC will help the hospital to resort to just in time systems and thereby reduce the overall inventory. It will enable him to ensure that the right supplies are available at the right time.
3. ***Economy in production time:*** PPC will help the hospital to reduce the cycle time and increase the turnover via proper scheduling.
4. ***Ensure quality:*** A good PPC will provide for adherence to the quality standards so that quality of output is ensured.

9.16 STEPS OF PRODUCTION PLANNING AND CONTROL

Production Planning and Control (PPC) is a process that comprises the performance of some critical functions of planning and control.

9.16.1 Production planning may be defined as the technique of foreseeing every step in a long series of separate operations, each step to be taken at the right time and right place and each operation to be performed with maximum efficiency. It helps hospital to work out the quantity of material manpower, machine and money required for producing predetermined level of output in given period of time.

9.16.2 Routing is the operation wherein path and sequence are established. To perform these operations the proper class of machines and personnel required are also worked out. The main aim of routing is to determine the best and cheapest sequence of operations and to ensure that this sequence is strictly followed.

9.16.3 Scheduling means working out of time that should be required to perform each operation and also the time necessary to perform the entire series as routed, making allowances for all factors concerned. It mainly concerns with time element and priorities of a job.

9.16.4 Loading is the execution of the schedule plan as per the route chalked out it includes the assignment of the work to the operators at their machines or workstation. So loading determines who will do the work as routing determines where and scheduling determines when it shall be done.

9.17 PRODUCTION CONTROL

Production control is the process of planning production in advance of operations, establishing the extract route of each individual item part or assembly, setting, starting and finishing for each important item, assembly or the finishing production and releasing the necessary orders of medicines, and initiating the necessary follow-up to have the smooth function of the enterprise.

9.17.1 Dispatching involves issue of production orders for starting the operations. Necessary authority and conformation is given for :

- Movement of materials to different workstations;
- Movement of tools and fixtures necessary for each operation;

- Beginning of work on each operation;
- Recording of time and cost involved in each operation;
- Movement of work from one operation to another in accordance with the route sheet; and
- Inspecting or supervision of work.

9.17.2 Follow up production programme involves determination of the progress of work, removing bottlenecks in the flow of work and ensuring that the productive operations are taking place in accordance with the plans. It spots delays or deviations from the production plans. It helps to reveal defects in routing and scheduling, misunderstanding of orders and instruction, under loading or overloading of work etc.

9.17.3 Inspection is mainly to ensure the quality of goods. It can be required as effective agency of production control.

9.17.4 Corrective measures involve any of those activities of adjusting the route, rescheduling of work changing the workloads, repairs and maintenance of machinery or equipment, control over inventories of the cause of deviation is the poor performance of the employees.

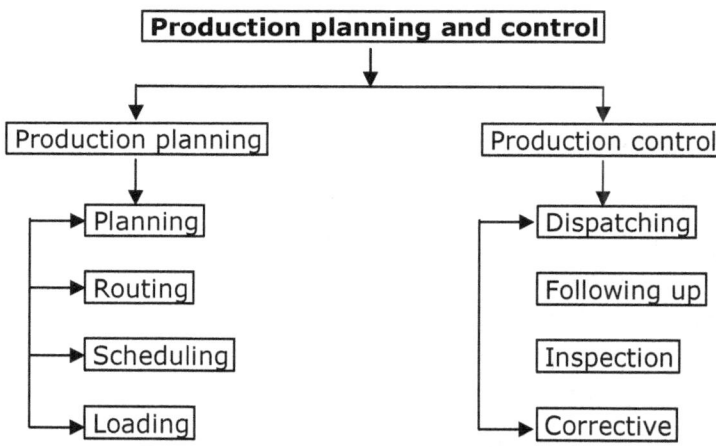

Fig. 9.1: Layout of PPC process

9.18 BATCH MANUFACTURING RECORDS

A Batch Manufacturing Record should be kept for each batch processed. It should be based on the relevant parts of the currently approved Manufacturing Formula and Processing Instructions. The method of preparation of such records should be designed to avoid transcription errors. The record should carry the number of the batch being manufactured. Before any processing begins, there should be recorded checks that the equipment and work station are clear of previous products, documents or materials not required for the planned process, and that equipment is clean and suitable for use. During processing, the following information should be recorded at the time each action is taken and, after completion; the record should be dated and signed in agreement by the person responsible for the processing operations:

1. The name of the product;
2. Dates and times of commencement, of significant intermediate stages; and of completion of production;
3. Name of the person responsible for each stage of production;
4. Initials of the operator of different significant steps of production and, where appropriate, of the person who checked each of these operations;
5. The batch number and/or analytical control number as well as the quantities of each starting material actually weighed;
6. Any relevant processing operation or event and major equipment used
7. A record of the in-process controls and the initials of the person(s) carrying them out, and the results obtained;
8. The amount of product yield obtained at different and pertinent stages of manufacture;
9. Notes on special problems including details, with signed authorization for any deviation from the manufacturing formula and processing instructions.

SUMMARY

Hospitals are creating cost effectiveness to self and patients by manufacturing the medicines of their own. Policies are framed including the type of medicine, its quantity as per the demand and costing of the hospital. The manufacture of medicines is a complex operation and must conform to GMP requirements which requires a system of QA designed to build quality into each product at all stages of its manufacture. To this end, pharmaceutical QA services work closely with production staff and provides a series of checks, tests and controls the throughout the manufacturing process like pharmaceutical quality systems, microbial and chemical testing of ingredients, labels and packaging components, checking approval of all SOPs and production documents, environmental monitoring in clean and aseptic areas, validating processes, equipments.

Manufacturing of the medicines is properly planned and controlled so that all measures of production can be implemented only to achieve the desired manufacturing results in terms of quality, quantity, time and place. All the records of the manufacturing like master formula card and batch manufacturing record are maintained to assure that all the quality checks have been made and transcriptions errors can be prevented.

A sterility test may be defined as a test that critically assesses whether a sterilized product is free from contaminating micro-organisms. Sterility testing can be done by membrane and direct transfer and direct inoculation. Pyrogen testing can be done by using the animals.

Production planning and control involve generally the organization and planning of manufacturing process. Especially, it consists of the planning of routing, scheduling, dispatching inspection; and coordination, control of materials, methods machines; tools and operating times. The ultimate objective is the organization of the supply and movement of materials and labour, machines utilization and related activities to bring about the desired manufacturing results in terms of quality, quantity, time and place.

✱✱✱

10

INCOMPATIBILITIES

10.1 INTRODUCTION

When two or more ingredients of a prescription are mixed together, the undesired change that may take place in the physical, chemical or therapeutic properties of the medicament is termed as incompatibility. Incompatibilities were frequent in earlier days when the prescription contained multiple ingredients. The modern trend towards simple prescription with only one or two specific medicines have reduced the frequency but not the importance of incompatibility and the present day pharmacist has to check all prescription carefully.

The primary function of physician is to diagnose and to prescribe and that of pharmacist is to compound and dispense a therapeutically effective medication. A very important ingredient of all the prescription is the skill with which they are compounded and this is particularly true in prescription originally containing an incompatibility. The most important step in dealing with incompatibility is recognizing an incompatibility before a prescription is filled. The pharmacist can take corrective measures to save time and material. It is better to prevent an incompatibility rather than correct it.

An incompatibility is not recognized until after the prescription has been compounded. The prescription should not be dispensed until the incompatibility has been corrected. If the problem can be sorted out in the filled prescription, it is fine, but it would be better to refill the prescription. Incompatibilities are of three types:

1. Physical incompatibility
2. Chemical incompatibility
3. Therapeutic incompatibility

10.2 PHYSICAL INCOMPATIBILITY

It may cause unsightly, non-uniform products from which removal of an accurate dose is very difficult. Physical incompatibilities are:

Immiscibility

Oils are immiscible with water.

Remedy: Emulsification or solubilization of the emulsion reduces the immiscibility, e.g.

1. Castor oil is not soluble in water. Hence, a third agent is added to prepare a stable emulsion. This third agent is called emulsifier.
2. Preparation of cresol soap solution Soap in high concentration in water forms micelles. The overall preparation is transparent.
3. Oil-soluble vitamins A, D are solubilized by Polysorbate (non-ionic surfactants).
4. Concentrated hydro alcoholic solutions of volatile oils such as spirits and concentrated aromatic water when used as adjunct (i.e. additive), e.g. as flavoring agents in aqueous preparations result in separation of large globules of oil.
    (i) The hydro alcoholic solution should be gradually diluted with the vehicle before mixing with the remaining ingredients.
    (ii) The hydro alcoholic solution should be poured slowly into the vehicle with constant stirring. Addition of high concentrations of electrolytes in which the vehicle is a saturated aqueous solution of a volatile oil.

Formulation: Potassium citrate (electrolyte), Citric acid, Lemon spirit, Syrup, Chloroform water DS, Water, and Quillaia Tincture 01%.

Remedy: When the lemon spirit used for flavoring is added, the lemon oil is thrown out of the solution, partly by the change of solvent and partly by the salting out effect of the high concentration of soluble salt (potassium citrate). To prevent separation of oil as surface layer, Quillaia tincture is included as an emulsifier.

Insolubility

1. Liquid preparations containing diffusible solids causes the formation of in diffusible solids suspension which settles quickly and thus uniform doses cannot be poured out.

Remedy: A thickening agent is necessary to increase the viscosity and reduce the rate of settling of particles. In diffusible solids e.g. chalk, aromatic chalk powder, succinic sulfathiazole and Sulphadimidine e.g. calamine and zinc-oxide, thickening agents like gum acacia, gum tragacanth, methylcellulose etc can be added.

2. Some insoluble powders like sulphur, and certain corticosteroids and antibiotics are difficult to wet with water because when water is added to this powder, slowly dispersing foam is formed on shaking. This foam is stabilized by fine solid particles.

Remedy: Wetting agents like saponins or Polysorbate can be incorporated in sulphur containing lotion, corticosteroid injections and antibiotic dry powder injections to avoid foaming.

3. *Claying of suspensions:* When large amount of wetting agents are used, a deflocculated suspension will be produced where all the particles will settle individually and will produce tightly packed sediment. This is called 'claying'. This tightly packed suspension is difficult to redisperse upon shaking.

Remedy: By reducing the amount of wetting agent smaller agglomerates of particles will form that will settle quickly but will be easily redispersed upon shaking.

4. When a resinous tincture is added to water the water insoluble resin agglomerates forming in diffusible clots.

Remedy: The undiluted tincture is added slowly to a diluted dispersion of a protective colloid with vigorous stirring. e.g., Preparation containing either Compound Benzoin tinctures, Benzoin Tincture, Lobelia Ethereal Tincture, Myrrh Tincture, and Tolu Tincture. When these tinctures are diluted with aqueous vehicle the resins precipitate and adhere to the side of the container and forms non-dispersible clots in the liquid. To prevent this, the tincture is mixed in a slow stream into the centre of Tragacanth Suspension and stirring rapidly. The hydrocolloids (acacia, tragacanth, and starch) are adsorbed over the surface of the resin particles and confer hydrophilic properties and prevent aggregation into clots.

5. Dispersions of hydrophilic colloids such as acacia or tragacanth mucilage are precipitated by high concentrations of alcohols or salts.

Remedy: Alcohols or salts are well diluted in the vehicle and then the electrolyte or alcohol solution is added slowly into mucilage with constant stirring to avoid local high concentration that might neutralize the effect of the protective colloid.

Lobelia Ethereal Tincture Resin solutions
- Stramonium Tincture
- Tragacanth Mucilage Hydrophilic colloid
- Potassium iodide Electrolyte
- Chloroform Water DS.
- Vehicle Water

Method of preparation
1. Half of the vehicle + Tragacanth power Triturated in a mortar and pestle. Tragacanth mucilage is formed.
2. Tincture is poured slowly into the centre of the mucilage with constant stirring.
3. Dissolve the electrolyte into half of the remaining vehicle. Added slowly and stirred to prevent local concentration.
4. The remaining vehicle is added to make up the volume.

Liquefaction

When certain low melting point solids are powdered (triturated in a mortar and pestle) together, a liquid or soft mass is produced due to lowering of melting point of the mixture to below room temperature. The medicaments those exhibits these behaviors are:
- Any pair among the following compounds: camphor, menthol, phenol, thymol, chloral hydrate.
- Sodium salicylate and phenazone.
- Aspirin and phenazone.

Method-I

If menthol and thymol are required to be dispensed as powder, they are triturated in a mortar to form the liquid mixture. The liquid is triturated with enough adsorbent powder e.g. light kaolin or light magnesium carbonate to give a free flowing product. Kaolin and magnesium carbonate are efficient absorbent and the light category of the powder has a very large specific surface area.

Method-II

If the final bulk volume of powder is very small, then menthol and thymol are triturated separately with small amount of adsorbent powder. Then the two powders are combined lightly and packing the resultant powder in capsules. The absorbent powders coat the particles and prevent contact between the medicaments and absorb any liquid that may be produced while triturating.

Methods for correction/prevention of physical incompatibility

Modified order of mixing

This method will vary often to overcome certain type of physical incompatibility. So this should be considered first. Example, if salt is not soluble in alcohol, prescribed in hydro alcoholic liquids: we dissolve salt first in water and then this solution should be mixed with the liquid prescribed.

Example : Alcohol soluble substances to be dispensed in hydro alcoholic liquids. First dissolve in small amount of alcohol, then mixed with the prescribed solution. A general rule is to dissolve the prescribed substance first in the solvent in which it is most soluble and then add to this solution slowly with constant stirring so as to effect the gradual dilution in the liquid in which it is least soluble.

Example of prescription:

        Magnesium carbonate ……….. 03.75g

        Citric acid ………………………….. . 07.5g

        Sodium bicarbonate ………….. 07.5g

        Boiled water ……………………….. q.s to make 250ml

Magnesium carbonate is insoluble and reacts with citric acid to from magnesium citrate in solution. Sodium bicarbonate is soluble in liquid. Citric acid is first dissolved in water, then sodium bicarbonate is added to this solution, and there after magnesium carbonate is added. A clean and complete solution is not produced because some of the magnesium carbonate remains unchanged. On the other hand a perfectly clean solution can be obtained by adding the magnesium carbonate to the solution of citric acid first and allow these 02 compounds to react completely to form solution of magnesium citrate and then adding the sodium bicarbonate. The reason for this order of mixing is that both magnesium carbonate and sodium bicarbonate will react with citric acid in solution. When bicarbonate ion is added first it uses some of citric acid so that not enough is left to convert all the magnesium carbonate to solubilized magnesium citrate. As a result the carbonate that is left will not dissolve by reacting the magnesium carbonate and citric acid. First all of the carbonate is converted to the citrate then the sodium bicarbonate which is water soluble is added to give a clean solution.

2. Solvents can be altered but to a limited extent, e.g. an alcohol soluble drug may be prescribed in elixir that does not have sufficient concentration of the alcohol to hold it in solution.

Alcohol: It is a good solvent for many organic compounds such as alkaloid, camphor, phenol; tannins, balsams, resins and some other organic acids.

Glycerin: It has solvent properties between those of alcohol and water. It is particularly good for dissolving tannins, boric acid, phenols, codeine and certain metallic salts. Example of alternate solvents to prepare clear solution is given by following prescription.

    Alcohol ……………………….. 15ml
    Terpene hydrate ………….. 02gm
    Glycerin ……………………….. 20ml
    Wild cherry syrup ………… q.s. to make 60ml

The prescription if filled as written will not give a clear solution. The alcohol concentration is not high enough to hold all the terpinehydrate in solution and small crystal settle out. This condition can be corrected by adjusting the alcohol concentration to 40%, which is same as that of the official terpene hydrate elixir.

3. *Changing the form of ingredients:* A change in the form of the ingredients is not able to obtain a better preparation. However it should be clearly understood that this action is applicable only when the therapeutic action of ingredients is not altered.

Example of prescription:

    Phenobarbital ………………............. 05 gm
    Sodium salicylate ………………….. 01gm
    Aqua mentha preparation ……. q.s. to make 50gm

Phenobarbital is insoluble in aqueous solution. Sodium slat of Phenobarbital, which has the same action and the same dose, may be used in its place to obtain a clear solution.

10.3 CHEMICAL INCOMPATIBILITY

It occurs as a result of interaction between ingredients of prescription. It is of two types:

1. *Usual chemical incompatibility* : It occurs immediately upon compounding, thus it is also called as immediate incompatibility. It occurs either due to precipitation or colour change.

2. *Delayed chemical incompatibility* : Mixture reacts at such a slow rate that no appropriate change occurs in delayed incompatibility. This may or may not result in loss of therapeutic activity.

Various types of chemical incompatibility are:

Racemization: It is the conversion of optically active form to the optically inactive active form without changing chemical constitution. It produces less pharmacological activity. Such reactions have been reported with adrenaline, ephedrine, and dextroamphetamine.

Precipitation: When O_2 or more pharmaceuticals are combined, a chemical change may take place with a formation of an insoluble substance, which precipitates from solution.

Examples are (a) Soluble inorganic salts except for the alkali metal react with basic hydroxide to yield water insoluble compounds; (b) Soluble salts of phenol, carboxylic acid and barbituric acid in an alkaline solution will yield the free acid in presence of relatively strong acid; precipitation depends upon the solubility of these acids in a particular solvent system; (c) Soluble salts of the amine drugs will release free base in presence of relatively strong base; precipitation will depend upon the solubility of this base in solvent system

Example of prescription:

    Cocaine HCl ……………… 0.3g
    Boric acid ………………… …01.2g
    Sodium borate ………… 01.2g
    Purified water ………….. .QS to make 60ml

The alkalinity of the solution because of the sodium borate causes the precipitates of the water insoluble cocaine base. Elimination of sodium borate prevents this difficulty.

Effervescence: Carbonate in the presence of acids, stronger than carbonic acid will form carbon dioxide. Weak acids such as boric acid will not react with carbonate.

Example of prescription: Suspension

    Sodium bicarbonate …………… 04gm
    Bismuth sub nitrate ……………. 04gm
    Purified water …………………….. QS to make 90 ml

Hydrolysis of bismuth sub nitrate yields nitric acid, which reacts with bicarbonate to give carbon dioxide. The gas formed would be sufficient to rupture the container. The completion of reaction is not feasible because of slow rate of acid production from the hydrolysis. A satisfactory remedy is to replace the nitrate salt with sub carbonate.

Colour change or formation of colour: Various types of chemical changes may result in alteration in colour. Occasionally the same mixture may have a slightly different colour, when compounded second time or by a different pharmacist. But the actual changing of the product colour is due to the chemical reaction.

Basically two parameters should be considered: (a) the change in colour of pharmaceutical preparation caused by age, exposure to light and temperature variation; (b) Colour change occurring immediately or after mixing. Most dyes or indicators in pharmacy are acidic or basic and generally form water-soluble ionized salts with anions or cations. The colour of these materials is influenced by their ionization and thus a change in pH of the solution that is sufficient to effect the ionization, which generally changes the colour. Phenolphthalein is a colourless acidic compound. On addition of an aqueous solution of base such as NaOH, a red ionized disodium salt is formed. Gentian violet is a basic purple compound. However on the addition of sufficient acid, the compound changes colour from green to yellow.

Oxidation reduction : Oxidation is defined as loss of electron and reduction as the gain of electron. Oxidation and reduction must occur together; it depends on the ability of the compound to accept the electron.

Examples:
(a) Phenothiazine tranquilizers are oxidized by ferric ion.
(b) Mercurous salts are easily reduced to free mercury in the presence of moisture, iron, light or heat.
(c) Stannous salts, of which the fluoride is most important, are readily oxidized by air and most mild oxidizing agents to stannic form.
(d) Bismuth compounds are easily reduced to metallic bismuth by organic compound such as glycerin and natural gums.
(e) Silver slats are reduced to metallic silver by light and compounds such as reducing sugars.
(f) Sugars are readily oxidized specially reducing sugars containing free ketonic group by bismuth, copper and silver.
(g) Aldehydes such as formaldehyde and chloral hydrate are subjected to the action of oxidizing agents, resulting in the formation of the corresponding acids.
(h) Oils and fats develop rancidity as a result of oxidization, generally catalyzed by light.
(i) Most of the vitamins are subjected to the oxidization process. The oxidization of ascorbic acid is catalyzed by traces of copper, iron. Thiamine is sensitive to both oxidizing and reducing agents and is converted to inactive form.
(j) Incompatibilities resulting from mixing of oxidants and reductant can be prevented only by removal of one of the specie from the system.

Hydrolysis: The reaction of the compound with the water divided into 2 broad categories,
- Ionic hydrolysis
- Molecular hydrolysis

Ionic hydrolysis: It involves the reaction of an ionized species or either hydrogen ion or hydroxyl ion to form unionized insoluble product. These hydrogen and hydroxyl ions result in the change in the pH of the solution. Both organic and inorganic salts may undergo this type of hydrolysis. Incompatibilities resulting from this type of hydrolysis generally manifest themselves as precipitates of basic salts or hydroxides.

Examples:

    (a) All zinc salts with the exception of sulfate and nitrate, hydrolyzed readily.

    (b) All aluminum slats hydrolyzed yielding insoluble basic salts and hydroxides.

    (c) The insoluble bismuth salts except sub carbonate, hydrolyzed to yield an acid. The sub nitrate and sub salicylates yield nitric acid and salicylic acid. The formation of these acids results in further incompatibilities due to acid base reaction.

    (d) Soluble salts of barbituric acid derivatives and sulfonamide, hydrolyzed slowly in water to yield the insoluble free acid.

Molecular hydrolysis: It is a reaction of water with organic compounds such as amides, esters and lacto. This type of hydrolysis proceeds at much slower rate and is often a function of hydrogen or hydroxyl ion. Because of the relatively slow rate of reaction, molecular hydrolysis is not of major concern to the dispensing pharmacist.

In most cases, the prescription will have been consumed before significant hydrolysis occurs, however this hydrolysis often reduces the therapeutic efficacy of drug and is not always detectable by a physical change. The pharmacist should aware of compounds that may exhibit this type of incompatibility.

Examples:

    (a) Disaccharides hydrolyzed in presence of hydrogen ion to yield monosaccharides. The inversion of sucrose to lactose and dextrose is a typical example of hydrogen ion catalyzed hydrolysis.

    (b) Esters are subjected to hydrolysis yielding the corresponding alcohols and acids. The hydrolysis is usually catalyzed by hydrogen or hydroxyl ion. The phenyl salicylates hydrolyzed in basic medium to phenol and salicylic acid.

    (c) Aspirin is readily hydrolyzed to acetic and salicylic acid in presence of moisture.

    (d) Some antibiotics tend to hydrolyze to inactive form in aqueous solution. The rate usually depends upon hydrogen and hydroxyl ion concentration.

Methods of correction/prevention of chemical incompatibilities

    1. *Replacement of reacting ingredient*: One of the commonest types of incompatibility is the formation of precipitate as a result of exchange of ions. If the solution is desired, it is frequently possible to replace one of the reacting substances with another of equal therapeutic value that will not cause precipitate.

Example of prescription:

    Sodium citrate   01g

    Calcium bromide   01g

    Simple isopril elixir   QS to make 120ml

    MFT solution

Although both sodium citrate and calcium bromide are soluble in aqueous liquid, they react in solution to form insoluble calcium citrate, which is precipitated. This incompatibility can be prevented by using sodium bromide in place of calcium bromide.

2. *Effervescence*: This technique is mainly used in compounding prescription in which effervescence takes place. Effervescence indicates a chemical reaction and is usually controlled by mixing the reacting ingredients in an open container such as mortar and pestle, combining them slowly and allows the reaction to go to completion before packing.

Example of prescription:

Ammonium carbonates	01gm
Ammonium chloride	02 gm
Dilute acetic acid	01 gm
Syrup cherry	QS to make 30 gm

In this prescription effervescence will occur by the reaction between ammonium carbonate and dilute acetic acid. The reaction happens at the time of mixing. This prescription could be mixed in a mortar or open container and boiled when the effervescence has stopped.

3. *Adding colour inhibiting agent*: Colour changes are sometimes important from the therapeutic point of view and at the same time, their influence upon the trust of customer and patient. Uniformity in the appearance of prescription and preparation in therefore highly considered. The order in which ingredients are mixed, affect the colour of finished preparation. Colour change may sometimes be prevented or modified by the addition of inhibiting agent.

Example of prescription:

Liquid phenol/phenol	02ml
Iron tincture	04ml
Glycerin	05ml
Aqua mentha preparation	QS to make 90ml

The phenol and iron chloride form an inky black colour in solution and the product is very unsightly. By adding citric acid or sodium citrate as an inhibitor, this colour formation is prevented and a pleasant solution is prepared.

4. *Oxidation-reduction*: Incompatibility resulting from mixing of oxidants and reductant can be minimized by removal of one of the species. Light catalyzed air oxidation can be minimized by storage in tight container or by the addition of materials, which will be preferentially oxidized such as sodium Met disulfide.

5. *Hydrolysis*: Ionic hydrolysis usually can be prevented or reversed by the addition of any of the species formed as a result of hydrolysis. Prevention of molecular hydrolysis is more involved and requires knowledge of conditions that effects stability of drug involved. Correction and prevention of incompatibility is essential.

Classification of inorganic incompatibilities
Metals and their salts
    Group IA : Sodium (Na), Potassium (K) and Ammonium (NH_4) salts.
    Group IB : Copper (Cu), Silver (Ag), Gold (Au).
    Group IIA : Magnesium (Mg), Calcium (Ca), Barium (Ba)
    Group IIB : Zinc (Zn), Mercury (Hg)
    Group IIIA : Aluminium(Al)
    Group IVA : Tin (Sn), Lead (Pb)
    Group IVB : Titanium (Ti), Zirconium (Zi)
    Group VA : Arsenic (As), Antimony (Sb), Bismuth (Bi)
    Group VII B : Manganese (Mn)
    Group VIII : Iron (Fe)

Non-metals
    Carbon (C), Sulphur (S), Iodine (I)
    Incompatibilities of acids
    Strong acids, Weak acids, Oxidizing acids and Reducing acids
    Incompatibilities of Metals and their Salts
    GROUP – I Alkali Metal Group [Na, K, NH_4]

Sodium
Sodium bicarbonate (NaHCO3) and Sodium perborate have lowest water solubility among the sodium salts. Example: A prescription contains sodium salicylate and potassium bicarbonate. Incompatibility: Sodium bicarbonate will be formed and precipitated. The solution will darken on standing due to the presence of salicylates in alkaline solution.

Incompatibilities: All the common salts of sodium are soluble in water. Many sodium salts are soluble in glycerin. Sodium salts are nearly insoluble in alcohol. The anionic part of a sodium salt may be precipitated from solution by other metals.

Potassium
The potassium salts are soluble in water. Only potassium Bitartarate (solubility 1 in 165 in water), form precipitates. Example: Potassium salts with acidic Bitartarate solution.

Incompatibility: Potassium Bitartarate will be formed which may precipitate.

Ammonium
Ammonium salts is ammonium chloride (NH_4Cl), ammonium nitrate (NH_4NO_3), ammonium nitrite (NH_4NO_2).

Incompatibilities
1. Ammonium salts form a white precipitate with tartaric acid.
2. In presence of alkalis ammonium salts liberates ammonia.
3. Ammonium salts are strong acids thus are acidic in reaction,
    e.g. $NH_4Cl + H_2O \rightarrow NH_4OH + HCl$

NH_4OH is a weak alkali while HCl is a strong acid hence in the solution number of H+ ion will exceed the number of OH− ion i.e. the solution will have an acidic pH.

GROUP – IB Coinage Metal Group

Copper

Salts: Cupric acetate [$Cu(CH_3COO)_2$], Cupric nitrate [$Cu(NO_3)_2$] are soluble in water while Cupric sulfate [$CuSO_4$] and Cupric chloride [$CuCl_2$] are insoluble.

Incompatibilities:

(a) Soluble copper salts give precipitates with solutions of tannic acid, arsenates, arsenates, alkalis, carbonates and phosphates.

(b) Soluble copper salts + alkali hydroxide → precipitate of cupric hydroxide [$Cu(OH)_2$] this precipitation can be prevented by organic hydroxy compounds like glycerin, tartrate, and citrates.

(c) Cupric salts (in solution) + Iodides → Precipitation of cuprous iodide + Iodine e.g. $2CuSO_4 + 4KI \rightarrow cCu_2I_2 + I_2 + K_2SO_4$.

(d) Cupric salts (in alkaline solution) + reducing agents (like glucose) → Cuprous oxide (Cu_2O). $Cu^{++} + Glucose + OH^- - Cu_2O^-$

Silver Salts

Silver nitrate [$AgNO_3$], Silver chlorate [$AgClO_3$] is soluble in water. Silver acetate [CH_3COOAg] and Silver sulfate [Ag_2SO_4] slightly soluble in water. Silver chloride [AgCl], Silver bromide [AgBr], Silver iodide [AgI], Silver arsenate, Silver arsenate, Silver borate, Silver carbonate [$AgCO_3$] and Silver phosphate are practically insoluble in water.

Incompatibilities

1. Many silver salts are decomposed by light with the formation of metallic silver.

2. Silver nitrate [$AgNO_3$] + Organic compounds → Metallic silver (Ag). When applied on the skin silver nitrate is reduced by some organic compound of the skin to form metallic silver, which is black. This silver causes the black stain on the skin.

$$Ag^+ + e \rightarrow Ag$$

Gold (Au)

Gold salts are unstable. They are reduced to metallic gold by even the weakest reducing gents such as organic matter or heat alone.

Gold salts : Gold dibromide

Gold sodium thiomalate Used as antiarthritic agents.

Gold sodium thiosulfate.

Incompatibility:

(a) Gold salts Au $(OH)_3$ $NaAuO_2$. Gold hydroxide Sodium laurite (Brown precipitation) (Soluble in water).

(b) Gold dibromide in aqueous solution → $Au + Br_2$.

(c) Gold sodium thiomalate : Both salts are soluble in water while Gold sodium thiosulfate is practically insoluble in alcohol and other organic solvents.

(d) Gold sodium thiosulfate darkens on exposure to air or light.

(e) Gold-Au[198] injection is a colloidal solution of radioactive gold. It is stabilized by the addition of gelatin and reducing agent.

GROUP-IIA (Alkaline earth group)

Magnesium salts: Magnesium Trisilicate ($Mg_2Si_3O_8$), Magnesium sulfate ($MgSO_4$), Magnesium oxide (MgO)

Incompatibilities : Magnesium oxide (MgO)

(a) MgO absorbs moisture and CO_2. It forms a cement-like mass with small amount of water. MgO in capsules sometimes causes the content to fuse into a hard insoluble mass.

(b) MgO is basic in nature. In solution it gives a pH ~ 10. Its alkalinity may cause destruction of certain drugs: aspirin and prednisolone.

(c) Liquid preparation containing sodium bicarbonate and magnesium oxide produces caking that cannot be broken by shaking the bottle.

Example:
- Mg $(OH)_2$ slowly reacts with $NaHCO_3$.
- Forms basic magnesium carbonate [$Mg_2(OH)_2CO_3$] which is a cement-like crystalline mass.
- Light MgO is more reactive than heavy MgO because light MgO has smaller particle size.

Calcium

Calcium compounds is sparingly soluble or insoluble in water, but soluble in acids (except $CaSO_4$).

Incompatibilities:

(a) Calcium: Hydroxide, Citrate, Arsenate, Carbonate, Oxalate, Tartrate and Phosphate precipitate in aqueous solution but remain soluble in acid except Ca Sulfate. In high concentration these salts precipitate and in very low concentration these salts are soluble.

(b) Soluble calcium salts reacts with free fatty acids to form precipitates of Ca salt of fatty acids.

$$Ca^{++} + RCOOH \rightarrow (RCOO)_2Ca^-$$

(c) Calcium chloride ($CaCl_2$) : $CaCl_2$ is deliquescent (i.e. it absorbs moisture and gets dissolved in it.)

(d) Calcium bromide ($CaBr_2$):

$CaBr_2$ + Sodium citrate → Ca-citrate $^-$

$CaBr_2$ + Sodium salicylate → Ca-salicylate $^-$

$CaBr_2$ + Sodium carbonate → Ca-carbonate $^-$

Remedy : Replace $CaBr_2$ with NaBr.

Barium

Barium sulfate is less soluble in water and forms suspension. It is used in diagnostic purpose.

Note: Soluble barium salts are extremely toxic.

Zinc and Mercury

Zinc (Zn) : Zinc chloride, $ZnCl_2$.

Zinc nitrate, $Zn(NO_3)_2$.

Zinc sulfate (ZnSO4)

Zinc acetate, $Zn(CH_3COO)_2$.

Zinc hydroxide, $Zn(OH)_2$.

Zinc carbonate, $ZnCO_3$.

Zinc phosphate $Zn(PO_4)_3$.

Zinc sulphide, $ZnSO_4$.

Incompatibilities:

1. Zinc salt + Fulgurated potash → $ZnSO^-$ (Zinc sulfide)

This incompatibility can be an advantage also in the preparation of lotion of zinc sulfide.

2. Solution of zinc salts undergo partial hydrolysis

$ZnCl_2 + H_2O → Zn(OH)Cl^- + HCl$

The basic salt [Zn(OH)Cl] may precipitate in weak aqueous solution, and form a cloudy solution. This problem is more acute if the solution contains any basic ingredient.

Remedy

In eye-washes (of Zinc iodide solution) the precipitation may be prevented by replacing part of the water by saturated solution of boric acid.

- Zinc salts + Fatty acids → Zinc salt of fatty acid, $^-$

e.g. Caprylic acid

Undecylenic acid

Stearic acid

Tannic acid

Mercury

Mercurous (Hg^+) salts are insoluble in water.

Mercuric (Hg^{2+}) salts are soluble in water.

Presently two mercury salts are used for their germicidal effect

(i) Ammoniated mercury.

(ii) Mercuric oxide (yellow in colour).

(iii) Mercuric chloride ($HgCl^2$), mercuric iodide (HgI^2).

(iv) Calomel (i.e. Mercurous chloride, Hg^2Cl^2).

Mercury

Mercurous (Hg^+) salts are insoluble in water, Mercuric (Hg^{2+}) salts are soluble in water.

Presently two mercury salts are used for their germicidal effect:

(i) Ammoniated mercury

(ii) Calomel (i.e. Mercurous chloride, Hg_2Cl_2)

Ammoniated mercury

Incompatibilities

(a) Ammoniated mercury is gritty and it is difficult to incorporate in an ointment base. Often it is triturated gently in a mortar and pestle. The frictional heat produced by heavy and vigorous grinding may reduce the compound into metallic mercury.

(b) The combined use of ammoniated mercury and salicylic acid in ointments frequently cause skin irritation due to the formation of mercuric salicylate. Mercuric chloride and Mercuric iodide Mercuric chloride slowly decomposes in aqueous solution, but is more stable in presence of excess chloride such as NH4Cl. Mercuric iodide is solubilized by the addition of potassium iodide (KI).

$$HgI_2 + 2KI \rightarrow K_2HgI_4$$

Mercurous chloride (Calomel, Hg_2Cl_2)

1. Some reducing agent reduces calomel to metallic mercury; e.g.

$$Hg_2Cl_2 + Sn^{2+} \rightarrow 2Hg^- + Sn^{4+} + 2Cl^-$$

2. Iodides and bromides convert Hg2Cl2 or Hg2I2 into mercuric compound and metallic mercury (Hg), e.g. An ointment containing calomel (Hg2Cl2) and potassium iodide (KI) is irritating because of the formation of mercuric salts.

$$Hg_2Cl_2 + 4KI \rightarrow Hg + K_2HgI_4 + 2KCl$$

Mercurous salts **(Hg+)**

Incompatibilities

(a) Hg+ salts are easily reduced to the free metal by light, moisture and triturating.

(b) Hg+ salt + Oxidizing agents (e.g. I_2) $\rightarrow Hg^{2+}$

(c) Since the dose of mercurous salts is high, they change to mercuric salts and the preparation becomes toxic.

GROUP-III A [Al]

Aluminium

Aluminium chloride, $AlCl_3$

Aluminimum sulfate, $Al_2(SO_4)_3$

Aluminium phosphate, $AlPO_4$

Aluminium carbonate $Al_2(CO_3)_3$.

Incompatibilities

1. Aqueous solutions of aluminium salts are acidic in reaction. It produces effervescence with any carbonate salts. e.g.

    $AlCl_3 + H_2O \rightarrow Al(OH)_3 + HCl$ (Strong acid)

    $CaCO_3 + 2HCl \rightarrow CaCl_2 + CO_2 + H_2O$

2. *Aluminium hydroxide gel* : Aluminium hydroxide gel is a suspension of aluminium hydroxide in water. The gel is destroyed by heat, freezing, electrolytes, acids, fixed alkalis and dehydration.

3. *Aluminium silicates*
    (a) Bentonite is a mixture of $[H_2O.(Al_2O_3.Fe_2O_3.3MgO).4SiO_2.nH_2O]$ and $[K_2O.Al_2O_3.6SiO_2]$.
    (b) Kaolin $[Al_2O_3.2SiO_2.2H_2O]$ adsorbs drugs and inactivates them, e.g. strychnine and atropine.

GROUP-IV A [Sn, Pb]

Tin (Sn)

Soluble salts of tin are precipitated by:

Fluoride

chloride

Hydroxides

Sulfides

Carbonates

Tannins

Phenols

Many organic acids

Plant extracts

Stannous fluoride is used in dentistry.

Incompatibility

(a) Stannous fluoride is water soluble, but may be oxidized and hydrolyzed.

(b) Stannous chloride Hydrolyzes Stannous hydroxide.

Remedy

Therefore only freshly prepared solutions are used in dentistry. Stannous chloride powder is also protected from moisture.

Lead (Pb)

Incompatibility

On exposure to air, solutions of lead salts absorb CO_2 and become cloudy due to the precipitation of basic lead carbonate.

$$Pb(CH_3COO)_2 + CO_2 + H_2O \rightarrow [PbCO_3, Pb(OH)_2]$$

Basic lead carbonate
Titanium

Titanium dioxide is used in sun-screen cream. It is neutral in action and is stable.

Zirconium

Zirconium carbonates and oxides are insoluble in water. They are used in ointments for external purpose and usually present no incompatibility.

Arsenic (As)

1. Arsenates and arsenates of alkali metals are soluble in water.
2. Arsenates are slowly oxidized to arsenates by oxidizing agents and are slowly oxidized by atmospheric oxygen in neutral solutions.
3. Arsenic trioxide is hydrolyzed in solution to arsenious acid [As (OH)3] and hydriodic acid.(HI). On standing the solution becomes yellow due to the liberation of iodine.

$$AsI_3 + 3H_2O \rightarrow As(OH)_3 + 3HI$$
$$4HI + O_2 \rightarrow 2I_2 + 2H_2O$$

Antimony (Sb)

Antimony salts hydrolyze in aqueous solution. Acid must be added to avoid the precipitation of basic salts. Tartar emetic (Antimony potassium tartrate, K (SbO) $C_4H_4O_6$) forms precipitates with the salt solution of any metal. It forms a precipitation of potassium Bitartarate with mineral acids.

$$K(SbO)C_4H_4O_6 + 3HCl \rightarrow KHC_4H_4O_6^- + SbCl_3 + H_2O$$

Bismuth (Bi)

1. Aqueous solutions of bismuth salts + Alkali hydroxide→Bi (OH) 3 $^-$.
2. Bismuth sub nitrate undergoes hydrolysis to yield an acidic suspension.

$$2BiONO_3 + H_2O \rightarrow (BiO)_2(OH) NO_3^- + HNO_3$$

Thus this aqueous suspension will present the incompatibilities of acids e.g.

(i) effervescence from carbonate salts.
(ii) Precipitation of salicylic acid from a solution of salicylate.

Remedy:

Bismuth sub nitrate is substituted with bismuth sub carbonate to avoid this problem.

Iron (Fe)

The common source of incompatibilities with iron salts are due to:

(i) Hydrolyses Iron salts in aqueous solution to produce acidic solution.
(ii) Various oxidation-reduction situations.

Incompatibilities

1. Ferric chloride hydrolyze into ferric hydroxide plus the free acid.

$$FeCl_3 + 3H_2O \rightarrow Fe(OH)_3^- + 3HCl$$

2. Fe₂+ salts + carbonates give precipitate of the corresponding ferrous salts:
   Arsenates
   Arsenates
   Oxalates
   Phosphates
3. Ferric salts are reduced to the ferrous state by iodides.

$$2Fe_3^+ + 2I^- \rightarrow 2Fe_2^+ + I_2$$

Salts of the metals in solution are incompatible with hydrates, carbonates, phosphates, oxalates and the corresponding acids; in many cases with proteins, tannins, acacia and often alkaloids and phenazone. Silver, mercurous, lead, and bismuth salts also with bromides and iodides: the same metals and calcium, barium and strontium, with sulphates and sulphuric acid.

Incompatibilities of non-metals

Carbon (C)

Activated charcoal

(a) It is easily oxidized so it is not triturated with oxidizing agents.

(b) It has adsorptive action hence, it should not be dispensed with potent drugs like alkaloids because the potent drugs will be adsorbed and become inactive.

Sulphur (S)

In pharmacy three forms of powdered- sulphur are available: precipitated, sublimed and washed.

These powders are soluble only in carbon-disulfide (CS_2), but insoluble in other solvents.

Iodine (I2)

Iodine is an oxidizing agent in alkaline solution.

1. I_2 + Arsenates Oxidizing Hypophosphates 2I and other reducing agents e.g. I_2 + H_2AsO_3 (Arsenious acid) + H_2O 2HI + H_3AsO_4 (Arsenic acid).

2. I_2 + Volatile oils Substitution e.g. Turpentine oil and oxidation: explosion may result from such combinations.

Incompatibilities of Acids

Acids, unless very dilute and in small amount, should be prescribed alone. They combine with bases to form salts, and are incompatible with oxides, alkalis, alkaline salts, hydrates and carbonates. They all precipitate albumin.

Categories of acids:

1. Strong acid: They are highly ionized in aqueous solution. e.g. Perchloric acid ($HCLO_4$), sulphuric acid (H_2SO_4), hydrochloric acid (HCl), Hydrobromic acid (HBr), Nitric acid (HNO_3), Phosphoric acid (H_3PO_4).

2. **Weak acid:** They are slightly ionized in aqueous solution, e.g. Acetic acid (CH_3COOH), Carbonic acid (H_2CO_3), and hydrogen sulfide (H_2S), hydrocyanic acid (HCN), boric acid (H_3BO_3).

3. **Oxidizing acid:** Nitric acid (HNO_3), Nitric acid + Hydrochloric acid mixture $HCl + HNO_3 + NaCl + Cl_2$. Permanganic acid ($KMNO_4$), Chromic acid ($H_2CrO_4$), Per boric acid ($HBO_3$) and Nitrous acid ($HNO_2$).

4. **Reducing acid:** Hypo phosphorous acid (H_3PO_2), sulphuric acid (H_2SO_3), hydriodic acid (HI), and thio sulphuric acid (H_2SO_3), thiocyanic acid (HSCN).

Nitric acid
(a) HNO_3 reacts with some alkaloids to form coloured compounds.
(b) It forms explosive nitroglycerin when rotated with sulphuric acid and glycerin.
(c) Fe++, arsenious and mercurous salts are oxidized by HNO3 into their oxidized state.

(a) Nitrates (like KNO_3) + Charcoal

Hypochlorous acid

HOCl is unstable. Hypo chlorites are decomposed by acids, even H_2CO_3 with the liberation of unstable HOCl. Solutions of hypochlorites must be prepared at room temperature, because heat converts them into chlorates and chlorides. Hydrogen peroxide (H_2O_2) Hydrogen peroxide decomposes slowly with the evolution of oxygen. Heat increases the role of reaction.

Hydriodic acid (HI)

HI and I– in acidic solution turn brown on standing, free iodine being released.

$$2HI \rightarrow H_2 + I_2$$
$$4I^- + O_2 + 2H^+ \rightarrow 2 I_2 + 2H_2O$$

Examples of acid preparations:
(i) **Fluid extract:** Ergot, ipecac, nux vomica, aconite.
(ii) **Elixir:** Compound pepsin, compound glycerophosphate, lactated pepsin.
(iii) **Solutions:** Ammonium acetate, ferric chloride, iron and ammonium acetate, ferrous sulfate, Hydrogen peroxide, magnesium citrate.
(iv) **Syrups:** Citric acid, hydriodic acid, cherry, ferrous iodide, orange, raspberry, squill, ipecac.

Glycerides: boroglycerin, pepsin
Tinctures: aconite, ferric chloride, camphorated opium, nux vomica, cinchona.
Miscellaneous: Squill vinegar

Organic incompatibilities

1. Hydrocarbons:
(a) They include both saturated and unsaturated compounds of C and H.
(b) Overexposure to volatile hydrocarbons may cause damage to the heart, liver or kidneys.
(c) A hydrocarbon may produce Vitamin A, D, E and K deficiency on prolonged use or exposure.

Saturated hydrocarbon: Saturated hydrocarbons used in pharmacy include:
- Petroleum ether ($C_5 - C_7$)
- Deodorized kerosene ($C_9 - C_{15}$)
- Light mineral oil ($C_{15} - C_{20}$)
- Mineral oil ($C_{18} - C_{24}$)
- Petrolatum ($C_{18} - C_{30}$), White petrolatum ($C_{18} - C_{30}$)
- Paraffin ($C_{24} - C_{30}$).

Sometimes unsaturated hydrocarbons may remain as impurities, which may degrade to rancidity. So dl-α-tocopherol is used as antioxidant.

Unsaturated hydrocarbons: Contains double bonds or triple bond(s) Reactions of unsaturated hydrocarbons:
- (a) addition type reactions : unsaturated bonds may add Br_2, HBr, H_2, H_2SO_4)
- (b) may be oxidized at instauration point
- (c) may be reduced at the instauration point
- (d) Aromatic hydrocarbon: Benzene, naphthalene, anthracene- these are not found in prescription.
- (e) Hydrogenated hydrocarbons, e.g. Chloroform ($CHCl_3$), ethyl bromide (C_2H_5Br) etc. They are immiscible with water, soluble in alcohol and organic solvents.
- (f) Alcohols: $C_2H_5OH + HI \rightarrow C_2H_5I + H_2O$.
  (Ethanol)   (Ethyl iodide)

Ethanol and methanol are incompatible with acacia, albumins and oxidizing agents such as chlorine, bromine, permanganate and chromic acid.

10.4 THERAPEUTIC INCOMPATIBILITY

It results when the response to one or more drugs in the patient is of different nature or the intensity then that intended by the prescriber. Therapeutic effectiveness maybe reduced or delayed as a result of physical or chemical reaction like hydrolysis or oxidation of a drug may result in loss of activity. Complexation or combination of a drug with protein, tannins, surfactants and other large molecule may result in delay in the release and absorption of drugs.

Physical and chemical incompatibility may lead to therapeutic incompatibility. Many therapeutic incompatibilities results from error in writing or interpreting the prescription order and the pharmacist is in the position to detect and help to avoid such problems. In such situations the pharmacist should revert to the prescriber.

Types of therapeutic incompatibility

Dosage error:

The overdose of medication is the most serious type of dosage error. Overdose can result from the administration of excessive single dose or too frequent administration of usual doses. The pharmacist in evaluating the prescription order should consider how much drug is given in each dose, how frequently the drug should be given, the age of patient, the sensitivity of the patient to a prescribed drug, the duration of activity and the possibility of synergism and antagonism.

The problem represented below is one that would cause harmful effect if not prescribed properly. The amounts indicated are those as included in each capsule.

Example of prescription:

    Atropine sulfate   0.006 gm
    Phenobarbital   0.015 gm
    Aspirin   0.300 gm

The quantity of Phenobarbital and aspirin represent single dose of these agents, however the quantity of atropine sulfate is in excess of usual and maximum recommended dose. Although in this particular case it appears that quantity of atropine sulfate specified might be reasonable for the entire 12 capsules. The pharmacist should contact the prescriber for clarification of matter.

Another type of preparation might be experienced if the below prescription is written slightly differently.

Example of prescription:

    Atropine sulfate   0.006 gm
    Phenobarbital   0.015 gm
    Aspirin   0.300 gm

If the prescription were filled as written, the dose of atropine sulfate would be reason reasonable but the dose of other two drugs would be small and probably with no therapeutic effect. Although the situation might not be as serious as occurring if the previous prescription was to be filled as written.

Overdosages are always accidental and usually result from error made in calculation or conversion from one system to another.

2. Wrong drug or dosage form:

This occurs occasionally when two drugs with different strength or actions have similar names and are easily confused. Mercurous chloride and mercuric chloride, arsenic acid and the solution of arsenic acid are the common examples. Many drugs are available in a variety of dosage form and when it is not clear which one should be dispensed, the prescriber should be consulted. A prescription order requesting 15gm tube of cordran that does not specify whether the ointment or cream should not be dispensed until the prescriber confirms it.

3. Contraindicated drugs:

A contraindicated drug is one which for some specific reason can't safely be given or in other words, in a situation where an individual has previously shown an allergic response to it.

Example:

    (i) Corticosteroids are contraindicated in patients with peptic ulcer.
    (ii) Vasoconstrictors are contraindicated in hypertensive patients.
    (iii) Some drugs should not be given to asthmatic patients, e.g. barbiturates, morphine etc.
    (iv) If a person is allergic to a drug, it should not be given to the patient.

(v) Certain combination of drugs are contraindicated:

Sulphadiazine	0.25 g
Sulphamerazine	0.25 g
Ammonium chloride	0.50 g

Prepare capsules

Label: Take two capsules six hourly for cough.

Comment: In this prescription ammonium chloride is a urinary acidifier and it could cause deposition of sulphonamide crystals in the kidney.

4. Antagonistic combination:

This results when two or more drugs whose action oppose or nullify each other are prescribed together. In such cases it is possible that resulting prescription will have no therapeutic effect, if the drug action cancels each other. Often this opposing action is the basis for the antidotes. In many cases the prescribing of an antagonistic combination is beneficial for example: if one drug has some desirable effect and some undesirable effects, it may be prescribed with the drug which oppose the undesirable effects but does not interfere with desired effects. Thus in prescribing morphine as an analgesic, a physician may use atropine to prevent an excessive depressant effect of morphine on respiratory center. A combination of opposite acting quinidine and digitalis is sometimes used.

5. Additive and synergistic combination:

Additives are substances meant to improve or preserve while synergists are substances meant to potentiate the action of additives. Additive and synergistic combinations are useful but sometimes they can be harmful too; hence, the prescriber has to be doubly sure while prescribing such a combination.

Example

(a) Combination of sulfonamides often shows less nephrite-toxicity than a single sulfonamide.

(b) Bromide, barbiturates combination reduces the bromide contents.

(c) Neomycin, erythromycin combination has a broad-spectrum action than either antibiotic alone.

(d) Aspirin, prednisolone or aspirin codeine combination may reduce the amount of prednisolone or codeine required.

Incompatibility involving Surface active agents

Types of surfactants:

(a) Anionic (−) eg: SLS, sodium stearate, potassium stearate.

(b) Cationic (+) eg: Cetrimide.

(c) Amphoteric (+&−) e.g. Betaines.

(d) Non ionic eg: span and tween.

Interaction between oppositely charged surfactants

The interaction occurs upon mixing anionic surfactants with cationic surfactants. This may be manifested, visually, as turbidity or formation of a precipitate. The surface activity of both materials will be drastically reduced. This occurs upon mixing sodium laurel sulphate with Cetrimide.

Interaction between surfactants and drugs

Drugs may interact with surfactants carrying opposite charge. The results of this type of interaction are:

Reduction of the therapeutic effectiveness of the drug

Reduction of the surface active property of the surfactant

SAA and acidic drug or excipients: It occurs with soap surfactants which are salts of weak fatty acids easily displaced by stronger acids, e.g. Na Stearate + Salicylic acid stearic acid (ppt) + sodium salicylate

It results in loss of surface activity.

SAA and Heavy metals: Na Stearate + Ca+2 Ca Stearate (insoluble in H_2O).

It can occur by hard water which contains divalent ions.

Incompatibilities of dyes

Colouring agents may be defined as compounds employed in pharmacy solely for the purpose of imparting colours. They may be classified in to organic or inorganic and natural or synthetic colours. These are used as colours for pharmaceutical preparation, cosmetics and foods and as bacteriological stains and diagnostic agents.

Dyes are mainly anionic (sodium salts) and hence are incompatible with cationic substances. Since the concentrations of these substances are generally very low no precipitate is evident. Polyvalent ions such as calcium, magnesium and aluminium also may form insoluble compounds with dyes. A pH change may cause the colour to change; acids may release the insoluble acid form of the dye.

Incompatibilities of anesthetics

Pharmaceutical interactions involve the drug incompatibilities that occur between the drug and anesthesia:

- Precipitation of thiopental may occur when it is injected together with succinylcholine into IV catheter line.
- Bicarbonate can decrease the solubility of bupivacaine and cause it to precipitate.
- Catecholamine solutions can be inactivated by the addition of sodium bicarbonate, a circumstance that could occur during cardiopulmonary resuscitation.

- The number of these incompatibilities is large and the anesthesiologist should avoid mixing drugs unless they are known to be compatible. Information on specific IV drug incompatibilities is readily available from most hospital pharmacist. Sometimes two drugs may interact chemically to form a toxic compound.
- The halogenated anesthetics like desflurane, enflurane and isoflurane have been shown to interact with dry soda lime or birdlime to produce carbon monoxide and heat. Desiccation of soda lime is most likely to occur when oxygen has been left flowing through the canister overnight.
- Nitric oxide is a selective pulmonary vasodilator that has been approved for treatment of primary pulmonary hypertension in the newborn. If NO is allowed more than fleeting connate with oxygen, it forms nitrogen dioxide (NO_2). The latter compound can be quite toxic and concentrations more than 10ppm can produce pulmonary edema and alveolar hemorrhage. The problem is circumvented by allowing oxygen and NO to mix in the breathing circuit must before administration.

SUMMARY

When two or more ingredients of a prescription are mixed together, the undesired change that may take place in the physical (It may cause unsightly, non-uniform products from which removal of an accurate dose is very difficult), chemical (It occurs as a result of interaction between ingredients of prescription) or therapeutic properties (It results when the response to one or more drugs in the patient is of different nature or the intensity then that intended by the prescriber. Therapeutic effectiveness maybe reduced or delayed as a result of physical or chemical reaction like hydrolysis or oxidation of a drug may result in loss of activity)of the medicament is termed as incompatibility.

Physical and chemical incompatibility may lead to therapeutic incompatibility. Many therapeutic incompatibilities results from error in writing or interpreting the prescription order and the pharmacist is in the position to detect and help to avoid such problems.

Physical incompatibility can be due to insolubility, immiscibility and liquefaction whereas chemical incompatibility can be usual chemical incompatibility (occurs immediately upon compounding and also called immediate incompatibility) or delayed chemical incompatibility (mixture reacts at such a slow rate that no appropriate change occurs in delayed incompatibility. This may or may not result in loss of therapeutic activity). Various types of chemical incompatibility are recemization, precipitation, effervescence, colour change or formation of colour, oxidation/reduction and hydrolysis (ionic and molecular hydrolysis).

Therapeutic incompatibility is due to dosage error (The overdose of medication is the most serious type of dosage error. Overdose can result from the administration of excessive single dose or too frequent administration of usual doses), wrong drug or dosage form (occurs occasionally when two drugs with different strength or actions have similar names and are easily confused) and contraindicated drugs (A contraindicated drug is one which for some specific reason can't safely be given or in other words, in a situation where an individual has previously shown an allergic response to it).

✱✱✱

11
COMMUNICABLE DISEASES

11.1 INTRODUCTION

A communicable disease is a disease that can pass from an infected person to another individual. Body excretions provide the mode for transmission. Some communicable diseases spread by casual contact, such as cold, flu and tuberculosis from respiratory droplets: coughing, sneezing or runny noses. Other communicable diseases require contact with blood from an infected individual, such as Hepatitis B and the Human Immunodeficiency Virus (the virus which causes AIDS). Other communicable diseases require intimate contact with an infected individuals body fluids or genitalia, such as Chlamydia, herpes and syphilis.

11.2 INFECTIOUS AGENTS

Infectious organisms, which can enter the human host (end parasites) belong to a wide range of classes and vary in size ranging from the 02-nm poliovirus to 10-m tapeworms. In addition, several types of arthropods are ectoparasites, cause damage only via the skin. These agents can be sorted into the following:

VIRUSES

All viruses depend on host cell metabolism for their replication, which means they are obligate parasites. They are classified by the nucleic acid content of their core (DNA or RNA) and by the shape of their protein coat or cased, which can be spherical if clasped proteins form and icosahedrons or cylindrical if they form a helix. Many of the more than 400 viral species known to inhabit humans do not cause any disease, but some are frequent causes of acute illness (e.g. cold, influenza). Others are capable of lifelong latency and of long-term reactivation (herpes viruses) or may engender chronic diseases (e.g. hepatitis B [HBV]). Together, viral pathogens are vectors of all human infections. Different viral species engender same clinical manifestations (e.g. upper respiratory infection) whereas; a single virus can cause different lesions depending on the age of the host or immune status (e.g. cytomegalovirus [CMV]).

BACTERIOPHAGES, PLASMIDS, TRANSPOSONS

These are mobile genetic elements that encode bacterial virulence factors (e.g. adhesions, toxin or enzymes that confer antibiotic resistance). They can infect bacteria and incorporate themselves into their genome, thus converting an otherwise harmless resistant bacterium into a virulent one or an antibiotic sensitive organism into a resistant one. Exchange of these elements between bacterial strains and species therefore endows the recipients with a survival advantage or with the capacity to cause disease or both.

BACTERIA

Bacterial cells are prokaryotes, which lack nuclei and endoplasmic reticulum. Their cell walls are relatively rigid, composed either of two phospholipids bilayer with a peptidoglycan layer sandwiched between (Gram-negative species) or of a single belayed covered by peptidoglycan (Gram-positive bacteria). Bacteria synthesize their own DNA, RNA and proteins but depend on the host for the favourable growth conditions. Some thrive mainly on the body's surface layers; normal person carry 10^{12} bacteria on the skin, including *Staphylococcus epidermoid* and *Propionibacterium acnes,* the agents responsible for adolescent pimples. Normally, 10^{14} bacteria reside inside the gastrointestinal tract, 99.9 per cent of which are anaerobic, including bactericide species. Many bacterial pathogens invade host tissue and are capable of extracellular division (e.g. *Pneumococci*) or of both extracellular and intracellular division (e.g. *Mycobacterium tuberculosis hominis*). Next to viruses, bacteria are the most frequent and diverse class of human pathogens and include many of the major pathogens.

CHLAMYDIAE, RICKETTSIAE, MYCOPLASMAS

These infectious agents are grouped together because they are similar to bacteria in that they divide by binary fission and susceptible to antibiotics but lack certain structures (e.g., Mycoplasma lacks a cell wall), or metabolic capabilities (e.g., Chlamydia lack adenosine triphosphate [ATP] synthesis. Chlamydia, are frequent causes of genitourinary infections, conjunctivitis and respiratory infections of newborn infants.

Most Rickettsia is transmitted by insect vectors, including lice (epidemic thymus), ticks (Rocky Mountain spotted fever [RMSF], Q fever) and mites (scrub thymus). Rickettsia are obligate intracellular agents that replicate in the cytoplasm of the endothelial cells; Rickettsia cause a hemorrhagic vacuities often visible as a skin rash but may also cause a transient pneumonia or hepatitis (Q fever) or injure the central nervous system and cause death.

Mycoplasma and the closely related genus Urea plasma are the tiniest free-living organisms known (125–300 nm). *Mycoplasma pneumonia* spreads from person to person by aerosols, binds to the surface of epithelial cells in the airways via an adhesion called P1 and causes an atypical pneumonia. Urea plasmas are transmitted venereal and may cause nongonococcal urethritis.

FUNGI

Fungi poses thick, ergosterol-containing cell walls and grow as perfect, sexually reproducing forms in nature and as imperfect forms *in vivo,* which include budding yeast cells and slender tubes (hyphae). Some produce spores, which are resistant to extreme environmental conditions, whereas hyphae may produce fruiting bodies called conidia. Some fungal species those of the Tinea group causing "athletes foot" are confined to the superficial layers of the human skin whereas other xerophytes preferentially damage the hair shafts and nails. Certain fungal species invade the subcutaneous tissue, causing abscesses or granuloma formation. Deep fungal infection can spread systemically, destroying vital organs in immunocompromised patients, whereas these fungal lesions heal spontaneously or remain latent in otherwise normal host.

PROTOZOA

Parasitic protozoa are unicellular organisms capable of motility, pliable plasma membranes and complex cytoplasm organelles. The flagellate *Trichomonas vaginalis* is transmitted sexually from person to person. The intestinal protozoa (e.g., *Entamoeba histolytica* and *Giardia lamblia*) are spread by the faecal-oral route. Blood borne protozoa (e.g., Plasmodium species and Leishmania species) are transmitted by blood-sucking insects, wherein they undergo a complex succession of life stages before being passed to new human hosts. *Tax plasma Gondi* is acquired either by contact with oocyst-shedding kittens or by eating cyst-ridden, undercooked meat.

HELMINTHS

Parasitic worms are highly differentiated multicellular organisms. Their life cycles are complex, most alternate between sexual reproduction in the definitive host and asexual multiplication in an intermediate host or vector. Thus, depending on parasite species, humans may harbour either adult worms (e.g., Ascaris) or immature stages (e.g., *Toxocara canis*) or asexual larval forms (e.g., Echinococcus). Adult worms, once resident in humans, do not multiply in number but generate eggs or larvae for the next phase of life cycle. There are two consequences of the lack of replication of adult worms: *(a)* Disease is often caused by the inflammatory responses to the eggs or larvae rather than adults (e.g., schistosomiasis) and *(b)* disease is in proportion to the number of organisms that have infected the individual (e.g., 10 hookworms cause little pathology, whereas 1000 hookworms cause severe anemia by consuming 100 ml of blood per day).

Parasitic worms are of three classes: first, *Roundworms* (nematodes), is characterized by a collagenous tegument and a non-segmented structure. These include Ascaris, hookworms and strongyloides among the intestinal worms and filaria and Trichinella among the tissue invader; Second, flatworms (cestodes), comprise gutless worms, whose head spouts a ribbon of flat segments covered by an absorptive tegument. This class includes the pork, beef, and fish tapeworm and the cystic tapeworm larva; Third, *Flukes*, which are primitive leaf like worms with syncytial integument, includes the oriental liver and lung flukes and the blood-dwelling schistosomiasis.

ECTOPARASITES

Ectoparasites are arthropods (lice, ticks, bedbugs, fleas) that attach to and live on the skin. In addition, skin lesions can be caused by the stings of mosquitoes and bees. Scabies is an example of severe dermatitis elicited by mites burrowing into the stratum cornea. Skin nodules caused by burrowing botfly larvae are intensely inflamed and eosinophil-enriched. In addition, attached arthropods can be vectors for other pathogens that make characteristic skin lesions (e.g., the expanding erythematous plaque caused by the Lyme disease spirochete Borreria *Burgdorferi*, which is transmitted by ticks).

11.3 FACTORS RELATED TO DISEASES

Infectious diseases are the consequences of interrelationship between disease-producing properties of microorganisms and host-defence capability against the invading organism. Briefly, factors determining this host-microorganism relationship are given below:

FACTORS RELATED TO INFECTIOUS AGENTS

Mode of entry: Microorganisms causing infectious disease may gain entry into the body by various routes:

1. Through ingestion (external route)
2. Inoculation (parenteral method)
3. Inhalation (respiration)
4. Prenatally (vertical transmission)
5. By direct contact (contagious infection)
6. By contaminated water, food, soil, environment or from an animal host

Spread of infection: Microorganism after entering into the body may spread further through the phagocyte cells, blood vessels and lymphatic's.

Production of toxin: Bacteria liberate toxins which affect the cell metabolism. Endotoxins are liberated on lyses of the bacterial cell while exotoxins are secreted by bacteria and have effects at distant sites too.

Virulence of organisms: Many species and strains of organisms may have varying virulence, e.g. the three strains of *C.diptheriae* (gravis, intermedia and mites) produce the same diphtheria Endotoxin but in different amounts

Products of organism: Some organisms produce enzymes that help in spread of infections, e.g. hyaluronidase by *Cl. Wallichii*, streptokinase by streptococci, staphylokinase and coagulate by staphylococci.

11.4 FACTORS RELATED TO HOST

Microorganism invades human body when defenses are not adequate. These factors include the following:

Physical Barrier: A break in the continuity of the skin and mucous membranes allows microorganisms to enter into the body.

Chemical barrier: Mucus secretions of the oral cavity and the alimentary tract and gastric acidity prevent bacterial colonization.

Effective drainage: The natural passage of the hollow organs like respiratory, gastrointestinal, urinary and genital system provide a way to drain the excretions effectively. Similarly, ducts of various glands are the conduits of drainage of secretions—obstructions in any of these passages promote infection.

Immune defence mechanism: These include the phagocyte leucocytes (polymorphs and monocytes), phagocytes of tissue (mononuclear-phagocyte system).

11.5 VARICELLA ZOSTER VIRUS INFECTION (CHICKEN POX AND SHINGLES)

Varicella zoster virus is a member of herpes virus family and causes chickenpox (Varicella) in non-immune individuals and herpes zoster (shingles) in those who had chickenpox in the past.

CAUSATIVE ORGANISM

Two of the herpes simplex viruses (HSV)—type 01 and type 02 cause 'fever blisters' and herpes genitals respectively.

HSV-1 causes vesicular lesions on the skin, lips and mucous membrane. The infection spreads by close contact. The condition is particularly severe in immunodeficient patients and neonates while milder attacks of infection cause fever blisters on the lips, oral mucosa and skin. Severe cases may develop complications such as meningoencephalitis and keratoconjuctivitis. Various stimuli such as fever, stress and respiratory infection reactivate latent virus lying in the ganglia and result in recurrent attacks of blisters.

HSV-2 causes herpes genitals. It is characterised by vesicular and necrotizing on the cervix, vagina and vulva. Like HSV-1infecction, lesions caused by HSV-2 are also recurrent and develop in non-immune individuals. Latency of HSV-2 infection is similar to the HSV-1 and organisms are reactivated by stimuli such as menstruation and sexual intercourse.

CHICKENPOX

Varicella or chickenpox is an acute vesicular exanthema occurring in non-immune persons, especially children. The condition begins as an infection of the nasopharynx. On entering the blood stream, viraemia is accompanied by onset of fever, malaise and anorexia, muculopapular skin rash, usually in upper trunk and face develops in one or two days. Each lesion progresses rapidly from a macula to a vesicle which resembles "a dewdrop on a rose petal". After a few days, most of the chickenpox vesicles rupture, crust over and heal by regeneration leaving no scars, whereas traumatic rupture of some vesicles with bacterial superinfection may lead to destruction of the basal epidermal layer and residual scarring. A few cases may develop complications, which include pneumonia, hepatitis, encephalitis, carditis, arthritis and haemorrhages.

HERPES ZOSTER

Herpes zoster or shingles is a recurrent, painful, vesicular eruption caused by reactivation of the dormant Varicella zoster virus in an individual who had chickenpox in earlier years. The condition is infectious and spreads to children. The virus during the latent period resides in the dorsal root spinal ganglia or in the cranial nerve ganglia; the activated virus infect sensory nerves which carry virus to one or more dermatomes. This causes vesicular lesions, differentiated from chickenpox by intense itching, burning or sharp pain. This pain is severe when trigeminal nerves are involved. Varicella zoster virus also causes interstitial pneumonia, encephalitis and necrotizing visceral lesions particularly in immunosuppressed patients.

11.6 MEASLES

Measles (rubella) virus is the cause of more than 02 million deaths per year. In the United States, the incidence of measles has decreased by 95 per cent since 1963, when measles vaccine was discovered, but miniepidemics of measles still occur among unvaccinated individuals and among vaccinated individuals who did not develop immunity.

CAUSATIVE ORGANISM

Measles virus is an RNA virus of the paramyxovirus family that includes mumps, respiratory syncytial virus (the major cause of lower respiratory tract infections in infants), and parainfluenza virus. There is only one strain of measles virus. It has an envelope that contains a hemagglutinin that binds the host cells and a small glycoprotein that has haemolytic activity and mediates penetration of the virus into the cytosol. Measles virus is spread by respiratory droplets and multiplies within the respiratory epithelial cells and mononuclear cells, including B and T lymphocytes and macrophages. A transient viraemia spreads the measles virus throughout the body and may cause croup, pneumonia, diarrhoea with protein-losing enteropathy, keratosis with scarring and blindness, encephalitis and haemorrhages. Most children, however, develop T cell-mediated immunity to measles to virus that controls the viral infection and produces the measles virus that controls the viral infection and produces measles rash, a hypersensitivity reaction to viral antigens in the skin. The rash does not occur in patients with deficiencies in cell-mediated immunity. Antibody-mediated immunity to measles virus protects against reinjection.

PATHOLPHYSIOLOGY

The blotchy, reddish-brown rash of measles virus infection on the face, trunk and proximal extremities is produced by dilated skin vessels, edema and a moderate, non-specific mononuclear per vascular infiltrate. Ulcerated mucosal lesions in the oral cavity are marked by necrosis, neutrophils exudates and neovascularizatrion. The lymphoid organs typically have marked follicular hyperplasia, large germinal centers and randomly distributed multinucleate giant cells. These are found in lungs and sputum. In severe or neglected cases, bacterial superinfection may be the cause of death.

11.7 INFLUENZA

Influenza viruses are RNA viruses in the family Orthomyxoviridae that can affect birds and mammals including humans. Influenza B and C viruses are maintained only in human populations. Influenza A viruses can affect many species, with the vast majority of these viruses occurring among birds. Waterfowl and shorebirds seem to the reservoir hosts for avian influenza viruses, which are usually carried asymptomatically in these populations. Avian influenza viruses can also become established among poultry, causing two forms of disease. Low pathogenicity avian influenza (LPAI) viruses, the form usually carried in wild birds, generally cause asymptomatic infections, mild respiratory disease or decreased egg production in poultry. A few influenza A viruses have become adapted to mammals including humans, swine, horses and dogs, and circulate in these populations. These viruses are called human influenza-A viruses, swine influenza viruses, equine influenza viruses and canine influenza viruses, respectively. In the mammalian species to which they are adapted, influenza viruses cause respiratory disease with high morbidity but low mortality rates. More severe cases can occur in conjunction with other diseases or debilitation, as well as in infancy or old age.

ETIOLOGY

Viruses in the family Orthomyxoviridae cause influenza. There are three genera of influenza viruses: influenza virus-A, influenza virus-B and influenza virus-C. Separate viral species are not recognized within these genera; the members of each genus belong to the three species "influenza-A virus," "influenza-B virus" or "influenza-C virus," respectively. These viruses are also called type A, type B and type C influenza viruses.

INFLUENZA A VIRUSES

Influenza-A viruses include avian, swine, equine and canine influenza viruses, as well as the human influenza A viruses. Influenza A viruses are classified into subtypes based on two surface antigens, the hemagglutinin (H) and neuraminidase (N) proteins. There are 16 hemagglutinin antigens (H1 to H16) and nine neuraminidase antigens (N1 to N9). These two proteins are involved in cell attachment and release from cells, and are also major targets for the immune response.

INFLUENZA B VIRUSES

Influenza-B viruses are known to circulate only in human populations. These viruses can cause epidemics, but to date they have not, been responsible for pandemics. They have also been found occasionally in animals. Influenza-B viruses are categorized into lineages rather than subtypes. They are also classified into strains. Influenza-B viruses undergo antigenic drift, though it occurs slower than in influenza-A viruses. Until recently, the B/Victoria/2/87 lineage predominated in human populations, and influenza-B viruses were said not to undergo antigenic shifts.

INFLUENZA-C VIRUSES

Influenza-C viruses circulate in human populations, and are mainly associated with disease in people. Until recently, they had never been linked to large-scale epidemics. However, a nationwide epidemic of influenza C was reported in Japan between January and July 2004. Influenza-C viruses have also been found in animals. Influenza-C viruses are not classified into subtypes, but they are classified into strains. Each strain is antigenic ally stable, and accumulates few changes over time. Recent evidence suggests that reassortment occurs frequently between different strains of influenza C viruses.

TRANSMISSION OF MAMMALIAN INFLUENZA VIRUSES

In mammals, influenza viruses are transmitted in aerosols created by coughing and sneezing, and by contact with nasal discharges, either directly or on fomites. Close contact and closed environments favor transmission.

PATHOGENESIS
INCUBATION PERIOD

The incubation period for seasonal human influenza is short; most infections appear after 01-04 days. Infections with the novel H1N1 virus circulating in humans usually become apparent in 02-07 days. The incubation period for avian influenza in humans is difficult to determine. Limited data from Asian lineage H5N1 infections suggest that, for this virus, it may range from 02-08 days and could be as long as 17 days. In most cases, the first symptoms occur 02-05 days. The World Health Organization (WHO) currently suggests using an incubation period of seven days for field investigations and monitoring patient contacts.

CLINICAL SIGNS

1. Fever;
2. Myalgia—painful condition of muscles, headache;
3. Malaise—An indefinite sensation of discomfort;
4. Dry cough;
5. Sore throat; and
6. Inflammation of nasal mucosa

Among children:

1. Vomiting;
2. Nausea;
3. Inflammation of the middle ear;

Influenza virus infection can cause:

1. Primary influenza viral pneumonia;
2. Secondary bacterial pneumonia;
3. Sinusitis; and
4. Co infection with other viral or bacterial pathogens.

Young children afflicted with influenza may become victims of bacterial sepsis with high fever, and the like.

11.8 DIPHTHERIA

Diphtheria is a highly infectious bacterial disease which causes inflammation of the throat, nose and tonsils with fever. It can cause dysphagia and may be cause suffocation. The infection may also produce toxins that circulate through the percent to blood damaging the heart, kidneys, and nervous system. Death occurs in 05-10 percent cases of diphtheria. Diphtheria is a bacterial disease in which the clinical manifestations result from the action of an extracellular substance (exotoxins) produced by *Cory bacterium diphtheriae*, a club-shaped bacterium. Diphtheria toxin, a protein with a molecular weight of 62 000, is known as an A-B type toxin, and consists of two fragments, i.e. A and B. Fragment B is necessary for binding to surface receptors and penetration into cells. Fragment A is responsible for its toxicity and exerts its action by interfering enzymatically with protein synthesis, finally producing the death of the cells. Diphtheria toxin exerts its effects on distant tissues and organs, especially the heart (myocarditis) and the peripheral and cranial nerves (weakness progressing to paralysis). All toxigenic strains of *C. diphtheria* produce an identical toxin. For a diphtheria strain to become toxigenic, it must be infected by a particular bacterial virus, the bacteriophage. This process is called lysogenic conversion. The introduction of a toxigenic strain of *C. diphtheria* into a community may initiate an outbreak of diphtheria by transfer of the bacteriophage to non-toxigenic strains carried in the respiratory tracts of its inhabitants. Both toxigenic and non-toxigenic strains of C. diphtheria may be isolated during such an outbreak.

Diphtheria is acquired through personal contact the incubation period is generally 02-05 days.

Signs and symptoms of Diphtheria:
1. A sore throat and hoarseness;
2. Dysphagia;
3. Swollen glands in the neck region;
4. A thick gray membrane covering the throat and tonsils;
5. Rapid breathing or dyspnoea;
6. Nasal discharge;
7. Fever and chills; and
8. Malaise.

In developing countries skin diphtheria is common, with lesions indistinguishable from, or a component of, impetigo. Laryngeal diphtheria is serious, while nasal diphtheria may be mild, often chronic. Late effects of diphtheria include cranial and peripheral motor and sensory palsies and myocarditis. The fatality rate is 05 -10 per cent. The main way that diphtheria is prevented is by receiving DTP vaccination (diphtheria, tetanus, and pertussis). The shot series starts with the first dose at 02 months of age and ends with a booster dose given before age seven with a total of five doses. Adults should receive a booster dose of Td (tetanus, diphtheria) every ten years.

11.9 TETANUS

Tetanus is caused by the action of a highly potent neurotoxin, tetanospasmin, which is produced during the growth of the anaerobic bacterium *Clostridium tetany*. *Cl. tetany* is not an invasive organism; infection with *Cl. tetany* remains localized. The disease usually occurs through infection of a skin injury with tetanus spores. Tetanus spores introduced into an area of injury convert to tetanus bacilli in the presence of necrotic tissue with reduced oxygen potential. Neonatal tetanus occurs through infection of the umbilicus when the cord is cut with an unclean instrument or when substances heavily contaminated with tetanus spores are applied to the umbilical stump. Tetanus toxin produced by *Cl. tetany* bacteria migrates to its site of action in the central nervous system by retrograde transport along nerves. Tetanus toxin is neurotoxic and it binds to ganglioside-containing receptors at the nerve termini. Once bound to neuronal tissue, tetanus toxin cannot be affected by tetanus antitoxin. Toxin accumulates in the central nervous system, where it blocks the release of inhibitory neurotransmitter substances, such as glycine and γ-aminobutyric acid, in neural synapses. Tetanus toxin is very toxic; the estimated human lethal dose is less than 2.5 nags per kg. Tetanus toxin is synthesized inside *Cl. tetany* bacterial cells as a single polypeptide chain of 150 000 molecular weight. In artificial laboratory conditions, the toxin obtained from the culture supernatant consists of light and heavy polypeptide chains connected by a disulphide bond. The toxin molecule can be degraded into polypeptide fragments by enzymes such as papain. Some of the polypeptide fragments are non-toxic and supposedly have potential for vaccines.

PATHOLOGY

Tetanus is a neurological disease caused by tetanus toxin. Three different clinical forms have been described; generalized (~80 per cent), local and cephalic tetanus. Symptoms of generalized tetanus include rigidity and painful spasms of skeletal muscles. Initial muscles affected are often in the jaw and neck (leading to the common name for the disease: "lockjaw") followed by involvement of larger muscles in a descending pattern. Seizures may occur. Less common forms of tetanus are local tetanus which is localized to the anatomic area of injury and cephalic tetanus which involves the cranial nerves. In countries with poor hygiene, neonatal tetanus causes significant mortality when infants born to unimmunized women have infection of the umbilical cord that was contaminated with soil or alternative medical treatment. Complications of tetanus include fractures, dyspnea, and abnormal heart rhythms. In addition, nosocomial infections related to prolonged hospitalization can occur. Death results in approximately 11 per cent of affected persons.

11.10 PERTUSSIS OR WHOOPING COUGH

Pertussis, commonly known as whooping cough, is a vaccine-preventable disease spread by close contact with the respiratory secretions of infected individuals. The clinical case definition for pertussis is a cough lasting for at least two weeks with paroxysms of coughing, aspiratory "whoop," or post-tussive vomiting, without other apparent causes. Complications include pneumonia, seizures, and encephalopathy. The incidence of pertussis is the maximum in infants under one year of age. Whooping cough or Pertussis has a significant mortality rate in infants.

Pertussis is an epidemic disease with 02—05 year cycle. Immunization reduced the total number of cases but did not change the cycles, suggesting that immunization controlled the disease but not the propagation of disease. Recent studies support the hypothesis that pertussis infection is very common among adults. IgA antibodies to pertussis antigens are only produced after a natural infection and not after immunization.

CAUSATIVE ORGANISM

Whooping cough (pertussis) is caused by the bacterium *Bordetella pertussis*. *B. pertussis* is a very small Gram- negative aerobic coccobacillus that appears singly or in pairs. *Bordetella pertussis, B. bronchiseptica, B. para pertussis* are responsible for mammalian pertussis; *Bordetella pertussis* are exclusively human pathogens. *B. para pertussis* does cause whooping cough but it is less severe than the one caused by *B. pertussis*... They can be grown in synthetic medium, however, which contains buffer, salts, an amino acid energy source, and growth factors such as nicotinamide (for which there is a strict requirement). Other species of Bordetella, including *B. para pertussis* and less commonly *B. bronchiseptica* or *B. holmesii*, are associated with cough illness; the clinical presentation of *B. para pertussis* can be similar to that of classic pertussis. Illnesses caused by species of *Bordetella* other than *B. pertussis* are not preventable by pertussis vaccines.

TRANSMISSION

Transmission most commonly occurs by the respiratory route through contact with respiratory droplets less than 5μ. These droplets are generated during coughing, sneezing, talking or singing. Transmission occurs less frequently by contact with freshly contaminated articles of an infected person. A carrier state is infrequent, transient in duration (less than six weeks), and probably of little importance in maintaining pertussis organisms in the community.

Communicability

Pertussis is highly communicable, as evidenced by secondary attack rates of 80 per cent among susceptible household contacts. Persons with pertussis are most infectious during the catarrhal period and the first two to three weeks after cough onset (21 days). Some undiagnosed and untreated cases may harbor *B. pertussis* and transmit to a maximum of six weeks. There are no long term carriers. Source: Pertussis is a human disease. No animal or insect source or vector is known to exist. Pertussis is predominantly a childhood disease with 75 per cent of the cases occurring in children less than five years of age. Adolescents and adults are an important reservoir for *B. pertussis* and are often the source of infection for infants.

PATHOGENESIS

Bordetella pertussis colonizes the cilia of the mammalian respiratory epithelium. Generally, it is thought that *B. pertussis* does not invade the tissues, but some recent work has shown the bacterium in alveolar macrophages.

The first stage, catarrhal stage, is an upper respiratory disease with fever, malaise and coughing, which increases in intensity over about a 10-day period. During this stage the organism can be recovered in large numbers from pharyngeal cultures, and the severity and duration of the disease can be reduced by antimicrobial treatment. Adherence mechanisms of *B. pertussis* involve a "filamentous hemagglutinin" (FHA), which is a fimbrial-like structure on the bacterial surface, and cell-bound pertussis toxin (PTx). The first stage, the catarrhal stage, is characterized by the insidious onset of Oryza (runny nose), sneezing, low-grade fever and a mild, occasional cough, similar to the common cold. The cough gradually becomes more severe, and after 01—02 weeks, the second, or paroxysmal stage, begins.

The second or toxemic stage of pertussis follows relatively nonspecific symptoms of the colonization stage. It begins gradually with prolonged and paroxysmal coughing that often ends in a characteristic aspiratory gasp (whoop).

It is during the paroxysmal stage that the diagnosis of pertussis is usually suspected. Characteristically, the patient has bursts, or paroxysms of numerous, rapid coughs. At the end of the paroxysm, a long aspiratory effort is usually accompanied by a characteristic high-pitched whoop. During such an attack, the patient may become cyanotic. Children and young infants, especially, appear very ill and distressed; vomiting and exhaustion is the sequel. Paroxysmal attacks occur more frequently at night, with an average of 15 attacks per 24 hours. During the first one or two weeks of this stage, the attacks increase in frequency, remain at the same level for 02-03 weeks and then gradually decrease. The paroxysmal stage usually lasts 01-06 weeks, but may persist for up to 10 weeks. Infants younger than six months of age may not have the strength to have a whoop, but they do have paroxysms of coughing. In the convalescent stage, recovery is gradual. The cough becomes less paroxysmal and disappears in 02-06 weeks. However, paroxysms often recur with subsequent respiratory infections for many months after the onset of pertussis. Fever is generally minimal throughout the course of pertussis. During the recovery period, a new viral respiratory infection can trigger a recurrence of paroxysms. During the second stage, *B. pertussis* can rarely be recovered, and antimicrobial agents have no effect on the progress of the disease.

11.11 TUBERCULOSIS

Tuberculosis (TB) is contagious and airborne. It is a disease of poverty affecting mostly young adults in their prime years. The vast majority of TB deaths are in the developing world. It is estimated by the World Health Organization (WHO) that one third of the global population is infected with TB and that 07-08 million new cases of

TB occur each year. Approximately, 01.75 million deaths resulted from TB in 2003 and 01.7 million people died of TB in 2009. WHO estimates that between 2000 and 2020 billion people will be newly infected: 200 million will get sick, and 35 million will die from TB if global control is not further strengthened.

CAUSATIVE ORGANISM

The *Mycobacterium tuberculosis* complex includes strains of five species—*M. tuberculosis*, *M. Canetti*, *M. africana*, *M. microti*, and *M. bovid* and two subspecies—*M. caprae* and *M. pinnipedii*. These mycobacterium are characterized by 99.9 per cent similarity at nucleotide level and virtually identical 16S rRNA sequences but differ widely in terms of host tropisms, phenotypes and pathogenicity. The most notable member of the complex is *M. tuberculosis* the causative agent of human tuberculosis which has an exclusive tropism for this host. In contrast *M. bovid*, the etiologic agent of bovine tuberculosis, causes only 05—10 per cent of human tuberculosis cases with a path biology indistinguishable from the one caused by *M. tuberculosis* and a wider host spectrum. The impact of *M. bovid* in human health declined sharply after the advent of pasteurization but there are records of new cases among immunocompromised individuals and re-activation cases amongst elderly individuals. The third member of the complex with an important, although geographically circumscribed, impact on human health is *M. africana* which is responsible for half of the TB cases in West Africa.

MODE OF TRANSMISSION

Human being acquires infection with tubercle bacilli by one of the following routes:

1. **Inhalation:** Inhalation of organisms presents in fresh cough droplets or dried sputum from an open case of pulmonary tuberculosis.
2. **Ingestion:** Ingestion of organisms leads to development of tonsil or intestinal tuberculosis. This mode of infection of human tubercle bacilli is from self-swallowing of infected sputum of an open case of pulmonary tuberculosis, or ingestion of bovine tubercle bacilli from milk of diseased cows.
3. **Inoculation:** Inoculation of organisms into the skin may rarely occur from infected postmortem tissue.
4. **Transplacental route:** This is responsible for congenital tuberculosis in foetus from infected mother; it is a rare mode of transmission.

SPREAD OF TUBERCULOSIS

The disease spreads in the body by various routes:

1. **Local spread:** This takes place by macrophages carrying the bacilli into the surrounding tissues.
2. **Lymphatic spread:** Tuberculosis is primarily an infection of lymphoid tissues. The bacilli may pass into lymphoid follicle of pharynx, bronchi, intestines or regional lymph nodes resulting in regional tuberculosis

lymphadenitis which is typical of childhood infections. Primary complex is primary focus with lymphangitis and lymphadenitis.

3. **Haematogenous spread:** This occurs either as a result of tuberculosis bacillaemia because of the drainage of lymphatic's into the venous system or due to gaseous material escaping through ulcerated wall of vein. This produced millet seed-sized lesions in different organs of the body like lungs, liver, kidneys, bones and other tissues and known as miliary tuberculosis.

By the natural passages
Infection from:
(a) Lung lesions into pleura (tuberculosis pleurisy)
(b) Tran bronchial spread into the adjacent lung segments
(c) Tuberculosis salpingitis into peritoneal cavity (tuberculosis peritonitis)
(d) Infected sputum into larynx (Tuberculosis laryngitis)
(e) Swallowing of the infected sputum (Ileocaecal tuberculosis)
(f) Renal lesions into ureter and down to trig one of the bladder.

PATHOGENESIS OF TUBERCULOSIS

Tuberculosis is an airborne disease, since the infectious bacilli are inhaled as droplets from the atmosphere. In the lung, the bacteria are phagocytosed by the alveolar macrophages. The interaction of mycobacterium components with macrophage receptors, such as Toll-like receptors (TLRs) results in the production of chemokines and cytokines that serve as infection signals. These signals result in migration of monocytes derived macrophages and dendrite cells from the blood stream to the site of infection in the lung. The dendrite cells that engulf bacteria then mature and migrate to the lymph nodes. Once there, CD4 and CD8 T cells are primed against mycobacterium antigens. Primed T cells expand and migrate back to the focus of infection in the lungs, probably in response to mediators produced by infected cells. This phenomenon of cell migration towards the infection focus culminates in the formation of a granuloma, the distinctive feature of TB. The granuloma is formed by T cells, macrophages, B cells, and dendrite cells, endothelial and epithelial cells, among others in a proportion that varies with its age. This granuloma prevents the spreading of bacilli resident within macrophages and generates an immune microenvironment which facilitates the interaction between cytokines secreted by macrophages and T cells. However, the granuloma also provides housing for M. tuberculosis during a long period of time. The latent bacilli can be later released if the cytokine balance is broken, triggering disease reactivation.

TYPES OF TUBERCULOSIS

Lung is the main organ affected in tuberculosis. Depending on the type of tissue response and age, the infection with tubercle bacilli is of two main types:
1. Primary tuberculosis
2. Secondary tuberculosis

Primary tuberculosis: The infection of an individual who has not been previously infected or immunized is called *primary tuberculosis* or *Goon's complex* or *childhood tuberculosis.*

Primary complex or Goon's complex is the lesion produced in the portal of entry with foci in the draining lymphatic vessels and lymph nodes. The most commonly involved tissues for primary complex are lungs and Hilar lymph nodes. The other tissues, primary complexes are tonsils and cervical lymph nodes, and in the case of ingested bacilli the lesions may be found in small intestine and mesenteric lymph nodes.

The incidence of disseminated form of progressive primary tuberculosis is particularly high in immunocompromised host such as AIDS.

Secondary Pulmonary Tuberculosis

The lesion in the secondary pulmonary tuberculosis usually begins as 01-02 cm apical area of consolidation of lungs, which may in time develop a small area of central necrosis and peripheral fibrosis. It occurs by haematogenous spread of infection from primary complex to the apex of the affected lung where the oxygen tension is very high and favourable for the growth of aerobic tubercle bacilli. Microscopically, it resembles tuberculosis granuloma with necrosis.

Patients with HIV infection previously exposed to tuberculosis infection have particularly high incidence of reactivation of primary tuberculosis and the pattern of lesions in such cases is similar to that of primary tuberculosis, i.e. with involvement of Hilary lymph nodes rather than cavitary and apical lesions in the lung. In addition, an opportunistic infection with *M. Avium*-intracellulare can occur in cases of AIDS.

11.12 POLIOMYELITIS

Poliomyelitis, often called polio or infantile paralysis, is a viral paralytic disease. The causative agent, a virus called poliovirus (PV), enters the body orally, infecting the intestinal wall. It may proceed to the blood stream and into the central nervous system causing muscle weakness and often paralysis. An ancient disease, it was first recognized as a medical entity by Jacob Heine in 1840. Eradication efforts led by the World Health Organization and the Rotary Foundation of Rotary International have reduced the rate of incidence of Polio from the hundreds of thousands to around a thousand a year.

Polio is a communicable disease which is categorized as a disease of civilization. Polio spreads through human to human contact, usually entering the body through the mouth due to fecally contaminated water or food. The poliovirus is a small RNA (ribonucleic acid) virus that has three different strains and is extremely infectious. The virus invades the nervous system, and the onset of paralysis can occur in a matter of hours. While polio can strike a person at any age, over fifty per cent of the cases occur in children between the ages of three and five.

CAUSATIVE ORGANISM

Poliovirus is a member of the enterovirus subgroup, family Picornaviridae. Enterovirus is transient inhabitants of the gastrointestinal tract, and is stable at acid pH. Picornaviruses are small, ether-insensitive viruses with an RNA genome. Humans are the only known reservoir of poliovirus, which is transmitted most frequently by persons with apparent infections. There is no asymptomatic carrier state except in immune deficient persons. Person to person spread of poliovirus via the fecal-oral route is the prime route of transmission, although the oral route may account for some cases. The incubation period of polio ranges from 03–35 days, thus Polio can spread widely before a polio outbreak is apparent. Most people infected with the poliovirus have no symptoms or outward signs of the illness and are thus never aware they have been infected. After initial infection with poliovirus, virus particles are excreted in the feces for several weeks and are highly transmissible to others in a community. In all forms of polio, the early symptoms of infection are fatigue, fever, vomiting; headache and pain in the neck and extremities. Around 01 per cent of unimmunized people develop paralytic complications, in some cases bulbar paralysis. Poliovirus infection typically peaks in the summer months in temperate climates. There is no seasonal pattern in tropical climates.

There are three poliovirus serotypes (P1, P2, and P3). There is minimal heterotypic immunity between the three serotypes. The poliovirus is rapidly inactivated by heat, formaldehyde, chlorine, and ultraviolet light. Poliovirus is highly infectious, with seroconversion rates in susceptible household contacts of children nearly 100 per cent and of adults over 90 per cent. Cases are most infectious from 07-10 days before and after the onset of symptoms, but poliovirus may be present in the stool from 03-06 weeks.

PATHOGENESIS

The mouth is the portal of entry of the virus and primary multiplication of the virus occurs at the site of implantation in the pharynx and gastrointestinal tract. The virus is usually present in the throat and in the stools before the onset of illness. One week after onset there is little virus in the throat, but virus continues to be excreted in the stools for several weeks. The virus invades local lymphoid tissue, enters the blood stream, and then may infect cells of the central nervous system. Replication of poliovirus in motor neurons of the anterior horn and brain stem results in cell destruction, causing the typical manifestations of poliomyelitis.

Various types of polio are:
1. 90 per cent have no or almost no symptoms or their disease is indistinguishable from influenza.
2. 09 per cent have non-paralytic polio.
3. 01 per cent has spinal or bulbar polio, of which:
4. 10 per cent are fatal
5. 50 per cent recover fully.
6. 40 per cent are left with only partial recovery or permanent paralysis.

Of that 0.4 per cent of polio patents who are left with permanent paralysis, the most affected locations are either or both lower limbs. Quadriplegia or respiratory paralysis occurs on only 0.01 per cent (01 in 10,000) of all polio patients.

NON-PARALYTIC POLIO

Non-paralytic polio may result in fever, vomiting, abdominal pain; lethargy, and irritability, and some muscles tender to the touch. In some cases there may be no significant symptoms are present.

SPINAL POLIO

The virus affects the anterior horn cells in the spinal column which control movement of the trunk and limb muscles including the intercostal muscles. An affected limb becomes floppy and poorly controlled—the condition of acute flaccid paralysis (AFP). This presentation can lead to permanent paralysis of the body yet it only occurs in 01 per cent of cases. The classic latter appearance is of muscle wasting in a leg. Destroyed motor neurons do not regenerate and the affected motor units of muscles are not being able to contract. However, some sprouting from nearby surviving neurons may reinervate the denervated muscle. This additional load on surviving motor neurons may precipitate the later developing symptoms of post-polio syndrome. The degree of paralysis is proportional to the extent of infection of the motor nuclei, which is likely to be proportional to the degree of viraemia, and inversely proportional to the degree of immunity. Extensive paralysis of the trunk and muscles of the thorax and abdomen (quadriplegia) may occur. If it affects the upper part of the cervical spinal cord (C3-4-5), the diaphragm paralysis requires ventilator support. Without respiratory support, polio affecting respiration is likely to result in death from failure of breathing, or aspiration of secretions and resulting pneumonia. The critical nerves are the Phrenic nerve (the cranial nerve driving the diaphragm to inflate the lungs) and the innervations to the muscles needed for swallowing. Skilled clearing of the airway with suction and tracheotomy are part of the care of such a patient. In Europe, the usual treatment is either mask ventilator or tracheal ventilator. Some patients use cuirass type mechanical ventilators worn over thorax and abdomen.

BULBAR POLIO

The brainstem is homologous to the spinal cord, but the motor neurons arising from there and passing in the various cranial nerves control the various muscles of eyeball movements; the trigeminal nerve and facial nerve which innervate cheeks, tears, gums, and muscles of the face, etc; the glossopharyngeal nerve which in part controls swallowing and functions in the throat, tongue movement and taste; the nerve that sends signals to the heart, intestines, and lungs; and the accessory nerve that controls upper neck movement. Thus, bulbar polio could affect any or all of these functions. Bulbar polio and spinal polio are part of a continuum of anatomy and disease (paralytic polio). Approximately, one in 1000 people who have had paralytic polio have permanent respiratory paralysis. Fulminating encephalitis (an overwhelming invasion of the virus into other parts of the brain) is rare, but is most often lethal.

11.13 CHOLERA

Cholera is a severe intestinal disease caused by the bacteria, *Vibrio cholerae*; the bacteria are typically found in water environments such as freshwater lakes and rivers. Cholera is usually transmitted to people or animals through contaminated water sources. Contamination comes from fecal material from infected individuals. Cholera can affect people and some animals and causes severe diarrhea, vomiting, dehydration, and shock. If untreated, death can occur within hours. Cholera is endemic in the Middle East, Africa, Central and South America, parts of Asia and the Gulf Coast of the United States but outbreaks can occur in any country. Major epidemics occur periodically in less developed countries; outbreaks in developed countries are usually localized due to better sanitation.

CAUSATIVE ORGANISM

Vibrio cholerae are Gram-negative bacteria. *V. cholerae* serogroups O1, O139 and O141 are the only known serogroups to produce the enterotoxin that causes cholera. Two serogroups, 01 and 0139 ("Bengal"), can cause disease. Serogroups O1 contains two serologically indistinguishable biotypes, classical and El Tor. Mild or asymptomatic infections are seen more often with the El Tor biotype. Cholera caused by serogroups 0139 emerged in 1992, in epidemics in India and Bangladesh Non-toxigenic *V. cholerae* can cause a diarrheal illness (fibrosis) but not cholera. Cholera is spread in contaminated water and food. The disease is not likely to spread directly from one person to another. Transmission is by the fecal–oral route. Infections are particularly common after ingesting contaminated water or food. Cases are occasionally seen in people who have eaten raw or undercooked shellfish, particularly oysters, from contaminated waters. *V. cholerae* is excreted in the feces and vomitus. Viable organisms can be found in feces for up to 50 days, on glass for up to a month, on coins for a week, in soil or dust for up to 16 days and on fingertips for 01-02 hours. Bacteria survive well in water and may remain viable in shellfish, algae or plankton in coastal regions.

The incubation period is a few hours to 05 days. Most infections -become apparent after 02-03 days.

PATHOGENESIS

Cholera is an acute bacterial enteric disease characterized in its severe form by sudden onset, profuse painless watery stools (rice water stool), nausea and vomiting early in the course of illness, and, in untreated cases, rapid dehydration, acidosis, and circulatory collapse. Asymptomatic or mild infection is frequent, especially with the El Tor biotype. Cholera appears abruptly with painless, watery diarrhea, sometimes accompanied by vomiting. Infections may be subclinical, mild and self-limiting, or fulminant and severe. Severe fluid loss can be seen in more serious cases; thirst, oliguria, severe dehydration, acidosis, muscle cramps and shock may result. Most cases last approximately 02–07 days but death may occur within a few cause of dehydration. A self-limiting gastroenteritis is seen after infection with pathogenic non O1/O139 strains. Death may occur within hours in severe untreated cases (cholera gravis), and the case-fatality rate may exceed 50 per cent; with proper treatment, the rate is less than 01 per cent. Differential diagnoses include other bacterial infections (including Non-toxigenic fibrosis, Shiga toxin-producing *E. coli*, salmonellosis, shigellosis), viral diarrhea, amebic dysentery and schistosomiasis).

11.14 RABIES

Rabies is a neurological disease of mammals that is almost invariably fatal once the clinical signs develop. Humans are usually infected when they are bitten by an infected animal, or exposed to its saliva or central nervous system (CNS) tissues. Although rabies is generally well controlled among domesticated animals in developed nations, canine rabies continues to be a serious problem in some areas of Africa, the Middle East, Asia and Latin America. Rabies can be effectively treated if the exposure is recognized before the symptoms develop. However, people in impoverished countries do not always have access to post-exposure prophylaxis, and even in nations with good medical care, cases occur occasionally in people who do not realize they were exposed.

ETIOLOGY

Rabies results from infection by the rabies virus, a neurotoxic virus in the genus Lyssavirus, family Rhabdoviridae. There are many strains of the rabies virus; each strain is maintained in particular reservoir host(s). Although these viruses can readily cause rabies in other species, they usually die out during serial passage in species to which they are not adapted. The reservoir host is sometimes used to describe a strain's origin. For example, if a virus from a skunk caused rabies in a dog, it would be described as skunk rabies in a dog, whereas a virus that is maintained in dog populations would be called canine rabies. Occasionally, a virus adapted to one species becomes established in another species. Closely related *lyssaviruses*, which are known as rabies-related *lyssaviruses* or no rabies *lyssaviruses*, can cause a neurological disease that is identical to rabies. Rabies and the rabies-related lyssaviruses have been classified into 02 phylogroups, based on how closely they are related. Phylogroups I contain the rabies virus, Duvenhage virus, EBLV1, EBLV2 and Australian bat virus, while phylogroups II consist of Lagos bat virus and Molokai virus.

TRANSMISSION

The rabies virus is readily transmitted between mammals, whether they are the same or different species. This virus is usually spread in the saliva, when an infected animal bites another. Less often, an animal or person is infected by contact with infectious saliva or neurological tissues, through mucous membranes or breaks in the skin. The rabies virus is not transmitted through intact skin. Rabies may be transmitted when saliva or other potentially infectious material (central nervous system tissue) penetrates the skin or contaminates the mucosa of a susceptible mammal. Although person to person transmission of rabies has been confirmed, transmission through bites or other mucous membrane exposure is possible—theoretically. In addition, four cases of rabies may have occurred as the result of exposure to large amounts of aerosolized rabies virus (e.g., exposure to millions of bats in a cave or through handling laboratory specimens). Rabies is not transmitted by contact with blood, urine or feces, by touching fur, or by being sprayed by a skunk. The virus becomes inactive with drying. There are also rare reports of transmission by other routes. A few cases have been reported after transplantation of organs, particularly corneas but also pancreas, kidneys and liver. Rabies viruses have been transmitted by ingestion in experimentally infected animals, and there is anecdotal evidence of transmission in milk to a lamb and a human infant. There is some speculation that ingestion could play a role in rabies transmission among wild animals.

INCUBATION PERIOD OF HUMAN RABIES

The incubation period of rabies in humans is typically 03-08 weeks but can range from 09 days to several years. Most cases become apparent after 01-03 months. In one study, approximately 04-10 per cent of cases had an incubation period of 06 months or more.

PERIOD OF COMMUNICABILITY

Rabies virus is present in saliva, CSF, and neurologic tissues of infected patients who are in the final (clinical) stage of disease. Rabid dogs, cats and ferrets are considered communicable no more than 10 days prior to symptom onset. Little or nothing is known about how early communicability starts in other species, including humans. Activities that could pose a risk for exposure include bites, kisses or other direct contact between saliva and mucous membranes or broken skin, sexual activity, and sharing eating or drinking utensils or cigarettes. It is not known how long humans can shed the virus before becoming symptomatic; the CDC recommends post-exposure prophylaxis for anyone who had at-risk contact with a person during the 14 days before the onset of clinical signs.

PATHOGENESIS

Immediately after infection, the rabies virus enters an eclipse phase during which it is not easily detected. During this phase, it replicates in non-nervous tissue such as muscle. It does not usually stimulate an immune response at this time, but it is susceptible to neutralization if antibodies are present. After several days or months, the virus enters the peripheral nerves and is transported to the central nervous system by retrograde flow in the axons. After dissemination within the CNS, where clinical signs develop as the neurons are infected, the virus is distributed to highly innervated tissues via the peripheral nerves. Most of the virus is found in nervous tissue, salivary glands, saliva and cerebrospinal fluid (CSF), which should all be handled with extreme caution.

Some virus has also been detected in other tissues and organs, including the lungs, adrenal glands, kidneys, bladder; heart, ovaries, testes; prostate, pancreas, intestinal tract; cornea, germinal cells of hair follicles in the skin, sebaceous glands, tongue papillae and the brown fat of bats. The rabies virus is found in the neurons, and handling most body fluids or intact organs is thought to carry a low risk of infection. However, a puncture could theoretically pierce a neuron, and health care personnel are given post-exposure prophylaxis after a needle-stick or other puncture wound received while caring for a rabies patient. Organ transplants also pose a (rare) risk, if the donor is not known to have been infected with rabies. Blood, urine and feces are not thought to be infectious; however, a few studies have suggested that viraemia might occur at some point during the infection. A recent study in mice, using a polymerase chain reaction (PCR) assay, found viral RNA in mice when they were clinically ill, but not during the asymptomatic stage when virus was migrating to the CNS.

CLINICAL SIGNS

Rabies is a rapidly progressive, acute viral encephalomyelitis. Initial symptoms may include headache, fever, and malaise. Initial neurologic symptoms may include parasthesias or pain often affecting the limb or at the site of inoculation. Subtle changes in personality have been observed. The early symptoms may include nonspecific prodromal signs such as malaise, fever or headache; discomfort, pain, pruritus or sensory alterations at the site of virus entry. After several days, anxiety, confusion and agitation may appear, and progress to insomnia, abnormal behaviour, hypersensitivity to light and sound; delirium, hallucinations, slight or partial paralysis; hyper salivation, dysphagia; pharyngeal spasms upon exposure to liquids, and convulsions. Either an encephalitic (furious) form with excessive excitability, autonomic dysfunction and hydrophobia, or a paralytic (dumb) form characterized by generalized paralysis, may predominate. Later neurologic symptoms can include seizures, excessive salivation, hydrophobia, delirium, agitation, and paralysis. Neurological deterioration is rapid; death is often due to cardiac arrest or respiratory paralysis. Death occurs 10 days after the onset of symptoms.

11.15 LEPROSY

Leprosy, also known as Hansen's disease, is a chronic, granulomatous infection caused by *Mycobacterium leprae,* an acid-fast bacillus (AFB) related to the bacteria causing tuberculosis. Leprosy is a stigmatized disease. It was discovered by the Norwegian, Gerhard A Hansen, in 1873 and principally affects the skin, mucous membranes of the nose, and peripheral nerves. It is an infectious disease that develops very slowly. It is caused by germs (bacilli) that affect mostly the skin and nerves. It can cause a variety of skin problems, loss of feeling, and paralysis of the hands and feet.

MODE OF TRANSMISSION

Transmission of *M. leprae* is primarily from untreated MB patients. The route of transmission is not however definitely known. Evidence suggests though that the main portals of entry are the skin and the upper respiratory tract. Nasal discharge from untreated patients with active leprosy has been shown to contain large numbers of acid-fast bacilli (AFB). Studies have shown experimental transmission of leprosy via aerosols to mice and some evidence of *M. leprae* entering through breaks in the skin barrier. It can spread only from some persons who have untreated leprosy, to other persons who have 'low resistance' to the disease. It is probably spread either through sneezing or coughing, or through skin contact. Most persons who come into contact with leprosy have a natural ability to resist it. Either they do not get it at all, or they get a small unnoticeable infection that soon goes away completely. From the time a person is first infected with leprosy germs, it often takes 03-04 years for the first signs of the disease to appear.

INCUBATION PERIOD

The average incubation period is probably four years for tuberculosis leprosy and twice that for lepromatous leprosy (nine months to 20 years). The disease is rarely seen in children under the age of three.

SUSCEPTIBILITY TO INFECTION

The overwhelming majority of people are not susceptible to leprosy and only a very small proportion of those exposed develop the disease. A number of factors however significantly increase the risk of developing leprosy.

These include old-age persons who may reflect both weaker immune systems and the increased likelihood of lifetime exposure, male sex, contact with a multibacillary (MB) as opposed to paucibacillary (PB) case, genetic closeness and increased proximity for a prolonged period to a patient. *M. leprae* reproduces at a very slow rate and few cases are diagnosed in infants less than 01 year of age. Leprosy can happen to people with exposure to past contacts of several years ago. The maximum incubation period is reported to be greater than 30 years in war veterans known to have been exposed for short periods in endemic areas but otherwise living in non-endemic areas. The average incubation time for tuberculosis and lepromatous cases, is supposedly 02—05 years, and 08—12 years, respectively. Contacts who develop leprosy may only have a single skin lesion (indeterminate leprosy), which often self-heals. Where self-healing or treatment does not occur, the disease may progress to active leprosy. Those who develop the disease demonstrate an impaired cell-mediated immune response to *M. leprae* and there is evidence to suggest that there may be a genetic predisposition in the host.

CLINICAL FEATURES OF LEPROSY

Early lesions and indeterminate leprosy represent an early form of the disease. Thereafter, it may manifest either as an area of numbness on the skin or as a visible skin lesion. The classic early skin lesion mainly occurs in children and is most commonly found on the face, extensor surfaces of the limbs, buttocks or trunk. Scalp, axillae, groins and lumbar skin tend to be spared and hair growth and nerve functions are unimpaired.

Skin lesions in this form tend to be either single or few in number and appear as small, flat, hypo pigmented or coppery with an irregular border. Biopsy may show the per neurovascular infiltrate with only scanty AFB. The majority of these cases will heal spontaneously, and the remainder, will persist in the indeterminate form indefinitely.

FEATURES OF ESTABLISHED LEPROSY

Presentation is often with signs of nerve damage such as weakness or anaesthesia due to a peripheral nerve lesion, or a blister, burn or ulcer in an anaesthetic hand or foot. Borderline patients may present with reversal reactions with nerve pain, sudden palsy, multiple new skin lesions, pain in the eye, or a systemic febrile illness.

Leprosy is a chronic bacterial disease of the skin, peripheral nerves and the upper airway. The manifestations of the disease vary in a continuous spectrum between the two forms which depends on the ability of the body to mount an immune response to the invading bacilli. It can be classified into two types broadly, lepromatous and tuberculosis.

TUBERCULOID LEPROSY (TT)

In the NT, TT has been the commonest form of leprosy in the past, making up more than a third of the cases. These cases have had a well-developed cell-mediated immunity and a very low bacillary load. TT may present as purely neural, with pain or swelling of the affected nerves followed by anaesthesia and possible muscle weakness and wasting. Alternatively, skin lesions may appear with or without evidence of nerve involvement. These are single or few in number and usually present as hypo-pigmented (never depigmented), erythematous coppery patches, with a well defined, but irregular and often slightly raised border. The lesions are non-sweating, have decreased hair and decreased sensation. Diagnosis depends on clinical examination and biopsy, as smears are usually negative. Palpation should be undertaken around the lesion for the possible palpation of a thickened nerve trunk. Tissues other than the skin and nerves are not affected.

LEPROMATOUS LEPROSY (LL)

Lepromatous leprosy is less common but is a more serious and disabling disease. There is loss of leprosy-specific mediated immunity with no check on multiplication and spread of bacilli. There is therefore wide dissemination and a very high bacillary load. Early symptoms include:

1. Skin lesions are usually the first clinical manifestation as early nerve involvement is asymptomatic. These are extensive and can be varied - macular, diffuse papules, nodular or infiltrative. Some may resemble urticaria. There is little Depigmentation, and usually no sensory loss in the lesions. In some cases the skin can be diffusely smooth and shiny (infiltration), with no discrete lesions.

2. Nasal symptoms of congestion can occur resulting from infiltration of the mucous membranes of the nose and mouth. Patients may complain of increased nasal discharge and papules and nodules on their lips, tongue, palate or larynx. Epistaxis is common and patients can develop a 'saddle nose deformity' resulting from destruction of the nasal septum and cartilage.

3. Leg and ankle oedema due to increased capillary stasis and permeability. Subsequent to this disease progression normally occurs with numbness and anaesthesia on the dorsal surfaces of the hands and feet and later on the extensor surfaces of the arms and legs and finally over the trunk. There may also be infiltration of the corneal nerves that may predispose to injury and blindness. Left untreated the forehead and earlobes become thickened (leonine facies), and the eyebrows become thin, particularly laterally, and are eventually lost (madarosis). The nose may collapse due to septal perforation and loss of the nasal spine and upper teeth may fall out. Skin becomes thickened with ulcers on the hands and legs (Figure 8) and development of a glove and stocking peripheral neuropathy. Muscle wasting can progress to deformities such as claw hand (ulnar nerve) and foot drop (common peroneal nerve).

11.16 TYPHOID FEVER

Typhoid or enteric fever is an ancient disease, which has afflicted mankind since human populations grew large enough to contaminate their water and food supplies. It is caused by *Salmonella enterica subspecies serovar typhi* (previously known as *Salmonella typhi*), a pathogen specific only to humans, as well as by certain non-typhoid salmonella (NTS), particularly Paratyphoid strains A, B, C. These waterborne Gram-negative aerobes are associated with poor sanitation and fecal contamination of water and food supplies. The syndrome needs to be distinguished from that caused by many other organisms. Today, there are as many as 16–30 million cases per year, almost exclusively in the developing world, with a mortality rate of 10 per cent. Recent developments in the mapping of the Salmonella genome have provided insights into its pathogenicity and how antibiotic resistance and human immunity develop. Typhoid fever is important surgically because abdominal complications such as intestinal perforation, bleeding, cholecystitis and pancreatitis typify most serious complications of the illness. Typhoid perforation of the ileum is one of the most common causes of bowel perforation in the developing world.

CAUSATIVE ORGANISM

Typhoid fever is caused by *Salmonella typhi* (full official designation is *S. enterica*—subspecies: *Enterica serovar Typhi*). It is a group D *Salmonella*, which is a *Salmonella* serogroups that also contains serotypes (serovar) that cause non-typhoid salmonellosis. Paratyphoid fever, a milder form of typhoid-like illness, can be caused by *S. Para typhi* (*S. enterica* subsp. *enterica* serovar Para typhi) serotypes A, B, and C. *S. Para typhi* B is the most common serotype. *S. Para typhi* A is less frequent and *S. Para typhi* C is rare. Many isolates of *S. Para typhi* B, particularly B variant L [+] tartrate + (previously known at *S. Java*) cause gastroenteritis rather than paratyphoid fever.

EPIDEMIOLOGY

SOURCE: Humans are the reservoir of *Salmonella Typhi*.

MODE OF TRANSMISSION

Ingestion of food or water contaminated with feces or urine from patients with typhoid fever or carriers of *S. Typhi*. Flies might help carry the bacteria from filth to food. Direct person to person transmission by the fecal-oral route may also occur.

PERIOD OF COMMUNICABILITY

The organism is shed in the stool during the acute illness and throughout convalescence. Approximately 02—05 per cent of typhoid patients become chronic carriers.

INCUBATION PERIOD

03 days to over 60 days, usually 08—14 days.

PATHOGENESIS

Much of the genetic and cellular studies on the path physiology of invasive Salmonella infection have been carried out in the marine model using *S. typhimurium*, which causes invasive disease in mice but not in humans. As opposed to the Salmonella spp. associated with human diarrheal illness, *S. typhi* and those strains that cause typhoid fever are able to achieve cellular invasion. The path physiology of typhoid fever is a complex process which proceeds through several stages. The disease begins with an asymptomatic incubation period of 07—14 days, (inversely related to the size of the infecting dose), during which bacteria invade macrophages and spread throughout the reticuloendothelial system. The first week of symptomatic disease is characterized by progressive elevation of the temperature followed by bacteremia. The second week begins with the development of rose spots, abdominal pain and splenomegaly. The third week is marked by a more intense intestinal inflammatory response particularly in the Peyer's patches with associated necrosis which can result in perforation and hemorrhage. These clinical stages are associated with complex cellular events just now being understood.

First, ingested bacteria must survive the acidic environment of the stomach. The known increased risk of typhoid fever with concomitant Helicobacter pylori infection may express itself *via* the hypochlorhydria associated with chronic *H. pylori* infection. Invading organisms pass through the intestinal epithelial cells and come into contact with phagocyte cells in the Peyer's patches of the intestinal wall. However, the macrophages do not kill the bacteria. Thence, bacterial replication is primarily intracellular. Salmonella avoids encapsulation in Lysosomes by diverting normal cellular mechanisms. Bacteria inject effector proteins into the cells of the innate immune system (macrophages and natural killer cells) though a type III protein secretion system (TTSS) which stimulates both pro and anti-inflammatory responses.

Over the asymptomatic incubation period of 07—14 days the bacteria proliferate and spread through the blood stream to other cells in the reticuloendothelial system in the liver, spleen, bone marrow and gall bladder. As replication inside phagocyte cells continues, bacteria are shed into the blood stream in sustained but low concentrations and the clinical syndrome of fever, headache and abdominal pain begins. The gallbladder is a significant site for ongoing exposure of intestinal epithelial cells to the pathogen. The inflammatory response to this process of repeated exposure engenders necrosis which is a prominent feature of the disease. This occurs in areas of greatest macrophage concentration such as the Peyer's patches and explains why intestinal bleeding and perforation are the most frequent complications; elsewhere typhoid nodules, foci of macrophages and lymphocytes proliferate. As the infection progresses the typical changes of sepsis accumulate in the heart, brain and kidneys. If not interrupted this process may lead to circulatory failure and death from overwhelming sepsis.

CLINICAL SYMPTOMS

Typhoid ("enteric") fever has a very different presentation than the more common kinds of salmonellosis. Vomiting and diarrhea are typically absent; indeed, constipation is frequently reported. As typhoid is a systemic illness, blood cultures are at least as likely to be positive as stool, particularly early in the course of the infection; bone marrow cultures may be most sensitive.

Initial symptoms typically include fever, anorexia, lethargy, malaise, headache, non-productive cough, abdominal pain, and constipation. As the illness progresses, there is protracted fever and mental dullness (stupor). Diarrhea may develop, particularly in children less than one year old. Many patients develop hepatosplenomegaly. After the first week, ~30 per cent of cases develop a salmon-colored muculopapular rash ("rose spots") on the trunk. Mild infections are common, particularly in endemic areas—as many as 10–20 per cent of untreated infections may be fatal, and relapses are not uncommon.

Paratyphoid fever is a similar but usually milder illness and is reported as Salmonellosis.

11.17 MALARIA

Malaria has been and is still a morbid disease. Although the disease has been eradicated in most temperate zones, it continues to be endemic throughout much of the tropics and subtropics. Forty per cent of the world's population lives in endemic areas. Epidemics have devastated large populations and malaria poses a serious barrier to economic progress in many developing countries. There are an estimated 300–500 million cases of clinical disease per year with 01.5–02.7 million deaths. Some of the earliest known medical writings from China, Assyria, and India accurately describe the malaria-like intermittent fevers. Hippocrates, the 'father of medicine', is generally credited with the first description of the clinical symptoms in 500 BC, more than 2000 years before the parasite was described.

CAUSATIVE ORGANISM

Malaria is caused by a single-celled parasite from the genus Plasmodium. More than 100 different species of Plasmodium exist. They produce malaria in many types of animals and birds, and humans. Four species of Plasmodium commonly infect humans. Each one has a distinctive appearance under the microscope, and each one produces a somewhat different pattern of symptoms. Two or more species can live in the same area and infect a single person at the same time.

1. *Plasmodium falciparum* is responsible for most malaria deaths, especially in Africa. The infection can develop suddenly and produce several life-threatening complications. With prompt, effective treatment, however, it is almost always curable.
2. *Plasmodium vivax*, the most widespread of the species, produces less severe symptoms. Relapses, however, can occur for up to 03 years, and chronic disease is debilitating. Once common in temperate climates, *P. vivax* is now found mostly in the tropics, especially throughout Asia.
3. *Plasmodium malaria* infections not only produce typical malaria symptoms but also can persist in the blood for very long periods, possibly decades, without ever producing symptoms. A person with asymptomatic (no symptoms) *P. malaria*, however, can infect others, either through blood donation or mosquito bites. *P. malariae* has been wiped out from temperate climates, but it persists in Africa.
4. *Plasmodium ovale* is rare, can cause relapses, and generally occurs in West Africa.

TRANSMISSION OF MALARIA

The malaria parasite typically is transmitted to people by mosquitoes belonging to the genus *Anopheles*. In rare cases, a person may contract malaria through contaminated blood, or fetes may become infected by its mother during pregnancy. Because the malarial parasite is found in RBCs, malaria can also be transmitted through blood transfusion, organ transplant, or the shared use of needles or syringes contaminated with blood. Malaria also may be transmitted from a mother to her foetus before or during delivery ("congenital" malaria).

PATHOGENESIS

The human malaria parasite has a complex life cycle that requires both a human host and an insect host. In Anopheles mosquitoes, Plasmodium reproduces sexually (by merging the parasite's sex cells). In people, the parasite reproduces asexually (by cell division), first in liver cells and then, repeatedly, in red blood cells (RBCs).

When an infected female Anopheles mosquito bites a human, it sucks blood. At the same time, it injects saliva that contains the infectious form of the parasite, the sporozoite, into a person's bloodstream. The thread-like sporozoite then invades a liver cell. There, during the next week or two (depending on the Plasmodium species), each sporozoite develops into a schizont, a structure that contains thousands of tiny rounded merozoites (another stage of the parasite). When the schizont matures, it ruptures and releases the merozoites into the bloodstream.

Alternatively, some *P. vivax* and *P. ovale* sporozoite turn into hypnozoites, a form that can remain dormant in the liver for months or years. If they become active again, the hypnozoites develop into schizont that then cause relapses in infected people.

Merozoites released from the liver upon rupture of schizont rapidly invade RBCs, where they grow by consuming hemoglobin. Within the RBC, most merozoites go through another round of asexual reproduction; again forming schizont filled with yet more merozoites. When the schizont matures, the cell ruptures and merozoites burst out. The newly released merozoites invade other RBCs, and the infection continues its cycle until it is brought under control, either by medicine or by the body's immune system defenses.

The Plasmodium parasite completes its life cycle through the mosquito when some of the merozoites that penetrate RBCs do not develop asexually into schizont, but instead change into male and female sexual forms known as gametocytes. These circulate in the person's bloodstream, awaiting the arrival of a blood-seeking female Anopheles mosquito.

When a female mosquito bites an infected person, it sucks up gametocytes along with blood. Once in the mosquito's stomach, the gametocytes develop into sperm-like male gametes or large, egg-like female gametes. Fertilization produces an oocyst filled with infectious sporozoite. When the oocyst matures, it ruptures and the thread-like sporozoite migrates, by the thousands, to the mosquito's salivary (saliva-producing) glands. The cycle starts over again when the mosquito bites its next victim.

CLINICAL MANIFESTATIONS

The pathology and clinical manifestations associated with malaria are exclusively due to the asexual erythrocyte stage parasites. Tissue schizont and gametocytes cause little, if any, pathology. Plasmodium infection causes an acute febrile illness which is most notable for its periodic fever paroxysms occurring at either 48 or 72 hour intervals. The severity of the attack depends on the Plasmodium species as well as other circumstances such as the state of immunity and the general health and nutritional status of the infected individual. Malaria is a chronic disease which has a tendency to relapse or recur over months or even years.

The most common way to catch malaria is through the natural transmission by mosquitoes. Malaria can also be transmitted via blood transfusions or sharing syringes. Mechanical transmission of infected blood will result in a shorter incubation period since there is no liver stage. There is also an increased risk of fatality with mechanically-transmitted *P. falciparum*. The lack of the liver stage infection also precludes relapses in *P. vivax* or *P. ovale* infections. Congenital transmission has also been documented, but its incidence is rare despite the heavy infection of the placenta.

Malaria typically produces a string of recurrent attacks, or paroxysms, each of which has three stages—chills, followed by fever, and then sweating. Along with chills, the person is likely to have headache, malaise, fatigue, and muscular pains, and occasionally nausea, vomiting, and diarrhea. Within an hour or two, the body temperature rises, and the skin feels hot and dry. Then, as the body temperature the patient sweats profusely; feeling tired and weak the patient, is likely to fall asleep.

The symptoms first appear some 10–16 days after the infectious mosquito bite and coincide with the bursting of infected RBCs. When many RBCs are infected and break at the same time, malaria attacks can recur at regular time periods — every 2 days for *P. vivax* malaria and *P. ovale*, and every 03 days for *P. malariae*.

11.18 SYPHILIS

Syphilis is an infectious venereal disease caused by the spirochete *Treponema pallidum*. Syphilis is transmissible by sexual contact with infectious lesions, from mother to foetus in uterus, via blood product transfusion, and occasionally through ruptures in the skin that come into contact with infectious lesions. Sexual transmission is probably by inoculation into tiny abrasions from sexual trauma causing a local response resulting in erosion, then an ulcer. This is followed by spread of the Treponema to the regional lymph nodes and haematogenous dissemination to other parts of the body. If untreated, it progresses through 04 stages: primary, secondary, latent, and tertiary. Syphilis first appears as an acute infectious disease, which appears to go away on its own. It may re-emerge a short while later, only to appear and disappear again. It may also come back as a chronic, non-contagious medical condition. Syphilis has an indefinitely number of presentations and can mimic many other infections and immune-mediated processes in advanced stages.

This means there are two distinct groups of people with syphilis:

(a) Those who are infectious but may recover spontaneously, and
(b) Those who are not infectious and won't get better without treatment.

Blood tests for syphilis in either group are positive.

Syphilis would be a leading cause of death and disability. It is believed that it reached Europe from the America by the early Spanish explorers. It spread throughout Europe and became a condition associated with sex. There was no treatment for syphilis until the availability of antibiotics in 1945 when penicillin was developed. Syphilis is becoming rare and rarer due to the widespread use of antibiotics.

CAUSATIVE ORGANISM

The cause of syphilis is infection with the spirochete *T pallidum,* which is solely a human pathogen and does not naturally occur in other species. *T pallidum* has, however, been cloned in *Escherichia coli* and has been used experimentally in rabbits. *T pallidum* is a fragile spiral bacterium 06–15 micrometers long by 0.25 micrometers in diameter. Its small size makes it invisible on light microscopy. It can survive only briefly outside of the body; thus, transmission almost always requires direct contact with the infectious lesion.

Transmission of *T pallidum* occurs via penetration of the spirochetes through mucosal membranes and abrasions on epithelial surfaces. It is primarily spread through sexual contact, but can spread by exposure to blood products and transferred in uterus. *T pallidum* is a labile organism that cannot survive drying or exposure to disinfectants; thus, formate transmission (egg, from toilet seats) is virtually impossible. In the vast majority of cases, syphilis is transmitted by sexual contact—conventional, oral and anal. Kissing too can cause syphilis. Syphilis produces a painless ulcer on the body part that's come into contact with an infected person. That sore slowly leaks a clear liquid, which contains many syphilis bacteria. If it touches someone else's ruptured skin or a mucous membrane (such as the inside of the vagina), it's likely to create a new sore passing on the infection. These initial sores cause no pain and are often located in hidden areas, so people can transmit syphilis without knowing they have it.

A few cases of syphilis are transmitted from infected mothers to their newborns, but with routine screening this form of transmission has almost vanished.

RISK FACTORS OF SYPHILIS INCLUDE THE FOLLOWING:
- Unprotected sex, promiscuity, and intravenous drug use are the major risk factors.
- Health care workers are at occupational risk.

Syphilis can be dichotomized into:

Acquired syphilis,

Congenital syphilis

Acquired syphilis can be divided into primary, secondary, latent, and tertiary stages. The infection can also be transmitted vertically resulting in congenital syphilis, and occasionally by blood transfusion and non-sexual contact. That is, it can be transmitted either by intimate contact with infectious lesions or via. blood transfusion—if the blood has been collected during early syphilis. Transplacental transmission, i.e. from an infected mother to her fetus is another potential source of syphilis.

ACQUIRED SYPHILIS

PRIMARY STAGE

T pallidum rapidly penetrates intact mucous membranes or microscopic dermal abrasions and, within a few hours, enters the lymphatic and blood to produce systemic infection. Incubation time from exposure to development of primary lesions, which occur at the primary site of inoculation, averages 03 weeks but can range from 10–90 days.

At first, it appears as a red dome and is where the bacteria initially multiply. It rapidly erodes to become a painless ulcer called a chancre (pronounced "shaker"). The chancre typically clears up and heals in a month or two whether the person is treated for the disease or not. A person is contagious during primary syphilis.

SECONDARY SYPHILIS

Secondary syphilis develops about 04-10 weeks after the appearance of the primary lesion. During this stage, the spirochetes multiply and spread throughout the body. Secondary syphilis lesions are quite variable in their manifestations. Systemic manifestations include malaise, fever, myalgia; arthralgias, lymphadenopathy, and rash. Widespread mucocutaneous lesions are observed over the entire body and may involve the palms, soles, and oral mucosa. Most often, the lesions are macular, discrete, reddish brown, and 05 mm or smaller in diameter; however, they can be pustule, annular, or scaling. All such lesions contain Treponema. Of these, wet mucous patches are the most contagious. Histologically, the inflammatory reaction is similar to, but less intense than that of the primary chancre.

Secondary syphilis presents with generalized rash affecting the palms and soles, generalized lymphadenopathy, or genital mucosal lesions, including snail tract ulcers. The rash which begins as macules becoming papules is usually non-itchy but pruritus may be present, particularly in dark skinned patients. It may be polymorphic, indolent, or transient but is not vesicular or bulbous. Less common presentations include patchy alopecia, anterior uveitis, retinitis; cranial nerve involvement, meningitis, laryngitis; gastritis, hepatosplenomegaly including hepatitis, glomerulonephritis, and periosteitis. The central nervous system (CNS) is invaded early in the infection; during the secondary stage; examinations demonstrate that more than 30 per cent of patients have abnormal findings in the cerebrospinal fluid (CSF). During the first 05-10 years after the onset of untreated primary infection, the disease principally involves the meninges and blood vessels, resulting in meningovascular neurosyphilis. Later, the parenchyma of the brain and spinal cord are damaged, resulting in parenchymatous neurosyphilis.

LATENT SYPHILIS

Latent syphilis is a stage at which the features of secondary syphilis have resolved, though patients remain seroreactive. Some patients experience recurrence of the infectious skin lesions of secondary syphilis during this period. About one third of untreated latent syphilis patients go on to develop tertiary syphilis whereas the rest remain asymptomatic.

TERTIARY SYPHILIS

Tertiary syphilis disease is rare. When it does occur, it mainly affects the cardiovascular system (80-85 per cent) and the CNS (05-10 per cent), developing over months to years and involving slow inflammatory damage to tissues. The 03 general categories of tertiary syphilis are gummatous syphilis (also called late benign), cardiovascular syphilis, and neurosyphilis. Gummatous syphilis (sometimes known as benign tertiary syphilis) can involve the organs or supporting structure and can result in infiltrative or destructive lesions leading to granulomatous lesions or ulcers, e.g., skin or perforation/collapse of structure, e.g. palate, nasal septum or organomegaly. Gumma of the tongue may be prone to leucoplakia leading to malignant change. Late neurosyphilis can cause meningovascular syphilis leading to stroke syndromes, parenchymal involvement leading to general paresis and tabs dorsalis. Cardiovascular syphilis involves the aortic arch which can lead to angina from coronary ostitis, aortic incompetence, and aortic aneurysm.

CONGENITAL SYPHILIS

Congenital syphilis is most severe when the mother's infection is recent. Because the Treponema do not invade the placental tissue or the foetus until the fifth month of gestation, syphilis causes late abortion, stillbirth or death soon after the delivery or it may persist in latent form to become apparent only during childhood or adult life. Within the first 02 years of life, symptoms are similar to severe adult secondary syphilis with widespread condylomata late and rash. In prenatal and infantile syphilis, a diffuse rash develops, which differs from that there is extensive sloughing of epithelium, particularly on the palms, soles and skin about the mouth and anus. Later manifestations of congenital syphilis include bone and teeth deformities, such as destruction of the nasal septum, inflammation and bowing of the tibia, (inflammation of the knee joints) and Hutchinson teeth (in which the upper incisors are widely spaced and notched). Tabes dorsalis and general paresis may develop as in adults, with eighth cranial nerve deafness and optic nerve atrophy as well as a variety of other ophthalmologic involvement leading to blindness being additional features.

11.19 FILARIASIS

Filaria or Filariasis is a chronic disease popularly known as Elephantiasis that typically affects the legs. This disease is caused by a worm spreads through the mosquitoes. The disease occurs due to the bite of an infected mosquito of the 'Culex' species. Filariasis occurs in different tropical regions and can be seen from mild to very severe stages of the condition. Usually, infection is established only with repeated and prolonged exposures to infective larvae. Since the clinical manifestations of filarial diseases develop relatively slowly, these infections should be considered chronic diseases with possible long-term debilitating effects. In terms of the nature, severity, and timing of clinical manifestations, patients with filarial infections who are native to endemic areas and undergo lifelong exposure may differ significantly from those who are travellers or who have recently moved to these areas. Characteristically, the disease is more acute and intense in newly exposed individuals than in natives of endemic areas. Filarial parasites infect approximately 170 million people worldwide, and are transmitted by specific species of mosquitoes or other arthropods (different in different countries).

CAUSATIVE ORGANISM

There are eight filarial species that can infect humans and out of these four cause most serious filarial infections and they are *Wuchereria Bancrofti, Bruges*

Malaya, Onchocerca volvulus, and *Loa* (the other 04 species are *B. tamari, Mansonella ozzardi, M. streptocerca and M. perstans*). The causative agents of filaria are nematodes; subcutaneous tissues and the lymphatic channels of humans are their habitat. Filarial parasites have a complex life cycle which include infective larval stages of insects and adult worms that reside in either lymphatic or subcutaneous tissues of humans. The microfilaria (offspring of adults) is about 200-250 μm (micrometer) long and 05-07 μm wide, with or without loose sheath. The microfilaria either circulates in the blood or migrates through the skin, and the circulating microfilaria is taken up by the arthropod vector (mosquito, midges, flies etc.) and develops over 01-02 weeks into new infective larvae. Microfilaria lives for 03 months to 03 years, whereas adult worms live for many years. Filarial infection generally occurs with repeated and prolonged exposures to infective larvae only. The clinical manifestations of Filariasis develop slowly; the infection can induce chronic disease with possible long-term debilitating effects. The adult parasites which are threadlike reside in lymphatic channels or lymph nodes. They can live there for more than two decades and cause lymphatic Filariasis. The nature and severity of clinical manifestations of Filariasis in individuals who are native to endemic areas may differ significantly from the travellers or who have recently moved to these areas and Filariasis is more acute and intense in newly exposed individuals than in natives of endemic areas.

TRANSMISSION OF FILARIASIS

Filariasis is mainly transmitted by mosquito (different species in different areas) bites and other insect bites like deerflies, black flies, midges etc.

For *W. Bancrofti* in cosmopolitan areas worldwide the mosquito involved is Culex. In India *Anopheles* mosquito is the main culprit and in China, Indonesia and Eastern Pacific it is the *Aedes* mosquito.

For *Bruges Malaya* in India, Indonesia and Southeast Asia the mosquitoes involved in transmission is *Ansonia* an *Anopheles* in nocturnal periodicity. In Indonesia mosquito involved in transmission is *B.timori*— *Anopheles*.

For *Loa* (found in West and Central Africa) the mosquito that causes Filaria is deerfly *Chrisoms*.

For *Onchocerca volvulus* found in Africa, South and Central America the causative organism is blackfly *Samarium*. For *M. perstans* found in Africa and South and Central America the insect involved in transmission is midge *Culicoides* and for *M. streptocerca* found in West and Central Africa the insect is the same midge *Culicoides*.

PATHOGENESIS

The main pathological changes in lymphatic Filariasis are seen in lymphatic's system which results from inflammatory damage due to the adult worms (not by the microfilaria). The adult worms live in afferent lymphatic or sinuses of lymph nodes and cause dilatation and thickening of the lymphatic vessels. Lymph valves are damaged or become incompetent due to tortuosity of the lymphatic's, which results from infiltration of plasma cells, eosinophil, and macrophages in and around the infected lymph vessels and also there is endothelial and connective tissue proliferation. Lymphedema and chronic-stasis occurs and the overlying skin becomes oedematous and brawny. All these changes in lymphatic Filariasis are due to direct effects of the adult worms and the inflammatory response of the host to the worms. Lymphatic obstruction occurs because of granulomatous and proliferative processes that occur due to inflammatory responses. The lymphatic vessels remain patent as long as the worm remains alive (viable) inside the vessels and death of the worm leads to enhanced granulomatous reaction and fibrosis which causes obstruction of lymph vessels. Collateral circulation of lymphatic occurs, but the lymphatic function is compromised despite development of collateral circulation.

CLINICAL SYMPTOMS

Most of the lymphatic Filariasis is asymptomatic (subclinical). The most common presenting manifestations of Filariasis are hydrocele, acute adenolymphangitis (ADL), and chronic lymphatic disease. In filaria endemic areas the large majority of infected individuals have a few overt clinical manifestations of filarial infection even if there are large numbers of circulating microfilaria in the peripheral blood. But all the individuals with filarial infection have some degree of subclinical manifestations like microscopic hematuria (blood in urine detectable under microscope only) and/or proteinuria (protein in urine), dilated and tortuous lymphatic's (visualized by imaging), and in men scrotal lymphangiectasia which can only be detected by ultrasound. But despite the subclinical findings most of the individuals with filarial infection remain asymptomatic for years and only a minority of them progress to acute or chronic disease.

Adenolymphangitis causes high fever, lymphatic inflammation (lymphangitis and lymphadenitis) and local edema. Lymphangitis extends from lymph nodes to the draining the area where the adult worms are present. Sometimes regional lymph nodes are enlarged, and the lymphatic channels can become indurate (hard) and inflamed. Lymphangitis and lymphadenitis can involve both the upper and lower extremities. Involvement of genital lymphatic occurs exclusively with *W. Bancroft* infection and with brugian Filariasis (*Bruges Malaya* and *B. tamari* infection). There may be a single local abscess along the involved lymphatic tract and subsequently rupture to the surface. The lymphadenitis and lymphangitis can involve both the upper and lower extremities in both bancroftian and brugian Filariasis, but involvement of the genital lymphatic occurs almost exclusively with *W. Bancroft* infection. This genital involvement can be manifested by funiculitis, epididymitis, and scrotal pain and tenderness. In endemic areas, another type of acute disease—dermatolymphangioadenitis (DLA)—is recognized as a syndrome that includes high fever, chills, myalgia, and headache. Edematous inflammatory plaques clearly demarcated from normal skin are seen. Vesicles, ulcers, and hyperpigmentation may also be noted.

There is often a history of trauma, burns, radiation, insect bites, punctiform lesions, or chemical injury. If lymphatic damage progresses, transient Lymphedema can develop into lymphatic obstruction and the permanent changes associated with elephantiasis. Brawny edema follows early pitting edema, and thickening of the subcutaneous tissues and hyperkeratosis occur. Fissuring of the skin develops, as do hyperplasic changes. Superinfection of these poorly vascularized tissues becomes a problem. In bancroftian Filariasis, in which genital involvement is common, hydrocele may develop; in advanced stages this condition may evolve into scrotal Lymphedema and scrotal elephantiasis. Furthermore, if there is obstruction of the retroperitoneal lymphatic, the increased renal lymphatic pressure leads to rupture of the renal lymphatic and the development of chyluria, which is usually intermittent and most prominent in the morning.

11.20 GONNORHEA

Gonorrhea is a very common sexually transmitted disease (STD). It is caused by the bacteria *Neisseria gonorrhoeae*. Gonorrhea is sometimes called "the clap". Gonorrhea can infect the vagina, cervix, rectum, penis, urethra, or sometimes the throat. Gonorrhea can be easily cured. Because gonorrhea usually has no signs or symptoms, many people don't realize they are infected. Without treatment, Gonorrhea may spread inside the body. There, it can cause pelvic inflammatory disease (PID) in women and epididymitis in men, two very serious illnesses. Rarely, the gonococcus bacteria can get into the blood and cause a kind of arthritis and other problems. Gonorrhea can cause a pregnant woman to go into labour early or deliver a low-birth weight baby. Gonorrhea can spread from mother to baby during birth and cause a serious infection in the baby's eyes that may lead to blindness. A pregnant woman can be treated to prevent transmission to the baby.

CAUSATIVE ORGANISM AND SPREAD OF GONORRHEA

It is caused by the bacteria *Neisseria gonorrhoeae*. Gonorrhea is spread through unprotected vaginal, anal or oral sex with an infected partner, even if that person has no symptoms. Ejaculation does not have to happen to get gonorrhea. It can also be passed from mother to baby during birth.

PATHOGENESIS

Extension of infection from the posterior urethra to the prostate, seminal vesicles and finally to the epididymis is the usual course of gonococcal infection. Inflammatory changes like cystitis, urethritis and epididymis occur with the development of frank abscesses in the epididymis resulting in extensive destruction of this organ. In the more neglected cases, the infection may spread to the testes and produce a suppurative orchitis.

1. **Pelvic Inflammatory Disease (PID)** can develop if Gonorrhea spreads to the uterus and fallopian tubes. PID can result in chronic pelvic pain, infertility, or tubal pregnancy (pregnancy outside the uterus). Symptoms of PID include pain in the lower abdomen or back, fever, spotting or bleeding

between menstrual periods, pain during sex, and increased vaginal discharge.
2. **Epididymitis** results when untreated infections in men spread into the testicles. This leads to pain or swelling in the scrotal area, which is a sign of inflammation of a part of the testicle called the epididymis. Epididymitis is often painful and, if it involves both testicles, it can lead to infertility.
3. **Disseminated Gonococcal Infection** occurs when Gonorrhea gets into the blood. This is rare but very serious. The main symptoms are joint pain and swelling, fever and skin rash.

CLINICAL SYMPTOMS

Most women (and some men) who have Gonorrhea don't notice anything wrong. If symptoms occur, they usually show up 01–02 weeks after infection. These are the main symptoms, listed from most common to less common:

Men
- Pain or burning while urinating.
- Itching inside the penis.
- Painful, swollen testicle.

Women
- Unusual vaginal discharge.
- Pain or burning while urinating.
- Bleeding between periods or after sex.
- Pain during sex.
- Stomach pain.

If gonorrhea is in the throat or rectum, there may be few or no symptoms. Some people feel a sore throat or itching and pain in the rectum. Even if you don't have symptoms, you can still have gonorrhea and pass it on to others.

11.21 HEPATITIS

Hepatitis means inflammation of the liver. The liver is a vital organ that processes nutrients, filters the blood, and fights infections. The term viral hepatitis is used to describe infection of liver caused by hepatotropic viruses. Hepatitis can be caused by a variety of different viruses such as hepatitis A, B, C, D and E. When the liver is inflamed or damaged, its function can be affected. Heavy alcohol use, toxins, some medications, and certain medical conditions can cause hepatitis. Since the development of jaundice is a characteristic feature of liver disease, a correct diagnosis can only be made by testing patients' sera for the presence of specific anti-viral antibodies.

Hepatitis A Virus (HAV), causing a fecally-spread self-limiting disease.

Hepatitis B Virus (HBV), causing a parenterally transmitted disease that may become chronic.

Hepatitis C Virus (HCV), previously termed non-A, non-B (NANB) hepatitis virus involved chiefly in transfusion-related hepatitis.

Hepatitis delta Virus (HDV) which is sometimes associated as superinfection with hepatitis B infection.

Hepatitis E Virus (HEV), causing water-borne infection

Hepatitis G Virus (HGV) is a recently discovered parenterally transmitted hepatotropic virus.

All these human hepatitis viruses are RNA viruses except HBV which is a DNAvirus.

HEPATITIS A

Hepatitis A, one of the oldest diseases known to humankind, is a self-limiting disease, which results in fulminant hepatitis and death in only a small proportion of patients. However, it is a significant cause of morbidity and socio-economic losses in many parts of the world. Infections occur early in life in areas where sanitation is poor and living conditions are crowded. With improved sanitation and hygiene, infections are delayed and consequently the number of persons susceptible to the disease increases. Such conditions can engender explosive epidemics from faecal contamination of a single source. Hepatitis A was formerly called Infectious hepatitis,

Epidemic hepatitis, Epidemic jaundice, Catarrhal jaundice, Type A hepatitis, HA.

CAUSATIVE ORGANISM

Hepatitis A is caused by infection with the hepatitis A virus (HAV), a non- enveloped, positive stranded RNA virus, first identified by electron microscopy in 1973, classified within the genus hepatovirus of the Picornaviruses family. HAV is a small, 27nm diameter, icosaherdal, non-enveloped, single-stranded RNA virus. The virus is present in the liver cells, bile, stool and blood during the incubation period and in pre-icteric phase but viral shedding diminishes after the onset of jaundice. HAV is known to produce disease in humans and non-human primates. The virus interferes with the liver's functions while replicating in hepatocytes. The individual's immune system is then activated to produce a specific reaction to combat and possibly eradicate the infectious agent. As a consequence of pathological damage, the liver becomes inflamed. Hepatitis A is responsible for 20–25 per cent of clinical hepatitis in the developing countries of the world but the incidence is far less in developed countries. Hepatitis A is usually a benign, self-limiting disease and has an incubation period of 15–45 days.

HAV infection induces lifelong protection against reinjection.

TRANSMISSION OF HEPATITIS A

HAV is transmitted from person to person via the faecal-oral route. As HAV is abundantly excreted in faeces, and can survive in the environment for prolonged periods of time, it is typically acquired by ingestion of faeces-contaminated food or water. High concentrations of virus are shed in the stools of patients during 03–10 days prior to the onset of illness till 01– 02 weeks after the onset of jaundice. Faecal excretion of HAV persists longer in children and in immunocompromised persons (up to 04-05 months after infection) than in otherwise healthy adults. Communicability is at peak during this interval. The spread is related to close personal contact such as in overcrowded places, poor hygiene and poor sanitation. Occasionally, HAV is also acquired through sexual contact (anal-oral) and blood transfusions. Infections occur early in life in areas where sanitation is poor and density of population is very high. With improved sanitation and hygiene, infections are delayed and consequently the number of persons susceptible to the disease increases. Under these conditions explosive epidemics can arise from faecal contamination of a single source.

PATHOGENESIS

The course of hepatitis A may be extremely variable. Patients with in apparent or subclinical hepatitis have neither symptoms nor jaundice. These asymptomatic cases can only be recognized by detecting biochemical or serologic alterations in the blood. Patients may develop anicteric or icteric hepatitis and have symptoms ranging from mild and transient to severe and prolonged, from which they recover completely or develop fulminant hepatitis and die. The severity of the disease increases with age at time of infection.

The course of acute hepatitis A can be divided into four clinical phases.

An incubation or preclinical period ranging from 10-50 days during which the patient remains asymptomatic despite active replication of the virus. In this phase, transmissibility is of greatest concern.

A prodromal or preicteric phase ranging from several days to more than a week, characterized by the appearance of symptoms like loss of appetite, fatigue, abdominal pain, nausea and vomiting, fever, diarrhea, dark urine and pale stools, followed by

In icteric phase, during which jaundice develops at total bilirubin levels— exceeding 20-40 mg/l— patients often seek medical help at this stage of their illness. The icteric phase generally begins within 10 days of the initial symptoms. Fever usually improves after the first few days of jaundice. Viraemia terminates shortly after hepatitis develops, although faeces remain infectious for another 01-02 weeks. Extra hepatic manifestations of hepatitis A are unusual. Physical examination of the patient by percussion can help to determine the size of the liver and possibly reveal massive necrosis. The mortality rate is low (0.2 per cent of icteric cases) and the disease ultimately resolves. Occasionally, extensive necrosis of the liver occurs during the first 06-08 weeks of illness. In this case, high fever, marked abdominal pain, vomiting, jaundice and the development of hepatic encephalopathy associated with coma and seizures, are the signs of fulminant hepatitis, leading to death in 70-90 per cent of the patients. In these cases mortality is highly correlated with increasing age, and survival is uncommon above 50 years of age. Among patients with chronic hepatitis B or C or underlying liver disease, who are super infected with HAV, the mortality rate increases considerably.

In convalescent period, resolution of the disease is slow, but patient's recovery is uneventful and complete. Relapsing hepatitis occurs in 03–20 per cent of patients 04–15 weeks after the initial symptoms have resolved. Cholestatic hepatitis with high bilirubin levels persisting for months is also occasionally observed. Sequel with persistence of HAV infection for more than 12 months has not been observed.

DIAGNOSIS

1. Since both clinically and biochemically, acute hepatitis due to HAV cannot be distinguished from that due to the other hepatitis viruses, serologic tests are necessary for a virus-specific diagnosis.
2. Diagnosis of hepatitis is made by biochemical assessment of liver function: laboratory evaluation of urine bilirubin and urobilinogen, total and direct serum bilirubin, ALT and/or AST; alkaline phosphatise, prothrombin time, total protein; serum albumin, IgG, IgA; IgM, and complete blood count.
3. The specific routine diagnosis of acute hepatitis A is made by finding anti-HAV IgM in the serum of patients. A second option is the detection of virus and/or antigen in the faeces.
4. Virus and antibody can be detected by commercially available RIA, EIA or ELISA kits. The commercially available assays for anti-HAV IgM and total anti-HAV (IgM and IgG) for assessment of immunity to HAV do not affect the passive administration of IG, because the prophylactic doses are below detection level.
5. At the onset of disease, the presence of IgG anti-HAV is always accompanied by the presence of IgM anti-HAV. As IgG anti-HAV persists lifelong after acute infection, detection of IgG anti-HAV alone indicates past infection.
6. Virus may still be present in the absence of detectable HAV antigen, as demonstrated by the use of more sensitive methods.
7. If laboratory tests are not available, epidemiologic evidence can help in establishing a diagnosis.

HEPATITIS B

Hepatitis B is responsible epidemics in parts of Asia and Africa; it is endemic in China. More then two billion people are infected with the infectious disease, including 350 million carriers of the infection. The transmission is a consequence of exposure of blood/body fluids. In developing countries prenatal route is the major source of infection. Health centres, dialysis, acupuncture, tattooing do transmit infection. Hepatitis B does not spread by breastfeeding, kissing, sneezing, and the like. Acute cases of Hepatitis B are marked by vomiting, jaundice and sometimes death. Cirrhosis of liver and fatal liver cancer are the sequel of chronic Hepatitis B.

CAUSATIVE ORGANISM

Hepatitis B is caused by the hepatitis B virus (HBV), is 42 nm, an enveloped virus containing a partially double stranded, circular DNA genome and classified within the family hepadnavirus. Electron microscopic studies on serum of patients infected with HBV show 03 forms of viral particles of 02 sizes- small spheres and tubules/filaments and large spheres .as under

PATHOGENESIS

The course of hepatitis B may be extremely variable. Hepatitis B virus infection has different clinical manifestations depending upon the patient's age at infection and immune status and the stage at which the disease is recognized.

During the incubation period of the disease (06-24 weeks), patients may feel unwell with possible nausea, vomiting, diarrhea, anorexia and headaches. Patients may then become jaundiced although a low grade fever and loss of appetite may improve. Sometimes HBV infection produces neither jaundice nor obvious symptoms. The asymptomatic cases can be identified by detecting biochemical or virus-specific serologic alterations in their blood. They may become silent carriers of the virus and constitute a reservoir for further transmission to others.

Most adult patients recover completely from their HBV infection, but about 05-10 per cent will not clear the virus and will progress to become asymptomatic carriers or develop chronic cover hepatitis possibly resulting in cirrhosis or liver cancer. Rarely, others may develop fulminant hepatitis and may die. Hepatitis B infection can be classified into acute hepatitis B infection and chronic hepatitis B infection.

ACUTE HEPATITIS B INFECTION

The acute form of the disease often resolves spontaneously after 04-08 weeks illness. However, a favourable prognosis is not certain, especially in the elderly who can develop fulminant, fatal cases of acute hepatic necrosis. Young children rarely develop acute clinical disease, but many of those infected before the age of seven will become chronic carriers.

The incubation period varies usually between 45-120 days, with an average of 60-90 days. The variation is related to the amount of virus inoculum, the mode of transmission and host factors.

The characteristic feature of acute viral hepatitis is the striking elevation in serum transaminase (aminotransferase) activity. The increase in aminotransferase, especially ALT, during acute hepatitis B varies from a mild/moderate increase of 03-10 fold of striking increase of >100 fold.

In patients with clinical illness, the onset is usually insidious with tiredness, anorexia, vague abdominal discomfort, nausea and vomiting, sometimes arthralgias and rash, often progressing to jaundice. Fever may be mild or absent.

The icteric phase of acute viral hepatitis begins usually within 10 days of the initial symptoms with the appearance of dark urine followed by pale stools and yellowish discoloration of the mucus membranes, conjunctivae, sclerae and skin. Jaundice becomes apparent clinically when the total bilirubin level exceeds 20-40 mg/l. it is accompanied by hepatomegaly and splenomegaly. About 04-12 weeks thereafter, the jaundice disappears and illness resolves with the development of natural, protective antibodies (anti-HBs) in 95 per cent of the adults.

Acute hepatitis B is characterized by the presence of anti-HBr IgM serum antibodies converting to IgG with convalescence and recovery and the transient (<6months) presence of HBsAg, HBsAg and viral DNA with clearance of these markers followed by seroconversion to anti-HBsAg and anti-HBsAg. More than 90 per cent of adult-onset infection cases fall into this category. The remaining 05-10 per cent of adult-onset infection and over 90 per cent of cases of neonatal infection become chronic and may continue for the life span of the patient.

A small percentage of patient die from acute hepatitis B.

CHRONIC HEPATITIS B

The presence of HBsAg in serum for at least 06 months or the presence of HBsAg and the absence of anti-HBr IgM meet the definition of chronic HBV infection. Risks associated with development of chronic HBV include the presence of 04 renal failure, diabetes, or HIV. The probability of developing chronic HBV is inversely proportional to age; infants have a 90 per cent risk while adolescents and adults have ~ 10 per cent risk. Patients who develop chronic HBV are subsequently predisposed to developing chronic liver disease, cirrhosis, and hepatocellular carcinoma (HCC). The progression from chronic HBV to HCC is also age dependent, with prospective studies indicating a 25 per cent risk in patients who acquire the disease as infants, compared to a 15 per cent risk if contracted as an adolescent. In addition, very high HBV DNA levels, normal ALT, and the presence of HBsAg characterize chronic HBV acquired through prenatal transmission. This immune-tolerant phase can last for 10-30 years, allowing for individuals with prenatal acquisition to be infectious in their adulthood and perpetuate vertical transmission of the disease. In contrast, children and adults who acquire chronic HBV infection present in the immune-clearance phase, which is marked by clearance of HBsAg, in 70 per cent of cases within 10 years.

Most patients who seroconvert remain HBsAg-negative and anti-He-positive with normal ALT and low HBV DNA, and are considered to be in an "inactive carrier state." Liver biopsies performed in patients with chronic HBV infection are classified as chronic persistent hepatitis, chronic active hepatitis, and cirrhosis. Histological results do not correlate with symptoms and often patients are asymptomatic until the development of cirrhosis. Cirrhosis is manifested by interlacing strands of fibrous tissue with nodules of regenerating cells resulting in a characteristic small and knobby-appearing liver; this form of injury is irreversible and can be exacerbated by heavy alcohol consumption and concomitant infection with HCV or HIV. The 05-year risk of decomposition after the development of cirrhosis is estimated to be 20 per cent.

SIGNS AND SYMPTOMS

- Easy fatigability, anxiety, anorexia, and malaise
- As cites, jaundice, varietal bleeding, and hepatic encephalopathy can manifest with liver decomposition

- Hepatic encephalopathy is associated with hyper excitability, impaired mutation, confusion, obtundation, and eventually coma
- Vomiting and seizures

PHYSICAL EXAMINATION
- Icteric sclera, skin, and secretions
- Decreased bowel sounds, increased girth, and detectable fluid wave
- Asterixis
- Spider angiomata

LABORATORY TESTS
- Presence of hepatitis B surface antigen for at least 06 months
- Intermittent elevations of hepatic transaminase (alanine transaminase [ALT] and aspartate transaminase [AST]) and hepatitis B virus DNA greater than 105 copies/mol
- Liver biopsies for pathologic classification as chronic persistent hepatitis, chronic active hepatitis, or cirrhosis.

HEPATITIS C

Hepatitis C is liver disease—usually transmitted by blood— caused by hepatitis C virus. The major cause of its spread is by having sex with an infected person. It is lifelong leading to liver carcinoma. Serious cases need a transplant. There is no vaccine for hepatitis c.

ACUTE HEPATITIS C

Hepatitis C infection has two phases. The first one, the acute phase, which last for 06 months from the time of exposure to the hepatitis C virus (HCV) till the onset of the symptoms. It is during the acute phase that the virus (HCV) finds its way to liver and reproduces inside of liver cells. Quite often it goes unrecognized because patients show flu-like symptoms. Patients with acute hepatitis C are often asymptomatic, but they may have malaise, anorexia, and jaundice, which occur in up to 25 per cent of cases. The mean incubation period of HCV is 50 days and viraemia can be detected within 03 weeks of initial exposure. Acute hepatitis C can be associated with severe symptoms, but fulminant disease is rare. An important feature of hepatitis C infection is that up to 70 per cent of cases develop chronic hepatitis. The patients with asymptomatic acute HCV infection are prone to HCV. Several diagnostic tests are available to detect acute HCV infection through detection of antibodies or viral target amplification. Antibody detection methods include enzyme immunoassay (EIA) and the recombinant immunoblot assay (RIBA). Specific antibodies to HCV by EIA are positive in only 50–70 per cent of patients during the initial onset of symptoms, but 90 per cent of patients have HCV antibodies after 03 months.

Qualitative tests are more sensitive with a detection limit 0f 100 copies/mol and should be the benchmark to determine spontaneous clearance of acute infection.

CHRONIC HEPATITIS

After contracting infection with hepatitis C, it takes 10–14 years to evidence chronic hepatitis. Once the hepatitis C infection afflicts the liver, the liver becomes inflamed, tender, and enlarged. In the inflamed liver scars replace the healthy tissue by diminishing the liver function; when the liver becomes excessively scarred, it cannot heal itself, developing into cirrhosis of liver. Once the liver is unable to function, it means liver failure.

PROGRESSION

Hepatitis C is a very slow progressive disease that affects people in different ways. Its progression, manifestation, and outcome can vary among people over a period of 20–30 years. Twenty-five per cent of people have no symptoms or serious liver damage with normal levels of liver enzymes (ALT). Usually liver biopsy shows some degree of chronic inflammation, but the degree of injury is usually mild, and the overall prognosis in these people is fairly good. Forty to fifty per cent of people may have few or mild symptoms, not detrimental to their health. In these people, progression of liver disease is difficult to predict. Up to 20 per cent of people will have severe hepatitis C symptoms at risk to develop cirrhosis of liver of which 01–05 per cent of develop liver cancer each year.

In the USA hepatitis C is the leading cause of liver transplant. Although it is difficult to prod, variety of rare extra hepatic clinical syndromes have been associated with chronic HCV infection. These syndromes include cryoglobulinemia, cutaneous vacuities, renal disease, neuropathy, lymphoma, and Sj¨ogren's syndrome. Cryoglobulinemia involves the presence of circulating immunoglobulin's that reversibly precipitate at ≤37°C. These cry globulins can precipitate in small blood vessels and induce vacuities. The cutaneous manifestation typically includes a palpable purpurea in the lower extremities, and is diagnosed as leukocytoclastic vacuities on biopsy of the lesions. Renal disease typically manifests as nephritic syndrome with pathology consistent with membranoproliferative glomerulonephritis.ict how someone will progress with chronic hepatitis C, researchers have identified factors that may influence and accelerate the progression of the disease. These factors include; male gender, age at time of exposure to the HCV (greater than 40 years old), consumption of alcohol, and co-infection with hepatitis B or HIV.

SYMPTOMS

Only about 20 per cent of infected people will develop acute symptoms, which a similar to those of hepatitis A and B e.g. loss of appetite, nausea, vomiting, diarrhea, fatigue, malaise, muscle and joint pain, dark ("coca-cola") urine, jaundice. Most people have no early illness and develop a chronic infection which can be passed on to others.

HEPATITIS D

The hepatitis D virus is the most virulent. Hepatitis D virus (HDV) cannot replicate and infect someone unless the person is already infected with the hepatitis

B virus (HBV). The hepatitis D virus requires the outer coating of the hepatitis B virus- called the surface antigen- in to reproduce itself in a human host. The virus currently infects 15 million people worldwide and it is most common among injecting drug user populations.

Hepatitis D symptoms are similar to other viral hepatitis diseases and include jaundice, fever, malaise, dark urine and nausea. Although symptoms are similar, patients are more ill with hepatitis D than with hepatitis B alone. Relatively severe chronic hepatitis, with or without cirrhosis, is the rule, and mild chronic hepatitis is the exception. Occasionally, mild hepatitis or even, rarely, inactive carriage occurs in patients with chronic hepatitis B plus D, and the disease may become indolent after several years of infection.

CAUSATIVE ORGANISM

The virus is defective single-stranded RNA virus. Hepatitis B virus is a formalin-sensitive, 35–37-nm virus with a hybrid structure. Its nucleocapsid expresses delta antigen, which bears no antigenic homology with any of the HBV antigens, and contains the virus genome. The virus has the smallest genome among all known animals' viruses. The hepatitis D virus requires a particle from the hepatitis B virus- the hepatitis B virus's outer coat called the surface antigen-to synthesize its own protein coat to encapsulate the genetic core. The hepatitis D virus can still successfully replicate in people whose hepatitis B surface antigen level has dropped below detectable levels. The hepatitis D virus inserts its genetic material into liver cells and uses the liver cells resource to replicate itself. HDV uniquely replicate in a way similar to how plant viruses replicate. When the virus's genetic material is assembled in the "host" liver cell, the virus completes itself by incorporating hepatitis B surface antigen into his cytoplasm, then it is released from the host cell as a whole hepatitis D virus capable of infecting a new cell.

TRANSMISSION

Hepatitis D is a blood borne disease and is transmitted primarily by exposure to an infected person's blood or by body fluids. As sexual transmission it is transmitted by barrier-free sexual activity. Vertical transmission (mother-to-infant) is rare.

PATHOGENESIS

HDV can either infect a person simultaneously with HBV (co-infection) or super-infect a person already infected with HBV (superinfection); when HDV infection is transmitted from a donor with one HBsAg subtype to an HBsAg- positive recipient with a different subtype, the HDV agent assumes the HBsAg subtype of the recipient, rather than the donor. Because HDV relies absolutely on HBV, the duration of HDV infection is determined by the duration of (and cannot outlast) HBV infection. HDV antigen is expressed primarily in hepatocytes nuclei and is occasionally detectable in serum. During acute HDV infection, anti-HDV of the IgM class predominates, and 30–40 days may elapse after symptoms appear before anti-HDV can be detected. In self-limited infection, anti-HDV is low titer and transient, rarely remaining detectable beyond the clearance of HBsAg and HDV antigen. In chronic HDV infection, anti-HDV circulates in high titer, and both IgM and IgG anti-HDV can be detected. HDV antigen in the liver and HDV RNA in serum and liver can be detected during HDV replication.

HEPATITIS E

Previously labeled epidemic or enteric ally transmitted non-non-B hepatitis, HEV is an enteric ally transmitted virus that occurs primarily in India, Asia, Africa, and Central America. This agent, with epidemiologic features resembling those of hepatitis A, is a 32–34-nm, non-enveloped, HAV-like virus with a 7600-nucleotide, single-stranded, positive-sense RNA genome. HEV has three open reading frames (genes), the largest of which encodes nonstructural proteins involved in virus replication. A middle-sized gene encodes the nucleocapsid protein, and the smallest, whose function is not known, encodes protein specificities to which antibodies appear in human serum. All HEV isolates appear to belong to a single serotype, despite genomic heterogeneity of up to 25 per cent. There is no genomic or antigenic homology, however, between HEV and HAV or other Picornaviruses; and HEV, although resembling calciviruses, appears to be sufficiently distinct from any known agent to merit a new classification of its own within the alphavirus group. The virus has been detected in stool, bile, and liver and is excreted in the stool during the late incubation period; immune responses to viral antigens occur very early during the course of acute infection. Both IgM anti-HEV and IgG anti-HEV can be detected, but both fall rapidly after acute infection, reaching low levels within 09–12 months. Currently, serologic testing for HEV infection is not available routinely.

PATHOGENESIS

This type of hepatitis, identified in India, Asia, Africa, and Central America, resembles hepatitis A in its primarily enteric mode of spread. The commonly recognized cases occur after contamination of water supplies such as after monsoon flooding, but sporadic, isolated cases occur. An epidemiologic feature that distinguishes HEV from other enteric agents is the rarity of secondary person to person spread from infected persons to their close contacts. Infections arise in populations that are immune to HAV and favour young adults. It is not known if hepatitis E occurs outside of recognized endemic areas, for example, in the United States, but preliminary studies suggest that HEV does not account for any of the sporadic "non-A, non-B" cases in no endemic areas. Cases imported from endemic areas have been found in the United States. Several reports suggest a zoonotic reservoir for HEV in swine.

HEPATITIS G

Hepatitis G virus (HGV): HGV is a single stranded RNA virus. At present HGV infection has been found in blood donors and is transmitted by blood transfusion. The virus has been identified by PCR amplification technique.

11.22 ACQUIRED IMMUNODEFICIENCY SYNDROME (AIDS)

The human immunodeficiency virus (HIV) was unknown until the early 1980's but since then has infected millions of persons in a worldwide pandemic. The result of HIV infection is relentless destruction of the immune system leading to onset of the acquired immunodeficiency syndrome (AIDS). The AIDS epidemic has already resulted in the deaths of over half its victims. All HIV-infected persons are at risk for illness and death from opportunistic infections and neoplastic complications because of the inevitable manifestations of AIDS. Once HIV infection became established in humans, the spread of HIV has been driven by multiple factors. The advent of quick air travel in the 20th century provided a means for spread, not present in past human pandemics.

DEFINITION

With the identification of HIV in 1983 and its proof as the etiologic agent of AIDS in 1984, and with the availability of sensitive and specific diagnostic tests for HIV infection, the case definition of AIDS has undergone several revisions over the years. The current CDC classification system for HIV-infected adolescents and adults categorizes persons on the basis of clinical conditions associated with HIV infection and CD4+ T lymphocyte counts. The system is based on three ranges of CD4+ T lymphocyte counts and three clinical categories and is represented by a matrix of nine mutually exclusive categories. Using this system, any HIV-infected individual with a CD4+ T cell count of <200/μL has AIDS by definition, regardless of the presence of symptoms or opportunistic diseases. Once individuals have had a clinical condition in category B, their disease cannot again be classified as category A, even if the condition resolves; the same holds true for category C in relation to category B.

CAUSATIVE ORGANISM

Human immunodeficiency virus (HIV) and its subtypes are retroviruses, and they are the etiologic agents of AIDS. Human retroviruses were unknown until the 1980's, though animal retroviruses such as feline leukemia virus had been detected previously. HIV belongs to a large family of ribonucleic acid (RNA) lent viruses. Lent viruses similar to HIV have been found in a variety of primate species, and some of these are associated with a disease process called simian AIDS.

The mature virus consists of a bar-shaped electron dense core containing the viral genome--two short strands of ribonucleic acid (RNA) about 9200 nucleotide bases long—along with the enzymes reverse transcriptase, protease, ribonuclease, and integrate, all encased in an outer lipid envelope derived from a host cell. This envelope has 72 surface projections, or spikes, containing an antigen, gp120 that aids in the binding of the virus to the target cells with CD4 receptors. A second glycoprotein, gp41, binds gp120 to the lipid envelope.

Retroviruses are unable to replicate outside of living host cells and do not contain DNA. The pathogenesis of HIV infection is a function of the virus life cycle, host cellular environment, and quantity of viruses in the infected individual. After entering the body, the viral particle is attracted to a cell with the appropriate CD4 receptor molecules where it attaches by fusion to a susceptible cell membrane or by endocytosis and then enters the cell. The probability of infection is a function of both the number of infective HIV virions in the body fluid which contacts the host as well as the number of cells available at the site of contact that have appropriate CD4 receptors.

HIV infection transmits through, pharyngeal, cervical, vaginal, and gastrointestinal mucosal surfaces, even in the absence of mucosal disruption. Routes of HIV entry into mucosal lamina propria include dendrite cells, epithelial cells, and micro fold (M) cells. Dendrite cells can bind to gp120 through a C type lection, suggesting that dendrite cells that squeeze between "tight" epithelium may capture HIV-1 and deliver it to underlying T cells, resulting in dissemination to lymphoid organs. HIV can cross a tight epithelial barrier by transcytosis during contact between HIV-infected cells and the apical surface of an epithelial cell.

TRANSMISSION

HIV is transmitted by both homosexual and heterosexual contact; by blood and blood products; and by infected mothers to infants either intrapartum, prenatally, or via breast milk.

SEXUAL TRANSMISSION

HIV infection is predominantly a sexually transmitted disease (STD) worldwide. Although in the United States ~42 per cent of new HIV infections are among homosexuals and ~33 per cent amongst heterosexuals'. Yet the most common mode of infection worldwide is heterosexual transmission. Furthermore, the yearly incidence of new cases of AIDS attributed to heterosexual transmission of HIV is steadily increasing in the United States, mainly among minorities, particularly women in minority groups.

TRANSMISSION BY BLOOD AND BLOOD PRODUCTS

HIV can be transmitted to individuals who receive HIV-tainted blood transfusions, blood products, or transplanted tissue as well as to IDUs who are exposed to HIV while sharing injection paraphernalia such as needles, syringes, the water in which drugs are mixed, or the cotton through which drugs are filtered.

Parenteral transmission of HIV during injection drug use does not require intravenous puncture; subcutaneous ("skin popping") or intramuscular ("muscling") injections can transmit HIV as well, even though these behaviors are sometimes erroneously perceived as low-risk.

OCCUPATIONAL TRANSMISSION OF HIV: HEALTH CARE WORKERS AND LABORATORY WORKERS

There is a small, but definite, occupational risk of HIV transmission to health care workers and laboratory personnel. Large, multi-institutional studies have indicated that the risk of HIV transmission following skin puncture from a needle or a sharp object that was contaminated with blood from a person with documented HIV infection is ~0.3 per cent and after a mucous membrane exposure it is 0.09 per cent.

MATERNAL-FETAL/INFANT TRANSMISSION

HIV infection can be transmitted from an infected mother to her fetus during pregnancy, during delivery, or by breastfeeding. This is an extremely important form of transmission of HIV infection in developing countries, where the proportion of infected women to infected men is ~1:1. Virology analysis of aborted fetuses indicates that HIV can be transmitted to the fetus as early as the first and second trimester of pregnancy. However, maternal transmission to the fetus occurs most commonly in the prenatal period.

TRANSMISSION BY OTHER BODY FLUIDS

Although HIV can be isolated typically in low titers from saliva, there is no convincing evidence that saliva can transmit HIV infection, either through kissing or through other exposures, such as occupationally to health care workers. Saliva contains endogenous antiviral factors; among these factors, HIV-specific immunoglobulin of IgA, IgG, and IgM isotopes are detected readily in salivary secretions of infected individuals.

PATHOGENESIS

1. HIV covered with cell membrane, antibodies from the infected donor enter the new host.
2. Infecting virus is immunologically recognized as antigen complex and is accosted by the CD4 + cells contact with protruding gp 160 causes infection.
3. The infected cell produces many virions not coated with antibodies, thereby spreading infection among CD4.
4. Lymphoid hyperplasia among B cells expansion and increasing levels humoral antibodies,
5. Then there is neutralized virus which is accumulation of HIV as viral immune complex on the surface of cell membrane. This virus is requisite for the progression of the disease.
6. Then the infected assumes a steady state wherein CD 4 becomes infected. Depending upon factors infected cells produce virus particles in the lymphoid or at distant sites.
7. The attrition of CD 4 cells exceeds formation marginally. This state can continue for quite a few years, and function of lymphoid tissue is interfered.
8. There is decrease in the immune function until the infection overpowers the patient.

CLINICAL SYMPTOMS

Clinical presentation of primary HIV infection may vary, but patients often have an acute retroviral syndrome or mononucleosis-like illness. Symptoms often last weeks, and hospitalization may be required for 15 per cent of patients. Primary infection is often associated with a high viral load and development of an immune response that for a period of time suppresses, but does not eliminate, viral replication. During this period, HIV is trapped by follicular dendrite cells in lymphoid tissue and replicates in the germinal centre. The amount of HIV RNA in plasma falls substantially at this point, and symptoms resolve gradually. This decline coincides with the development of an immune response to HIV. The clinically latent period, however, is not biologically latent because HIV replication and immune system deterioration are ongoing. A persistent decrease in CD4 cells is the most measurable aspect of this immune system destruction.

CLINICAL PRESENTATION OF PRIMARY HIV INFECTION IN ADULTS

Symptoms

- Fever, sore throat, fatigue, weight loss, and myalgia.
- 40–80 per cent of patients will also exhibit a morbilliform or muculopapular rash usually involving the trunk.
- Diarrhoea, nausea, and vomiting.
- Lymphadenopathy, night sweats.
- Aseptic meningitis (fever, headache, photophobia, and stiff neck) may be present in a quarter of presenting cases.

OTHER

Viral load in children and adults is different.

Most children born with HIV are asymptomatic. On physical examination, children often present with unexplained physical signs such as lymphadenopathy, hepatomegaly, splenomegaly, failure to thrive, weight loss or unexplained low birth weight (in prenatally exposed infants), and fever of unknown origin. Laboratory findings include anaemia, hypergammaglobulinemia (primarily IgA and IgM), altered mononuclear cell function, and altered T-cell subset ratios. Of note, the normal range for CD4 cell counts in young children is much different from that in adults. Bacterial infections, including Streptococcus pneumonia, Salmonella spp., and Mycobacterium tuberculosis, may be more prevalent in children with AIDS than in adults with the disease. Kaposi's sarcoma is rare in children.

SUMMARY

A communicable disease is a disease that can pass from an infected person to another individual. Body excretions provide the mode for transmission. Some communicable diseases spread by casual contact, such as cold, flu and tuberculosis from respiratory droplets: coughing, sneezing or runny noses. Other communicable diseases require contact with blood from an infected individual, such as Hepatitis B and the Human Immunodeficiency Virus (the virus which causes AIDS). Other communicable diseases require intimate contact with an infected individuals body fluids or genitalia, such as Chlamydia, herpes and syphilis.

Infectious organisms, which can enter the human host (end parasites) belong to a wide range of classes and vary in size ranging from the 02-nm poliovirus to 10-m tapeworms. e.g. virus, bacteria, fungi, protozoa, bacteriophages, plasmids, transposons, chlamydiae, rickettsiae, mycoplasmas, helminthes and ectoparasites.

Infectious diseases are the consequences of interrelationship between disease-producing properties of microorganisms and host-defence capability against the invading organism.

Chickenpox: Varicella or chickenpox is an acute vesicular exanthema occurring in non-immune persons, especially children. Varicella zoster virus is a member of herpes virus family and causes chickenpox (Varicella) in non-immune individuals and herpes zoster (shingles) in those who had chickenpox in the past. Two of the herpes simplex viruses (HSV)—type 01 and type 02 cause 'fever blisters' and herpes genitals respectively.

Measles: Measles virus is an RNA virus of the paramyxovirus family that includes mumps, respiratory syncytial virus (the major cause of lower respiratory tract infections in infants), and parainfluenza virus. The blotchy, reddish-brown rash of measles virus infection on the face, trunk and proximal extremities is produced by dilated skin vessels, edema and a moderate, non-specific mononuclear per vascular infiltrate.

Influenza: Influenza viruses are RNA viruses in the family Orthomyxoviridae that can affect birds and mammals including humans. Influenza B and C viruses are maintained only in human populations. Influenza A viruses can affect many species, with the vast majority of these viruses occurring among birds. In mammals, influenza viruses are transmitted in aerosols created by coughing and sneezing, and by contact with nasal discharges, either directly or on fomites. Close contact and closed environments favor transmission.

Diphtheria: Diphtheria is a highly infectious bacterial disease which causes inflammation of the throat, nose and tonsils with fever. It can cause dysphagia and may be cause suffocation. The infection may also produce toxins that circulate through the percent to blood damaging the heart, kidneys, and nervous system. Diphtheria is a bacterial disease, produced by *Cory bacterium diphtheriae.*

Tetanus: Tetanus is caused by the action of a highly potent neurotoxin, tetanospasmin, which is produced during the growth of the anaerobic bacterium *Clostridium tetany*. The disease usually occurs through infection of a skin injury with tetanus spores. Tetanus is a neurological disease caused by tetanus toxin. Complications of tetanus include fractures, dyspnea, and abnormal heart rhythms.

Pertussis or whooping cough: Pertussis, commonly known as whooping cough, is a vaccine-preventable disease spread by close contact with the respiratory secretions of infected individuals. Whooping cough (pertussis) is caused by the bacterium *Bordetella pertussis*. *B. pertussis* is a very small Gram- negative aerobic coccobacillus that appears singly or in pairs. Transmission most commonly occurs by the respiratory route through contact with respiratory droplets less than 5μ.

Tuberculosis: Tuberculosis (TB) is contagious and airborne and caused by Mycobacterium *tuberculosis.* This complex includes strains of five species—*M. tuberculosis, M. Canetti, M. africana, M. microti,* and *M. bovid* and two subspecies—*M. caprae* and *M. pinnipedii.* The mode of transmission includes inhalation, ingestion, inoculation and transplacental route. It can be primary and secondary tuberculosis.

Poliomyelitis: Poliomyelitis, often called polio or infantile paralysis, is a viral paralytic disease. The causative agent, a virus called poliovirus (PV), enters the body orally, infecting the intestinal wall. It may proceed to the blood stream and into the central nervous system causing muscle weakness and often paralysis. Polio is a communicable disease which is categorized as a disease of civilization. Polio spreads through human to human contact, usually entering the body through the mouth due to fecally contaminated water or food. Polio can be classified into three types, i) non-paralytic, ii) spinal and iii) bulbar polio.

Cholera: Cholera is a severe intestinal disease caused by the bacteria, *Vibrio cholerae;* the bacteria are typically found in water environments such as freshwater lakes and rivers. Cholera is usually transmitted to people or animals through contaminated. Cholera is an acute bacterial enteric disease characterized in its severe form by sudden onset, profuse painless watery stools (rice water stool), nausea and vomiting early in the course of illness, and, in untreated cases, rapid dehydration, acidosis, and circulatory collapse.

Rabies: Rabies results from infection by the rabies virus, a neurotoxic virus in the genus Lyssavirus, family Rhabdoviridae. There are many strains of the rabies virus; each strain is maintained in particular reservoir host(s). Rabies is a neurological disease of mammals that is almost invariably fatal once the clinical signs develop. Humans are usually infected when they are bitten by an infected animal, or exposed to its saliva or central nervous system (CNS) tissues. The early symptoms may include nonspecific prodromal signs such as malaise, fever or headache; discomfort, pain, pruritus or sensory alterations at the site of virus entry. After several days, anxiety, confusion and agitation may appear, and progress to insomnia, abnormal behaviour, hypersensitivity to light and sound; delirium, hallucinations, slight or partial paralysis; hyper salivation, dysphagia; pharyngeal spasms upon exposure to liquids, and convulsions.

Leprosy: Leprosy, also known as Hansen's disease, is a chronic, granulomatous infection caused by *Mycobacterium leprae,* an acid-fast bacillus (AFB) related to the bacteria causing tuberculosis. Transmission of *M. leprae* is primarily from untreated MB patients. The classic early skin lesion mainly occurs in children and is most commonly found on the face, extensor surfaces of the limbs, buttocks or trunk. Scalp, axillae, groins and lumbar skin tend to be spared and hair growth and nerve functions are unimpaired. Leprosy is of two types, tuberculoid leprosy and lepromatous leprosy.

Thypoid: Typhoid or enteric fever is an ancient disease and caused by *Salmonella enterica subspecies serovar typhi* (previously known as *Salmonella typhi*), a pathogen specific only to humans. Ingestion of food or water contaminated with feces or urine from patients with typhoid fever or carriers of *S. Typhi*. The first week of symptomatic disease is characterized by progressive elevation of the temperature followed by bacteremia. The second week begins with the development of rose spots, abdominal pain and splenomegaly. The third week is marked by a more intense intestinal inflammatory response particularly in the Peyer's patches with associated necrosis which can result in perforation and hemorrhage.

Malaria: Malaria is caused by a single-celled parasite from the genus Plasmodium. More than 100 different species of Plasmodium exist. The malaria parasite typically is transmitted to people by mosquitoes belonging to the genus *Anopheles*. The human malaria parasite has a complex life cycle that requires both a human host and an insect host. In Anopheles mosquitoes, Plasmodium reproduces sexually (by merging the parasite's sex cells). In people, the parasite reproduces asexually (by cell division), first in liver cells and then, repeatedly, in red blood cells (RBCs). Malaria typically produces a string of recurrent attacks, or paroxysms, each of which has three stages—chills, followed by fever, and then sweating. Along with chills, the person is likely to have headache, malaise, fatigue, and muscular pains, and occasionally nausea, vomiting, and diarrhea.

Syphilis: Syphilis is an infectious venereal disease caused by the spirochete *Treponema pallidum*. Syphilis is transmissible by sexual contact with infectious lesions, from mother to foetus in uterus, via blood product transfusion, and occasionally through ruptures in the skin that come into contact with infectious lesions. Acquired syphilis can be divided into primary, secondary, latent, and tertiary stages. *T pallidum* rapidly penetrates intact mucous membranes or microscopic dermal abrasions and, within a few hours, enters the lymphatic and blood to produce systemic infection.

Filariasis: Filaria or Filariasis is a chronic disease popularly known as Elephantiasis that typically affects the legs. This disease is caused by a worm spreads through the mosquitoes and caused by *Wuchereia bancrofti*. main pathological changes in lymphatic Filariasis are seen in lymphatic's system which results from inflammatory damage due to the adult worms.

Gonnorhea: Gonorrhea is a very common sexually transmitted disease (STD). It is caused by the bacteria *Neisseria gonorrhoeae*. Gonorrhea is sometimes called "the clap". Gonorrhea can infect the vagina, cervix, rectum, penis, urethra, or sometimes the throat. Most women (and some men) who have Gonorrhea don't notice anything wrong. If symptoms occur, they usually show up 01–02 weeks after infection.

Hepatitis: Hepatitis means inflammation of the liver. The liver is a vital organ that processes nutrients, filters the blood, and fights infections. The term viral hepatitis is used to describe infection of liver caused by hepatotropic viruses. Hepatitis can be caused by a variety of different viruses such as hepatitis A, B, C, D and E. When the liver is inflamed or damaged, its function can be affected. Heavy alcohol use, toxins, some medications, and certain medical conditions can cause hepatitis.

AIDS: AIDS is caused by human immunodeficiency virus (HIV). All HIV-infected persons are at risk for illness and death from opportunistic infections and neoplastic complications because of the inevitable manifestations of AIDS. HIV is transmitted by both homosexual and heterosexual contact; by blood and blood products; and by infected mothers to infants either intrapartum, prenatally, or via breast milk. HIV infection transmits through, pharyngeal, cervical, vaginal, and gastrointestinal mucosal surfaces, even in the absence of mucosal disruption. Symptoms of AIDS includes, fever, sore throat, fatigue, weight loss, myalgia, morbilliform or muculopapular rash usually involving the trunk, diarrhea, nausea, vomiting, lymphadenopathy, night sweats and aseptic meningitis (fever, headache, photophobia, and stiff neck).

12

DEFINITION OF DOSAGE FORMS

12.1 INTRODUCTION

Dosage forms are the means by which drug molecules are delivered to the seat of action within the body. The different forms in which drugs reach the site of action in a patient are explained in the sections below.

12.2 AEROSOLS

Aerosols consist of pressurized packs which contain the drugs in solution or suspension and a suitable propellant. They are most commonly used in the treatment of asthma. These devices are fitted with a metering valve which allows a metered dose to be delivered each time the device is used. Some aerosols are for topical use, which contain non-steroidal anti-inflammatory drugs as counterirritants.

12.3 APPLICATIONS

This is the name given to solutions, suspensions or emulsions which are for topical use. They contain substances such as acaricides or antiseptics.

12.4 CAPSULES

Capsules are solid dosage forms with hard or soft shells. They are of various shapes and sizes, and contain a single dose of one or more active ingredients. They are intended for oral administration as also for vaginal or rectal insertion. It is therefore important to inform the patient of their appropriate use. For both types of capsule, the drug is contained in a gelatin shell, usually as a powder or a liquid. Modified-release preparations are available where the drug is presented in a gelatin container as small pellets with different coatings.

12.5 COLLODIONS

Collodions are liquid preparations for external use. The liquid is painted on the skin, where it forms a flexible film. They contain substances such as salicylic acid which is useful in the treatment of corns.

12.6 CREAMS

Creams are semi-solid emulsions for external use. Because of water content they are susceptible to microbial contamination, and either includes a preservative or is given a short shelf life. Creams are easier to apply and are less greasy than ointments; so patients often prefer them.

12.7 DUSTING POWDER

Dusting powers are finely divided powders for external use. Their main uses are as lubricants to prevent friction between skins surfaces and for disinfection and antisepsis in minor wounds.

12.8 EAR DROPS

Ear drops are used topically to treat ear infections. The drops contain a drug, or mixture of drugs, and are presented as a solution or suspension in a suitable vehicle such as water, glycerol, propylene glycol or alcohol. The drops are dropped into the ear with a dropper. Some vehicles, such as alcohol, may cause a degree of stinging when applied to the ear. If patient find the degree of stinging unacceptable, they may have to be given ear drops with aqueous vehicle. Oil such as almond or olive is often recommended for the alleviation of the impacted earwax. It is usually suggested that such oils, before being dropped into the ear, should be warmed.

12.9 ELIXIRS

An elixir is a solution of one or more drugs for oral use. The vehicle generally contains a high proportion of sucrose or increasingly a sugar-free vehicle such as sorbitol solution, which is less likely to cause dental caries. The therapeutic action of drugs presented as elixirs varies widely and includes antihistamines, antibiotics and decongestants.

12.10 EMULSIONS

These are the mixtures of two immiscible liquids, usually oil and water. Emulsions refer to a preparation for oral use. The term 'oral emulsion' as an oral dosage form may be defined as 'a fine dispersion of droplets of an oily liquid in an aqueous liquid which forms the continuous phase'. Drugs may be dissolved in either of the phases or suspended in the emulsion.

12.11 ENEMAS

An enema is an oily or aqueous solution which is administered rectally. A variety of drugs is formulated as enemas and is used to treat conditions such as constipation or ulcerative colitis. They are also used in X-rays examination of the lower bowel and for systemic effects, such as the use of diazepam in status epileptics and febrile convulsions.

12.12 EYE DROPS

Eye drops are saline solutions containing drops used as medication in the eyes. Depending upon the infection eye drops may contain steroid, antihistamines, β-receptor blockers, parasympathomimetics, parasympatholytic, prostaglandins, non-steroidal anti-inflammatory drugs or topical anaesthetics.

12.13 GARGLES

Gargles are aqueous solutions used to treat infections of the throat. They are often presented in a concentrated form with instructions to the patient for dilution. Gargles should not be swallowed but held in the throat while exhaling through the liquid. After sometime, spit out the gargle.

12.14 GELS

Gels are semi-solid dosage forms for topical or other local use. They are usually transparent or translucent and have a variety of uses. Spermicidal and lubricants are often presented in a gel form. Preparations containing coal tar or other drugs used in the treatment of psoriasis and eczema are also presented in this formulation because it is non-greasy. The term 'gel' is also used to describe colloidal suspension of drugs such as aluminium and magnesium hydroxides.

12.15 GRANULES

This term is used to describe a drug which is presented in small irregularly shaped particles. Granules may be packed in individuals sachet containing a unit dose of medicament or may be provided in a bulk format where the dose is measured using a 05 ml spoon. Some laxatives are among the drugs currently presented in granules.

12.16 IMPLANTS

Implants are solid dosage forms which are inserted under the skin by small surgical incisions. Implants are designed to release or more medicaments over an extended period of time. They are more commonly used for hormonal replacement of contraceptive. Release of the drug from implants is generally slow and long-term therapy can be achieved.

12.17 INHALATIONS

Inhalations are preparations which contain volatile medicaments for beneficial effects in upper respiratory tract disorders such as nasal congestion. Some inhalations contain substances which are volatile at room temperature and patient can obtain a degree of relief by adding a few drops to a handkerchief or a pillowcase and breathing in the vapour. Other inhalations are added to hot water and the impregnated steam is then inhaled.. Pharmacists should advise against this, as the steam produced is so hot that can damage the delicate mucous membranes of the upper respiratory tract. Overuse of this type of preparation should also be avoided as it may cause a chronic condition to develop. The use of these strong aromatic decongestants is contraindicated in children less than 03 months owing to the risk of apnea.

12.18 INJECTIONS

Injections are sterile and used parenterally. These are subdivided into small and large volume parenteral fluids. Small-volume parenterals are sterile, pyrogen-free injectable products. They are packaged in volumes up to 100 ml Small-volume parenteral fluids are packed as:

- Single-dose ampoules
- Multiple-dose vials
- Prefilled syringes

12.19 INSUFFLATIONS

Insufflations are medicated powders designed to be blown into the ear, nose, throat or body cavities by means of a device known as an insufflators. The drugs are presented in a dry powder form, usually in capsule, which is inserted into a specially designed device where the capsule is broken, the contents are released and patient inhales the powder. Bulk insufflation has largely disappeared and has been replaced by individual doses of powdered drugs supplied in hard capsules. This type of insufflation is used mainly for drug delivery into the respiratory tract by inhalation.

12.20 IRRIGATION SOLUTIONS

Irrigation solutions are sterile, pyrogen-free solutions usually intended for irrigation of body cavities, operation cavities, wounds or the urinogenital system. Sterile solution of 0.9% is used to treat a wide range of common urinary tract pathogens. Antifungal drugs such as amphoteric and locally acting cytotoxic, e.g. doxorubicin and epirubicin are introduced into the bladder to treat mycotic infections and bladder tumors respectively.

12.21 LINCTUSES

Linctuses are viscous, liquid oral preparations that are usually prescribed for the relief of cough. They usually contain a high proportion of syrup and glycerol which have a demulcent effect on the membranes of the throat. The dose volume is small; for sustained demulcent action, they should be taken undiluted.

12.22 LINIMENTS

Liniments are fluid, semi-fluid or, occasionally, semi-solid preparations intended for application to the skin to alleviate the discomfort of muscle strain and injuries. They may be alcoholic or oily solutions or emulsions. Most are massaged into the skin but some are applied on a warm dressing or with a brush. Liniments should not be applied to broken skin. Examples of active ingredients found in liniments are turpentine oil and methyl salicylate.

12.23 LOTIONS

Lotions are fluid preparations for external application without friction and may be solutions, suspensions or emulsions. They are either dabbed on the skin or applied on a suitable dressing and covered with a waterproof dressing to reduce evaporation.

12.24 LOZENGES

Lozenges are large tablets designed to be sucked and remain in mouth for up to 15 minutes. Lozenges consist of sugar and gum, the latter giving strength and cohesiveness to the lozenge and facilitating slow release of the medicament. They do not disintegrate and active constituents are incorporated in a sugar base such as sucrose or glucose. They are used to medicate the mouth and throat and for the slow administration of indigestion or cough remedies.

12.25 MIXTURES

Mixtures are liquid oral preparations consisting of one or more ingredients dissolved or suspended in an aqueous vehicle. Official mixtures are not usually formulated for a long shelf-life.

12.26 MOUTHWASHES

Mouthwashes are similar to gargles but are used for oral hygiene and to treat infections of the mouth.

12.27 NASAL DROPS AND SPRAYS

Nasal drops and sprays are isotonic solutions used to treat conditions of the nose. Drugs in solution may be instilled into the nose from a dropper or from a plastic squeeze bottle. Locally acting decongestants are commonly presented in nasal drops. The drug may have a local effect, e.g. antihistamine, vasoconstrictor, decongestant. Alternatively the drug may be absorbed through the nasal mucosa to exert a systemic effect, e.g. the peptide hormones oxytocin and vasopressin. The use of oily nasal drops should be avoided because of possible damage to the cilia of the nasal mucosa. Prolonged use of nasal vasoconstrictors may result in rebound vasodilatation and further nasal congestion.

12.28 OINTMENTS

Ointments are semi-solid, greasy preparations for application to the skin, rectum or nasal mucosa. The base is usually anhydrous and immiscible with skin secretions. Ointments may be used as emollients or to apply suspended or dissolved medicaments to the skin. Ointments intended for application to large open wounds should be sterile.

12.29 ORAL EMULSIONS

Oral emulsions as an oral dosage form may be defined as 'a fine dispersion of droplets of an oily liquid in an aqueous liquid which forms the continuous phase'.

12.30 ORAL LIQUIDS

Oral liquids are homogeneous preparations containing one or more active ingredients dissolved or suspended in a suitable vehicle. Elixirs, linctuses, mixtures, oral drops, oral emulsions, oral solutions and oral suspensions are included in the general category of oral liquids.

12.31 PAINTS

Paints are solutions for application to the skin or mucous membranes. Skin paints often have a volatile solvent that evaporates quickly to leave a dry resinous film of medicament. Throat paints are more viscous due to a high content of glycerol, designed to prolong contact of the medicament with the affected site. Paints are used for their antiseptic, analgesic, caustic or astringent properties and should be applied with a brush to assist application.

12.32 PARENTERAL PREPARATIONS

Parenteral preparations are sterile dosage forms containing one or more medicaments and designed for parenteral administration. Injections are sterile solutions, suspensions or emulsions in a suitable aqueous or non-aqueous vehicle and are usually classified according to their route of administration.

12.33 PASTES

Pastes are semi-solid preparations for external application that differ from similar ointments and gels in that they contain a high proportion of finely powdered medicaments. The base may be anhydrous or water soluble. Their stiffness makes them useful protective coatings. Pastes intended for application to large open wounds should be sterile. Corrosive drugs such as dethrone are often formulated as pastes so that applied to the psoriatic lesion will not spread onto healthy skin and cause irritation.

12.34 PASTILLES

Pastilles are for oral use and like lozenges are designed to be sucked. They contain locally acting antiseptics, astringents or anesthetics and are used to treat or give symptomatic relief of conditions affecting the mouth and throat. They have a jelly-like consistency produced by their basis of gelatin or acacia.

12.35 PESSARIES

Pessaries are solid dosage forms for insertion into the vagina. They are used for both local and systemic action.

12.36 PILLS

These are oral dosage forms which consist of spherical masses prepared from one or more medicaments incorporated with inert excipients. The term 'pill' is used colloquially as a synonym for oral contraceptive tablets which are actually prepared by compression.

12.37 POULTICES

Poultices are paste-like preparations used externally to reduce pain and inflammation because they retain heat well. After heating, the preparation is spread thickly on a dressing and applied as hot as the patient can bear, to the affected area.

12.38 POWDERS (ORAL)

Powders (oral) are of two kinds intended for internal use: Bulk Powders usually contain non-potent medicaments such as antacids since the patient measures a dose by volume using a 05ml medicine spoon. The powder is then usually dispersed in water or, in the case of effervescent powders, dissolved before taking.

Divided powders are packaged individually and each dose is separately wrapped in paper or sealed into a sachet.

12.39 SUPPOSITORIES

Suppositories are solid preparations which may contain one or more active pharmaceutical ingredient(s) intended for rectal insertion. They are normally used for local action or systemic absorption of the active ingredient(s). They usually melt, soften, or dissolve at body temperature. Suppositories are usually prepared from excipients or bases such as cocoa butter, hard fat, glycerinated gelatin, hydrogenated vegetable oils and macrogols.

12.40 SUSPENSIONS

Suspensions are liquid dose forms where the active ingredient is insoluble. Suspensions are available for both oral and external use.

12.41 SYRUPS

Syrups are concentrated aqueous solutions of sugars such as sucrose. The term 'syrup' is frequently, but incorrectly, applied to certain sweetened liquids intended for oral use. The term 'syrup' should nowadays only be used to refer to flavouring vehicles. Sucrose is being replaced by sorbitol as the sweetening agent in many preparations to give 'sugar free' syrups to reduce the risk of dental caries.

12.42 TABLETS

Tablets are solid dosage forms containing one or more active ingredients. They are obtained by single or multiple compressions and may be uncoated or coated. They are usually intended for oral administration, but preparations for alternative applications, such as implants, solution-tablets for injections, irrigations, or for external use, vaginal tablets, etc.

13

LATIN

INTRODUCTION

Prescription written in the UK should be written in English and the use of Latin is strongly discouraged. However, the use of some Latin terms persists and abbreviations are often used, especially to indicate the frequency of dosage. Abbreviations may have different meanings in different countries. Great care is required to avoid errors arising through misunderstanding.

The following list includes terms which may be encountered in current practice.

Dosage forms

Latin name	Abbreviation	English name
Auristillae	*Aurist.*	ear drops
Capsular	*Caps.*	capsule
Cataplasm	*Cataplasm.*	poultice
Collunarium	*Collin.*	nose wash
Collutorium	*Collut.*	mouthwash
Collyrium	*Collyr.*	eye lotion
Cremer	*Cream.*	cream
Gutta	*gtt.*	drops
Haustus	*ht.*	draught
Liquor	*liq.*	solution
Lotio	*lot.*	lotion
Mixture	*mist.*	mixture
naristillae	*Narist.*	nose drops
Nebula	*Neb.*	spray solution
Oculentum	*Oculent.*	eye ointment
Pasta	*Past.*	paste
Pigmentum	*Pig.*	paint
Pulvis	*Pulv.*	powder
Pulvis conspersus	*Pulv. Consp.*	dusting powder
Trochiscus	*Troches.*	lozenge
Unguentum	*Ung.*	ointment
vapour	*vaps*	inhalation
Vitrella	*Vitrella*	glass capsule(crushable)

Terms used in prescriptions

Latin name	Abbreviation	English name
ante cibum	a.c.	before food
ante meridiem	a.m.	before noon
Ana	aa.	of each
Ad	ad	to
ad libitum	Ad lib.	as much as desired
alternus	alt.	alternate
ante	ante	before
applicandus	Applic.	apply
aqua	aq.	water
bis	b.	twice
bis die	b.d.	twice daily
bis in die	b.i.d.	twice daily
calidus	Calid.	warm
cibus	Cib.	food
composites	co.	compound
concentratus	conc.	concentrated
cum	c.	with
dies	d.	a day
destillatus	dest.	distilled
dilutus	dil.	diluted
duplex	dup.	doubale
ex aqua	ex aq.	in water
fiat	ft.	let it be made
fortis	fort.	strong
hora	h.	at the hour of
hora somnine	h.s.	at bedtime
inter cibos	ic.	between meals
inter	int.	between
mane	m.	in the morning
more dicto	m.d.	as directed
more dicto utendus	m.d.u.	to be used as directed
mittee	Mitt.	send

Latin name	Abbreviation	English name
nocte	n.	at night
nocte et mane	n.et m.	night and morning
nocte manqué	n.m.	night and morning
nomen propria	n.p.	the proper name
nocte	Nocte.	at night
omnibus alternis horis	o.alt.hor	every other hour
Omni die	o.d.	every day
Omni mane	o.m.	every morning
Omni nocte	o.n.	every night
parti affectae	p.a.	to the affected part
1. parti affectae applicandus	Parts affect.	apply to the affected part
prates aequales	p.aeq.	equal parts
post cibus	p.c.	after food
post meridiem	p.m.	after noon
pates	pp.	parts
pro re nata	p.r.n.	when required
parti dolente	Part. dolente.	to the painful part
quarter die	q.d.	four times daily
quarter die sumendus	q.d.s.	take four times daily
quarter in die	q.i.d.	four times daily
quaque	qq.	every
quaque hora	qQ	every hour
quarto quaque hora	q.qq.h.	every fourth hour
quantum sufficiat	q.s.	sufficient
recipe	R_x	take
secundum artem	Sec. Art.	with pharmaceutical skill
semisse	ss.	half
si opus sit	s.o.s.	if necessary
signa	sig.	label
statim	stat.	immediately
sumendus ter	sum.t	take thrice

Latin name	Abbreviation	English name
ter de die	t.d.d.	three times daily
ter die sumendus	t.d.s.	take three times daily
ter in die	t.i.d.	three times daily
tussis	Tuss.	a cough
tussive urgent	tuss.urg.	when the cough troubles
ut antea	u.a.	as before
ut dictum	ut.dict.	as directed
ut directum	Ut .direct.	as directed
utendus	Utend.	to be used

www.ingramcontent.com/pod-product-compliance
Lightning Source LLC
Chambersburg PA
CBHW081221170426
43198CB00017B/2680